TALL SHIPS
TO CATHAY

by Helen Augur

Exciting and charming and tumultuous, TALL SHIPS TO CATHAY is the story of the fabulous Low family of Salem and Brooklyn—who were part of the turmoil and vigor of the early stretchings of the giant, America.

The marvelous adventure started in 1829 when beautiful Harriet Low landed at Macao, headquarters for British and American merchants trading from Canton. Daring and high-spirited, she was the first American woman to set foot on Chinese soil. Harriet was soon followed by her brother Abbot, who joined the Boston firm of Russell & Co., which was beginning to break the British monopoly in the China trade. He was blessed with a genius for business, and became head of the firm and of the family, and earned respect for them throughout the East.

Growing up to be a daring and fearless sailor, Charles Low became the ship captain of the family. He sailed the ships that for years linked the Low enterprises with New York and Boston and Canton and skippered some of the most glamorous clippers that America ever boasted. Once, when a ship of his was caught by

(Continued on back flap)

TALL SHIPS TO CATHAY

DOUBLEDAY & COMPANY, INC., GARDEN CITY,

Tall Ships
TO CATHAY

NEW YORK, 1951

by Helen Augur

For Florence Wenner

. . . dulce ridentem Lalagen amabo,
dulce loquentem.

ACKNOWLEDGMENTS

For well over a century the Low family has recognized the importance of preserving its papers as an invaluable part of our national archives. As author I am grateful for this, the more so because the treasure has been opened to me without reservation.

I wish to thank Miss Elma Loines, herself an expert on the family history, for answering many queries and for permission to use material from various family letters and from the Macao journal of her bewitching grandmother, Harriet Low. Abbot Low's granddaughter, Mrs. William Raymond, was good enough to lend me a series of business letters from Seth Low to his oldest son in Canton. An especially rich collection of Captain Low's letters and ship logs turned up in Santa Barbara, where I received unstinted help from the clipper captain's youngest son, Mr. David Low, and from his grandchildren, Miss Alta Low, Miss Helen Low, and Mr. Thomas M. Low.

In gathering contemporary material I browsed for happy weeks in the Essex Institute of Salem, under the expert guidance of Miss Harriet Tapley and Miss Florence Osborne, now and then crossing the street to the Peabody Museum, where Colonel Lawrence W. Jenkins unearthed his own trove from Cathay.

The Manuscript Division of the New York Public Library, under the direction of Mr. Wilmer R. Leach and Mr. Robert W. Hill, has for years proved to have almost anything I hoped to find, and to my delight produced some of the best letters from William and Harriet Low included in the book.

The Library of Congress is slowly becoming the repository of Low papers, and there I received invaluable help from Mr. St. George L. Sioussat, chief of the Manuscript Division, and from Dr. Arthur W. Hummel, who as chief of the Orientalia Division has become the most instructed Low addict in the country. I was given my bearings on Antarctica and N. B. Palmer by the authority on both, Colonel Lawrence Martin, chief of the Cartographic Division.

The chapters on the clipper ships were written with two books constantly on tap: Arthur H. Clark's *The Clipper Ship Era* and the newer *Greyhounds of the Sea* by Carl C. Cutler. To all who know this blue-water classic my debt is obvious.

My gratitude to all these people does not implicate them in any blunders I may have made in handling the material. Conversely, I must disclaim credit for gathering the illustrations, for this complex operation was carried through in masterly fashion by Miss Barbara Zimmerman of Doubleday, to whom I am eternally grateful.

It is impossible to thank individually all the people who have helped to trace down the old paintings from which a selection was made. I am especially indebted to my good friend Helen Low of Santa Barbara, to Miss Loines and Mrs. Raymond, and to Mrs. William Emerson, Miss Harriette Low, Mrs. Benjamin R. C. Low, Mr. Bradford Boardman, Mr. Frederick Delano, Mrs. Alexander Grant, and Mrs. Joseph Pearman. Reproductions of clipper ships

8

and Chinese scenes were supplied by the Peabody Museum, the Frick Collection, the Marine Historical Association of Mystic, Connecticut and Mr. Harry Shaw Newman of the Old Print Shop.

And finally, I must thank the Metropolitan Museum of Art, not only for their steady counsel and several fine photographs, but for inspiring this book. Their 1941 exhibition, "The China Trade and Its Influences," evoked for me the exhilarating age which I have tried to recapture in these pages.

FOREWORD

To have a golden age, which really means a coming-of-age, is the lot of every great nation. But to have forgotten that luminous moment when national powers and temperament reached maturity is an amnesia wholly American.

A century ago we attained the climax of our long striving as colonies and young republic, and conquered the seas as a people of happy enterprise and boundless horizons. Our new clipper ships, beautiful as archangels, sped around the globe on missions of trade and friendship. This was the high point of our whole history as a salt-water people whose destiny lay on the seas. And since our first conquest in world trade was made on a little strip of the Canton water front, it was fitting that the China trade should evoke the clipper ships.

We can never forget the *Flying Cloud* or the *Great Republic*, but we do not remember what lay behind them. Having fulfilled our destiny as a maritime people, we were at that moment becoming a different race. Our national memories really begin with the forty-niners and the covered wagons surging west to settle a country which had suddenly exploded into a continent. In conquering the land we forgot the seas and the great world, we became parochial, and industrial too. The machine supplanted the winged sandals of world trade, in which for a dazzling moment we held first place.

This is a good time to remember our earliest conquest in the Orient, which evolved the pattern we have since followed: trade and friendship with all nations willing to receive us. Here, then, is an autobiography of the China trade, and of the Low family of Salem and New York who were for three generations at its heart. Typical Americans, they evolved with the nation into world traders and builders of clipper ships. As if conscious that they were living out a great adventure, the Lows wrote their story in countless letters, in journals and ship logs and books. They were charming young people with lively minds and warm sympathies, and since it is their story, they have been allowed to tell it themselves, with only a supporting trellis supplied by the author.

Helen Augur

CONTENTS

ILLUSTRATIONS

facing page

15

TALL SHIPS TO CATHAY

THE LOW FAMILY

David Low X Hannah Haskell   Thomas Porter X Ruth Allen

| | |

SETH (1782–1853)   X   MARY (1786–1872)

|

1. Mary Ann (1808–1851) m. 1833 George Archer
2. Harriet (1809–1877) m. 1836 John Hillard
3. Abiel Abbot (1811–1893) m. (1) 1841 Ellen Almira Dow
                                    (2) 1851 Ann Bedell Low
4. Seth Haskell (1812–1857) m. 1839 Rebecca Ann Cutler
5. William Henry (1816–1845) m. 1842 Ann Davison Bedell
6. Edward Allen (1817–1898) m. 1854 Lucy Elizabeth Haskell
7. Francis (1818–1836)
8. Josiah Orne (1821–1895) m. 1845 Martha Elizabeth Mills
9. Sarah Elizabeth (1822–1863) m. 1846 Edward Hutchinson
    Lyman
10. Charles Porter (1824–1913) m. 1852 Sarah Maria Tucker
11. Ellen Porter (1827–1898) m. 1849 Ethelbert Smith Mills

CHILDREN MENTIONED IN TEXT

Mary Ann's son, George Augustus
Harriet's daughters, Katherine, Frances, Mary, Sarah, Harriet
Abbot's children, Harriet, Abbot Augustus ("Gus"), Ellen, Seth
William's son, William Gilman ("Will")
Charles's children, Charles Palmer, Josiah Orne, Francis and
    Frances (twins), Samuel Percy, Rosalie Hunter, and David.

1

Lilacs

and

Pomegranates

It was almost typhoon weather, the seas an angry gray exploding white against the islands off Macao Roads, where the *Sumatra* was putting down her anchors. The long voyage from Salem was over, and Harriet Low stood at the postern gate of China.

The gate would not swing open for her; Macao was as much of the Flowery Kingdom as a foreign devil woman might enter in 1829. Harriet was poised at the rail like an impatient frigate bird; this almost typhoon, almost China did not suit her temperament. A soncy girl of twenty, a tangle of impulse and brightness, she yet longed for definition. And she had entered a realm of intangibles, an air half balm, half menace, an outpost of Cathay that was Portuguese and Chinese but stamped too with the omnipotent chop of the British East India Company.

Macao was to be her home for years to come. The anchor chains rattled to a standstill, the ship jerked at her tether and then lay quiet.

It was an overwhelming moment, like that May morning months ago when the *Sumatra* had sailed down the long Salem harbor, past the square-riggers still muffled in their dreams of the Celebes and the pepper coasts, past the green bastion of Marblehead, and out to Baker's Island, where the escort of half the small boats in Salem waved Harriet good-by and slowly turned back home. Her brothers and sisters had gone back to the crowded, happy house on Crombie Street and left her facing the great seas and the empire of the Son of Heaven, Tao Kwang.

Now she was in an oriental world that seemed composed of islands. Out at sea were Lantao and Lintin, far astern the Ladrones and what the Chinese called "the old ten thousand hills." Ahead, across three miles of shoal water, lay Macao. It looked like the tip of a peninsula, but it was an island, too, cut off from China proper by a strait guarded by a squat fortress.

The city was pyramided like a formal bouquet, each white house a camellia cupped in its own green foliage, each blossom set above the other so that all commanded the harbor. At the top of the bouquet bloomed the ancient Portuguese churches and fort; around its lower rim, like silver lace paper, were elegant waterfront buildings looped with the white ribbon of the Praya Grande.

In one of those houses Harriet and her beautiful young aunt would live the strange existence dictated by the Son of Heaven. He allowed foreign merchants a small foothold in Canton, but their families must live in Macao. During the tea season Canton was a gentlemen's club, Macao a city of female banality. Much as Harriet resented the Chinese ban on foreign women, it was responsible for her coming out with Uncle William Low and his wife. Abigail Low could never have faced the perils of living alone for most of the year in a community of heathens and Britishers.

Their house was waiting for them, their Chinese servants had been engaged. Now that they were actually about to land, Harriet and Aunt were full of domestic worries. Laundry was uppermost in their thoughts. Six dozen apiece of everything, a dozen dozen of every layer from chemises to the thin gowns they had worn during the stop in Manila, corsets, petticoats innumerable, garments unmentionable, with ruffles and laces and fine stitching, handkerchiefs, nightgowns, collars and fripperies—for four months they had been cramming them into trunks and boxes while the *Sumatra* plowed around Africa and past Java Head.

"Oh, dear suds!" Harriet wailed. It happened to be her favorite lament, but it sent them into gusts of laughter. They were still quivering with it when Uncle joined them. William Henry Low, the youngest brother of Harriet's father Seth, was slender and elegant like his wife, a dignified, rather somber man who was sometimes puzzled by what ladies chose to laugh about.

"I've been talking to Captain Roundy," he said. "A ladder's impossible in this sea. They're rigging a chair to swing you over the stern."

The ladies from Salem nodded. They had already estimated what this choppy sea would mean. They watched the tanka boats come up to take them off, fat little boats low in the water, with mats rounded over the seats making them look what the Chinese called them, egg-house boats. Chinese girls in loose nankeen trousers and tunics plied the oars, one with a baby strapped to her back, another with a flower in her hair.

Uncle William was swung over the stern with a rope around his middle, then Aunt was lashed in the bosun's chair, with an extra rope to hold her billowing skirts modestly below her knees, and lowered to her husband's arms. Then Harriet. It was nothing to be trussed up like a fowl and pitched into space toward a bobbing tanka boat. What she dreaded lay ahead. Three miles ahead were the ladies of the East India Company.

Seth Low brought up his seven sons and four daughters in a town that was a storeship loaded with riches from the wide seas— Russia leather, mother-of-pearl from cannibal isles, carved ivory picked up at Isle of France or Zanzibar, gauzes and humhums from India, cinnamon from Ceylon, silks and porcelains from

China. His boys watched the men pacing the ropewalks, and followed the procession when they marched with fife and drum bearing cordage for a new ship. They watched the sailmakers in their lofts, the riggers bending canvas on masts heaving gently as the tide filled. They dodged the drays carrying cargo to the ships and the sailors swarming off to the grogshops and the slaughter-houses where the fancy girls called from upper windows. And finally, in what had been the richest town in America, they watched the grass grow between the rough cobbles on Derby Street, and the clover pink and red creep along Derby Wharf.

With all his heart Seth Low prayed that none of his sons would ever go to sea. As a drug merchant he depended on the sea; it was and always had been America's life. But he and his wife Mary had both lost their fathers on trading voyages, and he was fully conscious of the deprivation this had meant, down to the second generation. Their hatred of the sea was nonetheless a strange attitude for a Salem woman and a man Gloucester-born.

Seth's father had been lost on a West Indies voyage, leaving him at fifteen as the virtual head of the family. He had managed to work his way nearly through Harvard, intending for the ministry, but an attack of measles had so damaged his eyesight that he left college in his third year and eventually settled in Salem as a middling, but highly respected, merchant.

The seas had thwarted his wife Mary Porter just as cruelly. By birth she was destined for Chestnut Street or Washington Square, but the early loss of her father on a coasting voyage had meant that she grew up as a poor relation in a prosperous uncle's house. She went to the famous Salem assemblies, where she danced with her Derby cousins, with the young Crowninshields and Salton-stalls and Peabodys, but the next morning was back at her needle-work and cookery lessons like any other undowered miss.

When they married and began bringing up their children the Lows saw what could happen to a town depending utterly upon the seas. First Jefferson the isolationist tied up Salem and all the ports with his Embargo. Then there was the War of 1812, and finally the slow death of a fabulously rich town into a pretty seaside village with a silting-up harbor.

Sensitive to the great tides, Seth Low decided to follow the migration of Yankee business brains down to New York City. Great fortunes had melted in New England, and the families who had weathered the long strangulation of shipping were now putting their money not into ships but into land enterprises—mills, water power, banking, and insurance—and sending their young men south. Before Harriet sailed for China her father had decided to move the family to New York, where he and his eldest son, Abiel Abbot, just eighteen, would go into business together.

This move was the result of good judgment, but it was also full of the peculiar fate that always put the Lows in the right place at the right moment. Whether judgment and happy fate agreed about Harriet's hegira to the Orient was a question, but it seemed logical to send a charming girl to the place where the most eligible young bachelors on earth were making money hand over fist in the China trade.

Besides, the China trade itself was beginning to interest Seth Low and his son Abbot.

The calls began before the Low ladies were settled in their white stone villa. The Company could not wait to see what these invaders were like, the first female Americans to broach the tight little colony at Macao.

From Elizabeth to Victoria the East India Company was to be the core of empire, in itself an empire ruling a hundred million souls, the greatest trade monopoly in human history, with its own navies, armies, forts, factories, palaces, and governors. Since the days of Charles I the Company had held a charter giving it the monopoly of Chinese trade. One after the other it had knocked down the other trading nations in Canton like bowling pins. Lately the Americans there had become "deeply annoying" as potential rivals, and Mr. Low, the new partner of the rapidly evolving Boston house of Russell & Co., was perhaps dangerous.

However, the Company ladies needed something new to gossip about, and the gentlemen called for reasons of business policy. These pampered and arrogant people were prepared to be civil, but hardly to accept the newcomers on an equal footing; they came to patronize and appraise. They found that amazingly enough the Salem ladies had social standards of their own, and received them with a certain reserve. The British were snobbish enough to like this, and showered them with invitations.

Mr. Low had gone up to Canton with the *Sumatra*, but the English merchants were lingering in Macao for the windup of the summer's gay season. The China trade was dominated by the monsoons, which happened to synchronize with the tea crops. It was early October, and the trading fleet was coming to China with the favorable southwest monsoon, while the fresh teas arrived in Canton from the interior. During the winter the ships were loaded and then the reversed monsoon blew them down the China Sea. When the northeast wind dropped in the late spring there was a general exodus of the trading colony down to Macao and female society.

Decidedly, the Salem ladies gave a fillip to the last balls and dinner parties. Abigail Low, dark-eyed and quiet, contributed an air of propriety; Harriet, one continual effervescence of charm. A madcap, a dynamo, she had more temperament than she knew what to do with, and more intelligence than was called for in the effete little world of Macao. In company, because she was struggling to overcome her shyness, her high spirits pretty well concealed the social drawback of her inquiring mind. Small, daintily rounded, with the brilliant rosiness and merry blue eyes of her clan, Harriet seemed created to lead a bevy of beaux like poodles on ribbons. She was provocative, her small, full lips were parted as if inviting a gallant or witty remark, and she loved both.

She was always getting into hobbles. On their third day in Macao Mr. George Vachell called, and set to work evoking Miss Low's dimples and quick laughter. Mr. Vachell was young, handsome, witty, and a great buck with his talk of racing and quadrilles. Harriet knew that the British gentlemen were free in their manners and also, alas, their morals, but she found the caller amusing, and assumed her most frivolous air.

After he had left, Apew, the comprador who ran their Chinese household, came running with the card he had neglected to give Mrs. Low when he announced the caller.

24

"Harriet! Mr. Vachell is the Company chaplain!"

"A parson," Harriet moaned. "Aunt, he was flirting with me, I swear it."

Abigail Low shook her head. "We must be careful, dear. This is a cruel place for gossip. And I'm afraid there's a great deal here to gossip about."

"Well, it won't be us, dearest. Oh, what beasts men are! A parson, betting on the races, dancing—what would dear Father think?"

Still, Harriet enjoyed the gaiety that ended the season. She danced and admired the fireworks at Captain Whitehead's fancy-dress ball, she enjoyed the amateur theatricals, and at Lady Claridge's quadrille had to take a different partner for each figure. She wore white muslin trimmed with yellow satin over white satin, a dress she had made herself, and that set off her golden-brown curls. She was the only spinster in the colony, but it was not for that reason the men flocked around her.

When their sedan chairs arrived from Canton, the Low ladies could see something of Macao itself, a bewildering town. One day the church bells pealed all over the island and the forts shot off volleys to salute the accession of Dom Miguel to the throne of Portugal. That reminded them that Macao was really Portuguese, and they made a pilgrimage to the cave where the poet Camoëns wrote his *Lusiads*, and watched the senhoritas promenade the Praya Grande on Saturday evenings wearing, shockingly enough, no bonnets. But sometimes they would see lily-foot ladies and remember that Macao was also Chinese, run jointly by a mandarin and a Portuguese judge. Hating chairs and the convention that forbade ladies to walk without a male escort, Harriet would sometimes rush out and climb to the Campo or Peña Hill, where she had a superb view of the harbor.

Her energy was boundless. For the first time in her life she had leisure, far too much of it. At home she and her beloved older sister, Mary Ann, made, and made over, the entire wardrobes for the family, including shirts and suits for the boys. Harriet could make ninety buttonholes in a day. In Macao there was no housekeeping. Apew the comprador alone understood how to run their domestic life. He was butler and steward, he supervised the marketing, he managed the China boys who, in their quarters belowstairs, jabbered in their southern singsong and slept at all hours. When their midafternoon snores became overpowering, Aunt Low would call to Apew.

"Turn them over!"

"Yes, Missy Lao."

They called Harriet Missy Ay-yee. She made no attempt to understand the Chinese: they were heathen, like the British.

For the Company paid calls on the Sabbath. In fact the favorite hour for visits was just after church. Harriet refused to go to the Company chapel, where Mr. Vachell was holding his last services before he went up to Canton. It was better to stay home and read a sermon. But she would just be deep in Buckminster when the gaily dressed callers arrived with the latest gossip.

She escaped finally to go down to the lower terrace of the garden, where a little observatory gave her a view of the harbor. There she would be entranced, as a Salem girl must be, by the shipping out in the Roads. At this season there was sure to be a pompous Indiaman or two, the huge, unwieldy vessels of the Company, ignoring the eager Yankee merchantmen, much smaller and faster, slipping ahead to enter the Pearl River. Coming down from China were great trading junks with matting sails and festoons of flags, an eye painted on either side of the bows so they could see where they were going—to Borneo, or down the coast for salt, or to Siam for teak. Far out, bound for the opium store-ships at Lintin Island, were the beautiful schooners bringing Benares and Malwa to be smuggled into ports all up the China coast. It was all fascinating, but on Sunday Harriet wanted to think of 17 Crombie Street.

Sunday morning at home in the yellow house flush with the street, she and Mary Ann sliding from their four-poster on the second-floor front, listening for sounds overhead that would assure them that Abbot was mobilizing his younger brothers—Seth Haskell, Edward, William, Francis, Josiah, down to five-year-old Charles. Abbot was the perfect oldest son of the Tribe of

Seth. He had a round, gentle face like a lion cub, he was firm and sunny and utterly dependable.

She and Mary Ann buttoned into their Sunday merinos, helping little Sarah with her hair, then running down the stairs with their arms around each other, to give Father a morning kiss. He was elegant on Sundays in his blue broadcloth coat and white stock, but then, he was always a dignified figure, and the town called him "Dr. Low" because he dispensed so much medical advice along with his drugs.

Father with his Bible, roly-poly Grandmother Porter in her black bombazine and widow's cap, with baby Ellen in her arms as usual, Mother in churchgoing black with a wide embroidered collar and colored ribbons on her matron's cap, tall, slender Mother who used to be called the May Pole. And the boys trooping down after Abbot, hastily scrubbed, but scrubbed rosy, in their roundabouts and broad linen collars. George Archer, Mary Ann's fiancé, apprenticed to Seth Low and living with the family. The Yankee dabster Hepzibah slipping in from the kitchen.

Father looks around the room, deciding which of the youngest children is more apt to make mischief, two-year-old Ellen or Charlie, bubbling with misdemeanor. He decides to pen his youngest son in the corner while he says the morning prayer, for Seth Low prays with his back to the room, keeping one eye on his Unitarian God, one on the rascal of the day.

Harriet very nearly worshiped her father, whose authority over her stemmed from love, the reverse of the old Puritan formula. She very nearly identified with her older sister; the pattern of the family, with Mary Ann and herself as the oldest children, followed by a train of boys, made her relation to her sister particularly close.

Together they mothered the boys, together, hour after hour, they sat in their room upstairs, cutting down suits, stitching shirts. Sometimes the seamstress Polly Jones worked with them, sometimes one of the boys, who had failed to keep the woodpile in the order Abbot demanded, sat beside them in penance, ripping out stitches in a hand-me-down. As they sewed, the sisters

27

discussed life, which of course meant men. Life was already decided for Mary Ann. But for Harriet—how could she decide, when there were so many youths to take her on berrying and nutting parties, and strolls in Harmony Grove? She must be entertained, she must have somebody who could talk well about any subject, and one after the other her Salem admirers had dulled. Not one of them could compare with brother Abbot, her loved "Botus."

It was hard to think herself back to Salem. Here was a drowsy impermanence, a pagan restlessness, like the wild little birds flying in from the terraced garden, circling the salon, flying out again to light briefly on a branch of scarlet pomegranate. Jeweled little birds—and not a song among them. Brilliant flowers—and not one with the fragrance of Salem lilacs. As for the British, they were dangerous.

Not Dr. Thomas Colledge, the Company's junior surgeon, who was kindness itself. "He is the best man I have seen yet," she had written Mary Ann. "Everybody loves him and speaks well of him. It is a shame he is a bachelor!"

But that oddest of mortals, Mr. Vachell, was no doubt as dangerous as he was diverting. In general, she thought the Company gentlemen a good-for-nothing set of rascals, and some of the ladies were no better. Friendly Mrs. Turner had confided a story that sent Harriet home feeling positively sick. A certain English lady, who had now mercifully left Macao . . .

"Well, my dear Miss Low! Of course in Canton the gentlemen are quite without female society—unless you believe the tales about the flower-boat girls—and come down to Macao quite *ravenous*. But, my dear, she belongs to an extremely good family at home——"

For years Harriet would have to live within the three square miles of Macao among people like that, and be civil to them for the sake of Uncle's business. There had been great strain in Canton because the Yankees were whittling down British trade. Now that the Americans were about to give the Company a real race, Uncle was counting on his ladies to play a diplomatic role,

28

enchanting the Company in Macao while he steadily stole its business in Canton.

She would do her best to help Uncle. He had been at great expense to bring her out, and had sent down an exquisite embroidered dress and fancy combs from Canton, wanting her to appear well. But she missed the dense, happy life of Salem, she could not talk to her dignified young aunt as she had to Mary Ann. And she longed for her brother Abbot to come out and make a fortune in the China trade. An impulse possessed her that she was to communicate to the family, as if she were its compass needle trembling to a stop. From now on the Low compass pointed east.

She thought of John Perkins Cushing, who had arrived in Canton at sixteen and had just now gone home a multimillionaire. Abbot could do as brilliantly. And for her family's sake she should find a potential Cushing as husband. It was silly to travel seventeen thousand miles and put Uncle to such expense if nothing was to come of it. But for months all the young Americans would be sealed up in Canton.

Harriet looked out at the Roads, where the early afternoon sun caught the topgallants of a trading ship making for the Pearl River. She began to dream of marrying a sea captain and making him take her all over the world. Wanting everything, she couldn't make up her mind what she wanted most. Just now she wanted her dinner.

2

Yankees

in

Cathay

William Low was only thirty-four, but if he had been a merchant with half a century of experience he would still have had to start all over again in Canton. The Old China Trade was like something on another planet, functioning without banks, post offices, or written contracts. Much as the Flowery Kingdom needed foreign commerce, it despised and feared foreign merchants, and kept them penned up in a row of hongs along the Pearl River. Their ships could not come up to Canton, but anchored at Whampoa a dozen miles down the river. Their point of contact with the vast empire was the Cohong, a little group of merchant princes who held the monopoly of foreign trade.

It was the Cohong that made the China trade delightful.

Half a dozen immensely rich Chinese with satin robes and

silken manners managed everything. Through their warehouses poured the stream of oriental goods: hyson, bohea, souchong, silks and porcelains, musk and cassia and camphor; everything Chinese reached the Western world through them. They were personally responsible for the personal conduct of the foreign devils, *Fanqui*, and kept them from being snared in the intricacies of Chinese officialdom. Such was their integrity that John Cushing could boast that in twenty-five years of doing tremendous business with the Cohong he never had a written contract, and never a dispute. He thought the hong merchants the most honorable people on earth, and the most accommodating.

Cushing was the link between the old romantic days when the Yankees first entered Cathay and the new era just now at hand, when after forty-five years of playing a flickering obbligato to the British the Yankees began to call the tunes. Anglo-American rivalry had deep roots. The Company had kept the thirteen colonies out of oriental trade, but once the Revolution was won the first American ship in the Pacific was the *Empress of China*, bound for Canton. Boston and Salem ships followed, and very early James and Thomas Handasyd Perkins, of Boston, set up their trading house on the Pearl River.

Their nephew John Cushing came out in 1803, and by a fluke became head of Perkins & Co. when he was only sixteen. A business genius, he immolated himself in work, living like a counting-house monk, with few intimates aside from his friend and mentor Houqua. As long as he lived Houqua was head of the Cohong, an astute and kindly gentleman who was probably the richest merchant in the world. Cushing was the first of several young American protégés to whom he revealed the art of making a fortune in China.

A few years before William Low arrived, John Cushing began to unload some of his business to the new Boston house of Russell & Co., the first American commission house in China, with a branch in Manila. Samuel Russell had only one partner, and when he retired home because of his wife's illness, William Low was invited to replace him.

It was a magnificent opportunity, though when the Lows sailed from Salem they had no inkling of what was in store: the sudden rocketing of Russell & Co. into the most powerful American house in the East. The Cushing-Perkins combination had held first place, spilling its surplus business to Russell. When John Cushing went home to Boston, he put his cousin Thomas Forbes in charge of his tremendous interests.

Thomas Forbes was drowned just before the Lows reached Manila. He had left Macao in a small yacht and been caught in a gale.

"What this tragedy is going to mean we don't know," Mr. Russell told William Low. "I believe Cushing will have to come back and rearrange his affairs. For the moment, Perkins & Co. is without a head, and since our houses are in close alliance, that will mean a busy winter for us, carrying on as best we can for both companies. Beyond that—we'll have to wait till Mr. Cushing gets back to Canton."

Beyond that was a shrewd guess as to what actually happened the next year: Mr. Cushing merged Perkins with Russell, and went home to stay.

With this dazzling prospect on the horizon, William Low arrived in Canton fairly staggering under his new responsibilities. Since Mr. Russell shuttled between China and the Philippines, Low was to be the virtual head of the Americans in Canton. He had been tossed without warning into a strategic and bewildering position as chief Yankee resident, directly vis-à-vis the Company. The British spent most of their energies expanding the clandestine trade in opium and wrangling with the Chinese authorities, but they were by no means oblivious to the threat that Russell & Co. now represented.

Down in Macao Harriet was already making remarks about the luxury in which the gentlemen lived in Canton. As far as creature comforts went, they were pampered like princes of the blood. It was a strange sort of nabob's life without women, and without the liberty to move outside the foreign quarter except on certain occasions. The British had the right temperament for living in a perpetual gentlemen's club, but the Americans missed family life.

Harriet Low in Macao. Portrait by George Chinnery. *Courtesy of Mrs. William Emerson.* Photograph by The Metropolitan Museum of Art.

William Henry Low I. Portrait by George Chinnery.
Courtesy of Miss Harriette Low. Photograph by The
Metropolitan Museum of Art.

The foreign quarter included the row of hongs, or factories, for Fanqui and Cohong, facing the river at the south and running back to Old China Street, where exporters had shops and display rooms. Several streets cut through from front to back, the one beloved of seamen, Hog Lane, where shops for grog and curios kept them happy on liberty days.

The hongs stood on made land, so swampy near "The Factory," as the Company arrogantly called its hong, that the British had recently filled it in so that chopboats could land at low tide. The Square before the hongs was theoretically reserved for the Fanqui, but a big fire in 1822 had burned down the fence around it, and now all the idlers and riffraff of the teeming city used it as an endless Bartholomew Fair. The Square was noisome in two senses; as the local British paper, the *Register*, complained, "it is a dunghill and a lazar house, and a burial ground for poor native wretches who died of leprosy." In fact the British boat crews who had removed the debris left from the fire had unearthed three corpses.

Originally each great trading nation had a hong apiece, but now the only important ones were the British, American, and, well behind them, the Dutch, who had spilled over into the hongs left vacant by their unsuccessful competitors. Under the British aegis were Parsee firms which carried on the "country trade" from India, largely opium. The Americans had two firms apiece from Boston, Philadelphia, and New York, one of them called Zion's Corner. The founder of this firm, David Washington Cincinnatus Olyphant, was a pious soul who refused to deal in opium and who was about to import the first American missionaries.

Russell & Co. was housed in Suy Hong in the middle of the row, which had been entirely rebuilt since the fire. Like the rest, it was a series of houses built one behind the other. As a Russell partner William Low had a front room in Number One hong with a view of the river, but the juniors lived in the three rear houses facing only blank walls. However, the living and bed rooms were comfortable with carpets and furniture brought from home.

On the ground floor, behind a gate with a porter always on

duty, was the godown where goods were stored on wooden frames raised above the floor and protected against the white ants. At this unloading season the godown was rapidly filling up with sheetings and drills from the new mills in New England, piles of tin, iron, copper, and steel, and furs—not the old sea otter now, but seal, beaver, and fox. There was just enough sandalwood still coming from the almost depleted forests in the Sandwich Islands to give the godowns a touch of fragrance. Later, when the Chinese goods replaced the American, they would be redolent of spice and teas.

Every morning at dawn Mr. Low was awakened by the pandemonium of a general market below his windows, yelling hawkers, poultry cackling, dogs barking, specialists bawling their virtues as ear cleaners, shampooers, barbers, and Jolly Toenail Cutters. Some worthies carried in portable kitchens to cook meals on the spot, others came to entertain the throng with juggling, fortune-telling, or music in some heathen form. When the crowd around an entertainer got too thick he took a cord with a bullet tied to one end and whirled it around his head in ever widening circles, keeping his eyes closed because he disliked to see the people he hit.

Then there were countless beggars, organized in the Heavenly Flower Society with a thousand dues-paying members and countless hangers-on. They were especially active about four in the afternoon when the Fanqui took their constitutional in the Square. About this time the blind beggars would arrive, strung together in a long line, howling lugubriously while they beat sticks together, belabored iron pots, and generally made themselves so obnoxious that the Fanqui, as expected, bribed them to go away.

The Fanqui themselves were a motley crew, a few Americans and Europeans scattered among the Parsees, Persians, Armenians, Malays, Hindus, Moors, Turks, and Jews from the "country ships." The British snubbed everybody, even their own Parsees.

Before the Square was the Canton of the river, a permanent floating city of houseboats ranged in close rows like streets, and in the avenues between them the scurrying sampans, the great canal boats from the interior, the Cohong's big chopboats (called "watermelons" because of their rounded sides and decks), the ferries running to the island of Honam, the stately mandarin boats, gay with plumes of flags, the boats for barbers and vendors of food and toys, the quarterboats coming up from the foreign ships at Whampoa full of tars on their liberty day. From the flower boats, painted and bedizened like the girls inside, came the tin-, kling music of *kin* or *pepa* and the rattle of dice and wine cups, while beside them in the houseboats the evening taper was lighted before the joss image, and blazing tinsel paper was thrown into the river.

Behind the hongs lay the crowded, odorous city within its walls, ringed by a low amphitheater of hills. But Canton was not William Low's business; it was bewildering enough to trace the intricacies of trade and appraise the weight of the pyramid of powers piled upon it—which really meant upon the shoulders of the Cohong.

Over all was the Manchu Emperor Tao Kwang, a luxury-loving despot embedded in wives, concubines, nobles, and ancient tradition.

Next, there was the viceroy of the two provinces of Kwantung and Kwangsi, who lived fifty miles up the river and appeared during any crisis worthy of his attention.

Next there was "Chow Tuck," Governor Le, of Kwantung, the guardian dragon who watched every misstep of the Cohong and the foreign demons.

Always and everywhere there were the mandarins, officials high and low, who fished in every troubled pool and were unbelievably childish when they fancied their dignity was outraged.

Then there was the Hoppo, Collector of Customs, perhaps the most fantastic figure of all. He existed to tap the wealth flowing into Canton, to satisfy the pampered appetites of Emperor, Manchu nobility, and the imperial concubines and eunuchs. The Hoppo was always a Manchu but never a noble or freeman, as he might then display too much independence. Instead, he was chosen from the Boyi, the hereditary bondsmen of the imperial family.

35

In Canton, however, he was outranked only by the governor and the viceroy. His authority was necessary for his task of squeezing the Cohong and commerce in general. The standing joke about the Hoppo, appointed like most Chinese officials for a three-year term, was that it took his first year's winnings to pay for his office, the second year's to keep it, and the third to amass enough to buy his way back to private life with a thumping big fortune. He took in every year ten times what the official customs receipts indicated.

His inspectors, posted in chophouses near the hongs, were supposed to tax every boatload of goods entering or leaving Canton. They could get more for the Hoppo and themselves by accepting informal presents from the shippers. Even a fat bribe was cheaper than the duty, for instance, on a boatload of precious silks. Thus the Hoppo was able to milk the foreign trade to an extent far beyond anything known in the world of commerce.

At Russell & Co. there were high hopes of the new Hoppo, Chung Tseang. While they understood the giant, even imperial, squeeze to which he was subjected, they hoped he would bring about needed reforms and increase the number of the Cohong, depleted by the recent bankruptcy of two members. Not that it was easy to persuade a rich merchant to join the Cohong. Chung's predecessor had been forced to use torture to bring in a new member, and then he had been released after an appeal to Governor Le.

"Why don't merchants want to join the Cohong?" William Low asked the juniors at dinner one day. "Isn't there a fortune in it?"

"Certainly there is," said Charles Talbot. "But consider the squeeze, Mr. Low. Take Houqua. He was a very rich young man when he started in this business nearly forty years ago. I suppose he paid a quarter of a million for his seat in the Cohong. A while ago he bought Houqua, Jr., the rank of mandarin to the tune of a hundred thousand taels."

"And a tael is a dollar and sixty-six cents. That's a lot of money."

"A whopping amount. But that's only the beginning. Whatever

36

happens in the Flowery Kingdom, Houqua must bear the brunt. Every time the Hwang Ho floods it costs him personally about a hundred thousand dollars. He was fined three times that when pirates boarded an English ship down the river, and six hundred thousand dollars when there was a rebellion in Kashgar.

"Now there's a new Hoppo. First he taps each hong merchant for two thousand taels to buy a pearl for the cap of his infant grandson. Next his birthday is around the corner, and that will mean about ten thousand taels apiece from the Cohong. And after that he'll simply milk the hong merchants, on one pretext or another. They have to stand security for the foreign ships, and of course somebody is always breaking the rules. Houqua is the richest, and he detests wrangles, so he's the easiest target. He'd like to resign, but God help us all if he succeeds, Mr. Low. The China trade would be in rags."

Wu Ping-ch'ien, whose business name was Houqua, was a man of peace. For many years he had been the Company's chief hong merchant, and every year this relation had bred more complications for him. The British were restless and rebellious, they were forever creating incidents which Houqua could not conceal from the authorities, since the English were extremely conspicuous in their displays of bad temper. The Cohong, and Houqua especially, paid for these displays; theirs was a role of vicarious atonement. The hong merchants might be deprived of their mandarin rank or banished to Tartary for their own sins, of which bankruptcy was the unforgivable one. But if a Fanqui misbehaved, the authorities might imprison his hong merchant's relatives, put them to the torture, or strangle them to death.

Where was all this leading? Was the day coming when there would be a fatal clash between the English and the Chinese? Houqua watched; his aristocratic mind, kept free of small distractions, appraised the deeper currents. His maneuvers were far too subtle to attract notice, and only in the end was it plain that his strategy for saving China from grave trouble was to build up the Americans as an equipoise to the British.

He also liked the Americans for their own sakes.

William Low was fascinated by his first encounter with Houqua. He had heard about the famous chops of congo, grown on Houqua's ancestral estates in Fukien; about the fabulous gardens and palaces of his home across the river on Honam; about his princely generosity to his friends.

"You and I belong Number One olo flen," he had told a bankrupt American heavily in his debt, as he gently tore his note across.

Mr. Low had heard many tales of Houqua's shrewdness in driving a bargain or seeing a chance for a profit. He knew that three hundred coolies were kept busy in Houqua's hong at the west end of the row, and many more in his warehouse on Honam.

Expecting a rather overpowering creature, he saw instead a frail man of sixty, his bald skull tapering to a narrow chin which bore a wisp of goatee. He had the face of a medieval monk and the great somber eyes of a poet. It was a wonderful face, and whenever the Macao portraitest, George Chinnery, painted it he must have gloated over the opportunity El Greco had missed.

Houqua, who gave away fortunes all his life and still died richer than John Jacob Astor, was an ascetic Kublai Khan. His personal habits were simple and even frugal; there was no ostentation about his business establishment; if his dress was rich, that was prescribed by his mandarin rank. Over his brocade robe he wore a dark gown lined with white silk, with flowing sleeves folded back from his exquisite hands and a square embroidered panel across the front. He wore long chains of precious jade, and white-soled shoes turned up at the toes. His cap was topped by a blue button, symbol of his rank and the barometer of Fanqui behavior; if there was serious trouble he would be "unbuttoned" and in disgrace.

A few days after this chin-chin, Houqua sent a houseboat to bring Mr. Low and various other guests to dine with him at his villa on Honam Island, where several of the wealthiest Cantonese lived. Here was a blending of simplicity with the artifice of Xanadu, of order and airiness with the jewel-box richness of houses and gardens set within a five-acre space on the river. All

38

South China had this air of happy contrivance; there was formality even in the landscape, the hills looked sculptured, the rivers looked like canals, the trees like anything the gardener fancied, clipped and pruned in a thousand shapes.

Houqua's establishment was walled around with sun-baked brick, and the river was let in to wander through the gardens in little streams and toy waterfalls and ponds paved with lilies, ending in a wide tidal pool before the main house, where mandarin ducks and swans and ibises played. Houqua showed his guests through the principal house: marble floors covered with silk and velvet carpets, columns of marble and the native light gray granite, furniture of the finest japanned work, libraries with shelves of scrolls, incense burners, bronzes, porcelains, paintings —yet nothing too much. Scattered through the grounds were houses, pavilions, and courtyards, temples and shrines.

He enjoyed most leading the way through his famous gardens, an intricate mosaic of waterways with light bamboo bridges, marble benches, and parapets bearing potted flowers and shrubs in bloom, the chrysanthemums now at their peak and arranged in pyramids of color, for the Chinese liked to pot their flowers so they could shift and group them at will. It was all a picture that changed slowly with the falling light, that moved with the stately pace of a peacock along a mossy stream.

Within the walls was the hidden life of Cathay, the jewellike women enclosed in airy little palaces, the enameled birds drifting on the ponds, time itself moving gently. Hour after hour their banquet moved through thirty courses as the Fanqui watched the light change on the tidal pond and sampled plovers' eggs and bêche-de-mer and drank green-pea wine from tiny silver cups. Until Houqua, in a jovial mood, proposed the final toast:

"Catchee one tousand per cent plofit. Ayah!"

Dinner at the Factory was a revelation of another sort to William Low. It was a tall building at the east end of the row with a pediment proclaiming: *"Pro Regis et Senatus Angliae,"* and recently, in defiance of the mandarins, fenced off from the Square. Mr. Low climbed the broad stone steps past the chapel where young Mr. Vachell held his services, up to the long book-lined library.

The famous dining room opened on a terrace overlooking the river. At one end was a portrait of King George IV, at the other one of Lord Amherst, the unhappy reminders of the British attempt several years before to open diplomatic relations with the Son of Heaven. Amherst's embassy to Peking had begun with a serious blunder in court etiquette, and ended just there. The Factory had inherited the King's portrait intended for the Emperor.

Guests were expected to bring their personal servants to a Company dinner; there must be a man behind each chair. William Low's boy was waiting with the Factory servants at the far end of the room and when everybody was seated he took his stand behind his master. The illumination was as lavish as the service: myriads of wax candles burned in the chandeliers and silver candelabra were spaced down the long table. It was all very heavy; catties and taels of food, pounds of silver plate.

The sheer weight of silver and beef was lightened by the music of a band borrowed from an Indiaman down the river, by madeira shipped around the world to mellow, and finally by the jokes that came with the Manila cheroots and port. The jokes, being British, male, and concerned with the peccadilloes of the colony, were not always light.

However, William Low felt at home with the British, being rather English himself in his love of decorum and his matter-of-fact view of the world. He got on well with the chief, Mr. William Baynes; at least they could agree in enjoying rather indifferent health. If he had known more of the real pitfalls in the China trade, he would have been disturbed at the highhanded course Mr. Baynes was taking with the Chinese.

"This antiquated, heathenish, preposterous system is going to blow up one of these days," he said. "It's all based on the silly pride of the mandarins. They resent us because by now they know we're greater gentlemen than they are. But they must keep up the pretense that we're uncouth barbarians, so they forbid us to have sedan chairs or Chinese servants."

William Low smiled. "But we have plenty of both, Mr. Baynes."

"Yes, we've set them in their place on that score. But we're still prisoners, Mr. Low. We can't go about the city, or sail for pleasure on the river, or make a move in any direction, without a linguist along, like a blasted nursery governess. Linguist, indeed! They know nothing but pidgin, they're spies and snoops and a confounded nuisance. As for the iniquitous notion that they're going to keep our wives out of Canton much longer——"

"Now there," said William Low, "you've brought up a most interesting subject."

At Suy Hong the old hands assured William Low that Mr. Baynes was creating most of his own troubles. They insisted that there was no more delightful place on earth to trade than Canton. True, the mechanism was complicated, but the highly trained servants of the Cohong took care of all details.

"The hong merchants relieve us from all the drudgery," they said, "and they're buffers between us and the officials. As long as we behave ourselves, everything's as smooth as wax. The Consoo House exists mostly to iron out troubles with the Factory."

Consoo House, headquarters of the Cohong, was a handsome building on Old China Street, the empire's coronary artery of foreign trade. It had many suites for business conversations with the Fanqui, and when anything critical came up the Cohong invited the taipans, the chiefs of the foreign houses, to a formal conference in the main hall.

Mr. Low could see the dignity and order expressed in Consoo House, and the vigilance with which the Fanqui were guarded. Strictly speaking, the Chinese were not obliged to protect the merchants, since they were in China at their own risk and had no diplomats or accredited consuls. But the Fanqui were assured the most careful protection. A guardhouse with a dozen Chinese soldiers stood at the rear corner of the American hong and Old China Street, partly to see that the Fanqui did not stray off their premises, but mainly to keep them safe. All the streets back in the city were closed at night by wickets at the end of each block with a watchman on duty.

Fires were a constant menace, and it was literally true that the Chinese were more careful of Fanqui property than of their own. More than once the hong merchants had sent armed coolies to a Fanqui hong threatened by fire, to carry papers and valuables to boats and then stand guard over them. One of John Cushing's stories concerned Yee-shing, an independent merchant licensed by the Cohong to sell silks to the foreigners. In the great fire of 1822 Yee-shing had in his shop waiting to be dyed fifty thousand dollars' worth of crapes belonging to Cushing. He let the fire destroy his house and all his own property while he saved Cushing's silks—and then was apologetic because a fraction of them had been burned.

Within Suy Hong there was the same security. The house comprador, Ah-kee, square and powerful as a wrestler and noonday honest, had all the keys. But keys and safes were superfluous, even at this season when the godowns were full of porters bringing in the green hysons and the black boheas, souchongs, and congos. The Chinese were determined to keep the Fanqui and their property safe.

Where else on earth could a young merchant find a system like this? You worked hard for a few months in the winter, and then were required by law to go to Macao for a long summer vacation. A few years of this, and you went home with a competence, perhaps a fortune. Meanwhile, you were housed and fed luxuriously, you never had to hang up a garment or light your own cheroot. You dressed as carelessly as you liked, and swore when you felt like it, and could get drunk every night if your liver held out, because there were no ladies to reckon with.

Where else on earth would a merchant be invited to a banquet like one of Chinqua's or Puankeiqua's? Their colleague Houqua's little thirty-course dinners were monastic by comparison. Puankeiqua was apt to hire an entire company of actors, along with an orchestra, to present any play you chose in an outdoor pavilion. Chinqua's singsongs lasted as long as the dinner, that is, from three in the afternoon until ten, a combined circus, pageant, and theater.

The fat and jovial Chinqua loved variety in his feasts. He

offered his guests English, French, and Chinese dishes, and each course was served on a different set of priceless ware. After the three dessert courses the white tablecloths were removed and scented flowers were strewn on the polished tables. Meanwhile actors, jugglers, tumblers, and musicians had been presenting several short plays. Then there was a pageant of mandarins, warriors, elephants, tigers, and children dressed as birds, then heroic battle scenes and duels between monsters and demons, with drums, gongs, and cymbals crashing. Then boys came on dressed as mandarin ladies attended by maids carrying their bandboxes, parasols, and wraps, and you could hear the real ladies of the house giggling softly behind their screen of latticework.

The women? What were they like? If you were a very young man at Suy Hong you would think about them on sultry nights, listening to the tap-tap of bamboo canes as the night guard marked the half hour, to a crying child out on the river, to the muted laughter from the flower boats. Yes, you could imagine what the boat girls were like, little white swans behind their gaily painted screens, priestesses of exotic rites. There were men who had smuggled river girls ashore and into the hongs, and they told a little, and yet perhaps too much.

But the wives and young concubines of the mandarins and merchants were really mysterious. You caught glimpses of them sometimes, swaying on their little feet like spicy carnations, nodding, bowing, giggling softly, making eyes behind their fans. They were positively not for you, and you didn't even want them. What would you do with a highborn Chinese lady? You could no more read her than you could read an ancient scroll. Scented, painted, lovely creatures, you thought about them when you were sick of the smell of matting around the boxes of tea. But not too much; you were here in an enclave, you weren't really in China at all.

3

Wicked

Innovation

In spite of her resolve not to be influenced by the Company ladies or, as she put it, "to vie with them in anything but good conduct," Harriet absorbed their attitude toward the Chinese. They were a necessary evil, quaint and amusing when they obliged you, despicable when they did not. To Harriet the most disobliging thing about the Chinese was their ban on Fanqui women, classed as lethal weapons.

"Neither women, guns, spears, nor arms of any kind can be brought to the factories," said the ancient edict.

Harriet decided to break it down. She had only a faint notion of the size of China or the strength of its traditions, but she set to work to clear up its misunderstanding of fair ladies.

Soon after her arrival Mouqua, second in the Cohong, came down to Macao and made a Sabbath call on the Low ladies.

Harriet knew that the Cohong did not use their honorable names in the low pursuit of business but adopted trade names, usually ending in *qua*, which meant "sir." But she called him Mr. Mouqua, and cutting short the preliminary compliments, got down to her crusade.

"Why you no let ladies go along Canton?" she ventured in her shaky pidgin.

"Too muchy men want to look," said Mouqua, emphasizing the compliment with a bow.

When Harriet persisted, the merchant displayed his knowledge of foreign devil women, who had the horrid habit of taking exercise.

"Canton too small, no walky," he said blandly.

She fared little better at a dinner party later for four members of the Cohong, managing to insult the venerable Chinqua by assuring him he didn't look a day over thirty-five. In oblique fashion he returned her shock for shock, discussing his five wives. "Number One I no likee," he said. "Too muchy ugly."

That sounded like Mr. George Chinnery. After years in India the great portraitest had deserted his debts there because they bored him, and his wife, as he loved to explain, because she was too hideous to abide. She had once pursued him to Macao, but he had taken refuge in Canton, thanking a merciful providence for the ban on women which preserved him from having to look at her ever again.

"It's horrible enough," he said, "looking at my own face when I shave."

Mr. Chinnery was indeed a fascinatingly ugly man with the sort of face, Harriet decided, to go along with his droll stories. A prodigious eater, he drank nothing but tea, and that cold by preference. He had the great virtue of being a fixture in Macao, like Dr. Colledge.

The Company kept the senior surgeon in Canton, and paid Thomas Colledge, who was thirty-four, the fat salary of a thousand sterling to look after the health of the Macaons. He was also given an allowance which enabled him to expand his ophthalmic clinic for poor Chinese and save thousands of them from blindness.

Another non-migratory gentleman was the wealthy bachelor, James P. Sturgis, Mr. Russell's partner in the Manila firm. He belonged to the Boston clan of Cushing, Perkins, and Forbes, the greatest family constellation in China. Like his cousin John Cushing, he was a recluse. But one day he astonished himself by calling at the Low villa.

"I have lived in Macao for twenty years," he anounced to Mrs. Low, "and this is the first call I have ever made on a lady."

He promptly went back into his shell, but they were to see a great deal of him later.

Harriet managed to fill her days. She studied Spanish and French, and read improving books. She developed friendships with several of the English ladies, and taught them the harmless game of Old Maid as a diversion from their endless whist and loo. There were picnics at Casilla's Bay and sails to the little islands near the city. She wrote her sister that she was plump, and more like "the frigate" than ever, but perhaps that was the enormous cushioned sleeves that were all the rage that year. She kept expecting that Abbot would come out to China, but he was too busy helping their father get established in New York.

The British took Christmas more seriously than the Yankees, and many of the men, including Mr. Vachell, came down for a holiday that stretched into February. She and Aunt were invited to Christmas dinner at the beautiful Factory on the Praya Grande.

"These dinners are amazing stiff," she wrote Mary Ann, "but I shall rig myself in a white satin under-dress, with a wrought muslin petticoat, and a pink satin bodice to set neatly to my neat little form, and made by my own neat little hands."

She sat next Mr. Vachell; somehow the Company hostesses were always putting them together. He called often to take her walking, always providing an escort for Mrs. Low. One windy day they climbed a hill, "where, I am sure," she told her sister, "it would have been much more safe to scud than to go as we did with royals and studding sails set. Although I kept crying 'Stand by topgallant halyards!' it was of no avail. We were beating

46

against the wind and, when we were at the height of the hill, my dress tangled around Mr. V.'s legs, and in trying to extricate himself, he caught his foot in the trimming, which came very near throwing both of us over the precipice into the sea. But after much labor we weathered the gale."

In three years the Company's charter in China would be renewed by Act of Parliament—or else rescinded. Never before had the Factory worried about losing its monopoly of the China trade. But there was criticism at home about the perpetual wrangles which stemmed from Mr. Baynes's bellicose policies, and pressure at home from shippers and merchants who wanted the Company's hold broken.

In this period of uncertainty and strain Mr. Baynes went back to Canton in February, taking his wife and children with him. Before this shocking act of defiance embroiled the higher official circles the Cohong quietly threatened a trade embargo, and Mrs. Baynes, and two other Company ladies who had followed her to the forbidden city, returned to Macao, where the air, they said, was purer.

Mrs. Baynes assured Harriet that Canton was much better than she had expected. Naturally, the Chinese were tremendously excited at their first glimpse of female Fanqui. Enterprising Cantonese had stationed boats near the Factory and charged all comers three cash for a look. When the ladies took their exercise in the Square immense crowds gathered, but they had been most respectful, retreating to either side as the ladies advanced, and merely voicing what Mrs. Baynes described as a buzz of admiration. The Fanqui never dreamed how revolting they appeared to the Chinese.

Harriet would have been tortured with envy at all this but for the excitement of moving to the new house up near the Portuguese cathedral. It was cooler and more elegant than their old villa, and so high that from the big terrace at the back they could see the whole sweep of the Macao Roads.

They were settled in their vast high-domed rooms by April, when Mr. Low at last came down, bringing "Uncle Russell" as guest. One day Mr. Russell called Harriet to the terrace to see a remarkable sight, the first steamship in Chinese waters. It was the English steamer *Forbes*, towing the lovely opium clipper *Jamesina* from Calcutta to the storeships at Lintin Island.

"Steam towing sail," Harriet marveled. "How very odd!"

"They're dangerous contraptions," said Mr. Russell. "Every now and then they blow up. A passing fad, in my opinion."

And so most Americans were to think, for a long time to come. The British, bolstered by their Navigation Acts which protected them from foreign competition, were remarkably slow to evolve good sailing ships—except for their opium fleet. Now they were getting interested in steam and experimenting with it in the lucrative opium traffic. They were selling about twelve million dollars' worth of the drug to Chinese smugglers every year, a good deal more than half their total imports. The Americans sold less than a million dollars' worth in 1830, most of it Turkish, which they often dropped at Singapore for the British to pick up and smuggle.

Nobody worried about the imperial decrees banning the opium traffic because too many Chinese high and low were in the game.

John Cushing had been taking a holiday in Europe when he received word of the death of his cousin Thomas Forbes. At once he wrote to Boston inviting the younger Forbes brothers, Robert and John, to go out to Canton, along with the seasoned merchant and sea captain, Augustine Heard. The three of them arrived about the time Cushing himself was back in Canton, and for weeks the Yankee taipans were in a ferment of reorganizing. The house of Perkins was liquidated, and its interests merged with Russell & Co., which now had as partners Mr. Russell, William Low, and Augustine Heard.

As for the charming Forbes brothers, Mr. Cushing put John, a boy still in his teens, in the new company as clerk, with a partnership promised in four years. Robert Bennet Forbes, his older brother, begged off from life in a countinghouse. "Black Ben," whose very dark hair was to go gray by the time he was thirty, was a salt-water man. At thirteen he had sailed to China before

ABOVE, The Praya Grande at Macao. Painting by a Chinese artist. BELOW, The Foreign Hongs in Canton. Painting by a Chinese artist. *Courtesy of the Peabody Museum.*

Wu Ping-ch'ien (Houqua). Portrait by George Chinnery.
Courtesy of Mr. Frederic Delano. Photograph by The
Metropolitan Museum of Art.

the mast in a Perkins ship, at twenty he had commanded another in a voyage around the world. He had just arrived on the new barque *Lintin*, which his Perkins uncles had built for use as a storeship off Macao. It was finally agreed that he should take charge of the barque, and he spent the next two years anchored at Lintin Island.

While the Americans were busy setting up the enlarged company, the British continued their defiance of the sacred traditions. Mr. Baynes came up to Canton for the fall season, and again his wife was with him. Now the viceroy intervened and had Mouqua on the carpet. Mouqua explained that Mr. Baynes was very ill, and his wife had come up to take care of him. Both knew this was false, as Mr. Baynes was extremely in evidence, but it saved official face for the moment.

Then Mrs. Turner arrived. Mouqua was again summoned, his precious button trembling on his cap. As he told the Lows later, he did his best, explaining to the viceroy that Mrs. Turner was Mr. Baynes's cousin and, ill as he was, "he wanchy too much to see he." That was brave, considering that former members of the Cohong were now in Tartary for much lighter crimes than admitting Fanqui women.

The viceroy now issued a mandate to the Cohong to expel the females, "or hereafter there will be a confused bustle and worse imitation, which will be a great and wicked innovation on the laws and regulations of the Celestial Empire." He ordered them also to stop the foreigners using sedan chairs: "they must all, as of old, walk on foot—they must not overstep their station." He ended with a threat to degrade and punish the hong merchants without mercy if this order was not carried out.

The British were furious enough at this, but even more at the viceroy's proclamation posted on the Factory walls. Every year with the new teas there was such a proclamation, reiterating the ban against the Fanqui being allowed women, sedan chairs, and Chinese servants. But this chop also accused the Cohong of pandering to the British, bringing them young boys in the guise of servants, and procuring for them prostitutes from the flower boats.

The hong merchants and linguists, said the chop, "ought continually to instruct and direct the foreigners to repress their pride and profligacy, and to insist on causing them to turn, with all their hearts, towards renovation, that both parties may enjoy the repose of gladness and of gain." It ended sternly, "Let everybody yield a trembling obedience."

The Cohong had reason to tremble. One of them, Goqua, was at that moment being persecuted by the Hoppo because he had been caught smuggling opium, but especially because he was resisting the Hoppo's demand for a present of ten thousand dollars. The British tried to help him, but when the mandarins discovered that Goqua's uncle Woo-yay had procured a sedan chair for an Englishman—and a green one, the color allowed only to grandees —they imprisoned and tortured the old man, and threatened to strangle him. Goqua could not ransom him at any price, and finally Woo-yay poisoned himself in prison.

There was a spate of British protests at the insults loaded upon them, but soon affairs went beyond the stage of verbal warfare. There was a murder in the hongs. The captain of a Dutch ship got into a quarrel one night with three Parsee servants of his hong, and they beat him to death. The Fanqui tried to settle this matter themselves and after holding an inquest delivered the Parsees to the British, who locked them up in the Factory. The viceroy at once demanded that the murderers be surrendered to him. He also ordered the ladies to leave within three days, or he would send soldiers to seize them.

Thereupon the British flouted another sacred rule. They sent down to Whampoa for a hundred armed marines and two quarterdeck cannon, which they placed at the Factory gates. It was now a powder magazine holding two ladies, three murderers, and a hundred soldiers.

The Chinese art of accommodation which had kept trade going for centuries now came into play. Governor Le backed down and said the officials had been too hasty. The British managed to smuggle the Parsees out to the authorities in Bombay, but the forbidden ladies remained with the forbidden redcoats to guard them.

At this tense moment William Low decided to make a dangerous move and bring his own ladies up to Canton. Mouqua was in favor of it, admitting that the officials would not listen to reason and must be bullied. He promised that if the Low ladies arrived the Cohong would "shutty eye and shutty ear."

A delicate matter of commercial diplomacy was involved. Russell & Co. had now emerged as a powerful rival to the Factory; a show of solidarity with the British would be a tactful move. Moreover, it would be a big step forward if the new regime could be inaugurated with a blasting of Old Custom.

Mr. Cushing lent Mr. Low his little brig *Terrier* to go down and bring the first American women to China, and on November 5, after hasty packing, they scrambled aboard in Macao Roads. There was a cold piercing wind dead ahead from the north, and the ladies began to droop.

"I'm not seasick," Harriet insisted. "But I wish, if Britannia rules the waves, she'd rule 'em straighter."

Beating against the wind, it was two in the afternoon when they reached Lintin Island, where fifteen opium smugglers were at anchor. It was Harriet's first sight of Lintin, whose high peak protected ships from the northeast monsoon. Auctioned off in the Company's godowns in Bombay and Calcutta, the opium chests were brought here by the elegant barque-rigged vessels, *Sylph*, *Water Witch*, *Jamesina*, *Red Rover*, and the fine Parsee, *The Cowasjee Family*. They unloaded to the storeships, and then the chests were taken by the smugglers, called "centipedes" because of their fifty oars, for fast delivery up the China coast. There was an amicable arrangement between the authorities and the "smug boats," and often the mandarin junks themselves undertook delivery. The system was disrupted when new Chinese officials came into the picture, especially at New Year's, and fresh bargains had to be arranged.

The Lows found their old friend the *Sumatra* at anchor, and Captain Roundy lent them a longboat with four seamen to go along in tow, in case the wind failed and they had to row up the river. Waiting at Lintin till the tide turned at ten, Harriet went below to the luxurious little cabin she shared with her aunt, and found herself in her first battle with the Flowery Kingdom. Regiments, battalions, of cockroaches were waiting for her. She couldn't bear to crawl into her berth behind the red silk curtains, so lay down on the transom across the sternpost. Aunt Abigail came in, philosophically draped herself in the mosquito curtains, and stretched out on the floor. Harriet considered this a brilliant solution and wished there were room for two. The *Terrier* was beating up the river, and every time the brig tacked, Harriet had to tack with it. It was a long time till daylight.

By then they were anchored a safe distance below Bocca Tigris, the military gateway to South China, guarded by forts on either side. Here they were to transfer to the opium schooner *Sylph*, and disguised their feminine silhouettes in men's long velvet cloaks and wore velvet caps instead of their bonnets. This picaresque touch helped make up for the cockroaches.

It was dark by the time they reached Whampoa, and Harriet could just see the outlines of many ships at anchor, but soon the moon came up and she stayed on deck, entranced by the pagodas and then by the sleeping village of the river boats. They landed after midnight, still muffled in their men's cloaks.

"Now I can walk directly to the factory," Harriet announced, and indeed she knew the American hong so well from descriptions that she walked straight to the door. The porter opened, and for the first time she was under a Chinese roof.

Young William Hunter was about Abbot Low's age. He had come out to China at thirteen and was the first American to master Chinese. A junior purser and interpreter for Russell & Co., he was too young and obscure to receive more than sisterly attention from Harriet. That left him free to record the impact of the female invasion with a degree of asperity.

"What will Canton turn into, and where will the bachelors find rest? Nowhere," he confided to his journal a few days after the midnight occupation of Suy Hong. "The second day after they arrived several old codgers were seen in immense coats, which had been stowed away in camphor trunks for ten or fifteen years, and with huge cravats on, and with what once were gloves, on their way to make visits!"

But the next day Hunter himself paid his respects and found the ladies holding a perpetual salon in their front rooms of Suy Hong, quite transformed by the domestic trifles they had brought along from Macao. The British called, emphasizing the entente cordiale. Mr. Vachell was frequently in attendance.

And Mouqua arrived, with the profound hope that if he explained the situation he might after all save his button. He recounted his conversations with the viceroy about Mr. Baynes's severe illness that required the presence of the British ladies.

"But now," he sighed, "I can no talky sick any more. Now I know not what talky."

That should have warned them, but they were horrified when on November 14, ten days after their arrival, an official chop was issued, saying that trade would be stopped "if one Low did not immediately remove his family to Macao."

"These despicable Chinese aren't worth our notice," Harriet stormed.

But the Chinese were adroit. The threatened embargo was not on all American trade, but on Russell & Co., at the busiest time of the year. No daughter of a merchant family could fail to see the deadly import of this threat.

"I suppose we shall have to budge," she admitted. "But they are letting the English ladies stay, because the British are a body and can threaten the Chinese. Now we shall have to go back to Macao while Mrs. Baynes and Mrs. Turner stay here and enjoy themselves. Why don't they forbid all ladies, not just us?"

"They do, and always have," her uncle reminded her. "The Chinese know what they're about. They don't want to start a war with England. Remember how Governor Le backed down when the Factory brought up the marines?"

There was no answer to this that Harriet could make aloud. Those gallant tars guarding her friends in the Factory! The Americans had no marines to bring up from Whampoa; she and Aunt were decidedly in a second-rate position. Not that she wanted bloodshed . . .

53

"We're not sure," Mr. Low said, "that this chop comes from the viceroy. Possibly it is a little forgery by the Cohong, a move to scare us just enough to send you home, without kicking up any official dust."

For a day or two neither side made a move, while Harriet brooded over the disappointing tendency of the situation to flatten out. One of the Yankees tried to comfort her.

"Think of the *éclat* you'll have, Miss Low, if the trade of the vast Celestial Empire is stopped on your account!"

"But I don't want the Russell trade stopped."

That was the worst of it. If the viceroy had threatened a general embargo against American trade all the gallant youths would have ringed Suy Hong, not, alas, in beautiful scarlet coats like Mrs. Baynes's marines, but at any rate a personal guard of honor.

Word seeped through from the Cohong that it would be wise for Mr. Low to announce the date of his ladies' departure. And then, if they were not ready to leave, "putty off a little, that have mandarin fashion."

They learned to procrastinate mandarin fashion, sitting on an active volcano, keeping their salon alive at the expense of a certain strain on the men. One night Hunter's roommate came back from a call on the ladies, ripped off coat, gloves, and cravat, called for his comfortable jacket and neck ribbon, lighted a cheroot, and sighed, "Thank God that is over!" And when Hunter returned from a bachelor dinner, rather haphazard in tracking down his room in one of the back hongs, his first prayer on awakening was that the ladies had not observed his wild careenings.

Harriet's reports to Mary Ann were in a sweetly unconscious vein. "About dark it grew rather cool," she wrote of November 26, "and a fire was proposed; and you have no idea how cozy we looked, with our carpets down and a blazing coal fire. Our circle round the 'wee bit ingle' was composed of Aunt, Uncle, Messrs. Russell, Heard, Latimer, and Blight and my own dear self. After a social cup of tea, Mr. Russell left us for the office, and shortly came back with budgets of news. The *Ann Amelia* had arrived from England, bringing Mr. Majoribanks and others, to supersede Mr. Baynes and his assistants. So they are turned out. . . ."

The Company directors at home had seen the perils in Mr. Baynes's mailed-fist policies, and the new regime was to ease the situation considerably. After the Americans had digested the news the whole party ventured out for a walk in the moonlight in front of the hongs, then to the streets in the rear. The Chinese called for torches so that they could see the Fanqui women, and then followed them into the Square. At once the marines took over and dispersed the mob, which had been perfectly well behaved. Still, the evening was a high point of the Canton adventure.

A day or so later Mr. Low took his ladies back to Macao. The grateful Cohong gave them a chopboat for the journey, and the entire American colony took boats and escorted them as far as Jackass Point. That done, one crusty old bachelor sighed, "I hope we shall never be bothered with ladies in Canton again."

So did the Son of Heaven. The matter had gone up to the Emperor himself, and a chop was posted in Canton:

"And if the foreign boats again bring up foreign women, I have ordered naval officers immediately to stop, seize and conduct them back to Macao, and if they with presumptuous barbarism oppose, instantly to open their guns and make a thundering attack on them."

Having called down the wrath of Tao Kwang, Harriet was glad to be back in Macao. Three weeks of Canton was delightful, she wrote her sister, "but to be constantly subject, morning, noon and night, to visits from people we care nothing about, but are obliged to treat civilly, I assure you, fond as I am of society and company, it was too much for me."

Besides, a most amusing young man had just arrived from Philadelphia.

4

Tribe

of

Seth

Seth Low was prospering in New York. In his wholesale house on Fletcher Street he built up his business of importing myrrh and aloes from Africa, musk in pods, gum benzoin, peppers, asafetida, Bombay arrowroot, Mocha gum arabic, a profitable and odorous assortment. Abbot was proving himself as a born merchant, and Mr. Low was soon to take in as second partner Mary Ann's fiancé, George Archer.

For all his conservatism Seth Low could smell a wind before most people, and therefore he settled his family in Brooklyn Heights across the East River. It had as many pigs rooting in the rich mire of the streets as Manhattan itself, but was slowly acquiring a tone, and within another decade was to become the home of many important merchants. Already several ferry lines ministered to Brooklyn, and the new Fulton Market near by was patronized by the commuters.

Starting with a comfortable three-story house on Nassau Street, Mr. Low was a pioneer in developing the choicest section of Brooklyn. One of his earliest investments was building up two blocks on Concord and Washington streets, with two houses to the block, and back of them a large school, Classical Hall, for boys of the better families. Always faithful to Salem, Mr. Low imported Messrs. Eames and Putnam as schoolmasters.

They had their problems with his youngest son, who displayed ingenuity and leadership in the pursuit of mischief. Charles commanded the infants of Classical Hall in their standing feuds with two other schools in the neighborhood. A rosy boy with bright blue eyes and rollicking good humor, he would come home from a hand-to-hand engagement to be patched up by his adoring mother and grandmother, who seldom remembered to report Charlie's sins when his father came home. Many of them were concealed from the entire family, for when Mr. Putnam locked him up in the hat room to ponder his wickedness, Charles learned to unscrew the hasp of the lock and go home for dinner and then lock himself in again.

When Mr. Low took stock of his seven sons, Charles was always the puzzle. In animal spirits and sturdiness he was a little outside the family pattern. It was plain from the start that he had inherited the essence of Gloucester and Salem. He was like Seth Low's brother James, who had run away to sea at ten and was now a captain. Charles would bear watching.

Abbot represented balm and hope; he was, as a personality, the most successful of the family. He had an instinctive moderation, and yet he was lightning-quick to see an opportunity and fearless in leaping ahead. Seth Low sometimes thought that Abbot could make a fine career in public life with his persuasive, melodious voice, his gifts for strategy and swift sound judgment. But Abbot was not interested in politics. It was his father who paced the floor, furiously snapping his fingers at President Jackson's notions.

No, Abbot was clearly meant for a brilliant career in business, and Josiah, now ten, had much the same steady industry. Josiah was the droll one of the family, always making them laugh, but Mr. Low could see he was going to grow up like Abbot.

The sons between—Seth Haskell, William, Edward, and Francis —presented problems. Twelve-year-old Francis was far from robust, he was a health problem. The older trio were dashing, high-spirited, and inclined to take life joyously. Mr. Low and Abbot took much pains guiding these young blades in the sober ways of business.

Not that the lower tip of Manhattan was at all a dull place during the thirties. The port was being transformed by the fresh blood coming down from New England. The old days of the Huguenots, the LeRoys, Bayards, and Rays, were giving way to the era of the shrewd, dynamic Yankee. Junius Spencer Morgan had come down from Hartford to start his banking business. Jonathan Goodhue, of Salem, the Minturns, Grinnells, and Stevenses were making things hum.

In the China trade, which the Lows now watched closely, there was a growing activity. The chief houses were a branch of the pious Olyphants, the Griswolds, and Howland & Aspinwall. The Griswolds had arrived some time before from Old Lyme, Connecticut, and were the tea specialists. Their house was called Great Gain and No Loss Griswolds from the initials of its heads, George and Nathaniel L. For no definite reason N. L. Griswold wore a slouch hat in frontier style, which made him conspicuous in this age when merchants wore high silk hats and closely buttoned frock coats.

The Griswolds had good ships and good captains, driving both hard. By accident they hit upon a merchandising trick which they exploited to the limit. Their tea chests from China bore the firm name and the name of the ship that brought them, and an early consignment of teas on the *Panama* happened to be so excellent that "Panama teas" became a byword in the retail stores. The Griswolds were to have three successive ships with the magic name.

The house of Howland & Aspinwall was less rugged in style and its heads were important in society. The Howlands were a *Mayflower* family allied with the powerful Bayards, who were still leading in the Indian and spice island trade, importing their Calcutta cloths, sooty or frocketsay romals, beerboom gurrahs, and gauzipore baftas, prized by ladies of fashion. Now in the South American trade with occasional ships to Canton, Howland & Aspinwall were one day to become the chief competitors of the Low brothers.

Grinnell, Minturn was coming up as a shipping firm to succeed the house of Fish & Grinnell, still dominated by Preserved Fish, one of the oddest characters of the merchant world. His fantastic name, inherited from his Huguenot father, was the source of many a tale. A revenue cutter once hailed him at sea.

"What's the name of that brig?" called the officer.

"Flying Fish."

"What's your cargo?"

"Pickled fish."

"Who's your captain?"

"Preserved Fish."

The officer boarded the brig ready to commit murder, but found he had a story to last him a lifetime.

Downtown New York was accumulating its folklore, but often when Abbot walked along the cluttered waterfront where the canawlers and coasters and China traders unloaded, he could feel mightier days coming for the port of New York, and for himself, too.

Young Mr. William Wightman Wood, who arrived in Macao soon after Harriet's return from Canton, provided just the diversion she needed at that moment. His rapidity and staying powers as a talker may have been too much for most people, but not for Harriet the insatiable listener. She found this talented monologist from Philadelphia had wit, intelligence, and considerable dramatic talent. This was not surprising, since his parents were both famous on the stage and had their own company, which included the first Joseph Jefferson and Edwin Forrest.

Since he was far from handsome and deeply pock-marked, Mr. Wood was denied the boards, and released his talents in a bit of writing and drawing. He was now making a stab at business and

59

was bound for a small job with Russell and an attempt to start an American newspaper in Canton. There were still only a handful of Americans there, but he expected all the English to subscribe too.

There was a good deal of dissatisfaction with the *Register*, which was the Factory mouthpiece and went further than necessary in abusing the Chinese. The weekly sheet was filled with the wildest tales of piracy, arson, kidnapings, the slave traffic in women and children, cases of incest or depravity—anything to make out the orientals as lurid barbarians and to provide spice. The *Register* doted on naughty stories.

While Mr. Wood was not at all sentimental about the Chinese, he considered himself something of an authority, and had just published a little book growing out of a previous visit to China, and illustrated with his own spidery sketches. Harriet pulled many a plum from this opus, and was forever quoting his masterpiece about the egg boats being "*manned* by a brace of Chinese *ladies.*"

Mr. Chinnery loved puns, too, and he and Mr. Wood were destined to become great friends. At once a rivalry began between them as to which was the ugliest man in Macao. When Mr. Chinnery met the younger man on the street he scowled and shook his fist.

"Oh, you wicked man," he cried. "I was someone until you came. You are marked, it is true, but I was remarked. Passers-by would say, 'There goes old Chinnery, what an ugly fellow.' Poco poco my title became undisputed. What a triumph! Now you carry off the palm. Oh, you ugly piece of wood!"

Harriet had never had time to take drawing lessons from Mr. Chinnery, but now she developed an intense interest in art, with Mr. Wood to guide her. When he went up to Canton he kept sending her drawing materials and advice. Just as he had divined her need for a drawing master, Mr. Vachell understood her need for long conversations about religion. As the spring advanced and Harriet made her gingham and chintz gowns for the hot days ahead, Mr. Vachell advanced, too, from the worthless creature she had thought him; he was her best, her only friend among the English.

Her uncle was ignorant of Harriet's new interest in religion. Both Mr. Cushing and Mr. Russell had sailed home, and William Low had his hands full in Canton. But the Macao ladies had not failed to note Harriet's pink bonnet at every service of Mr. Vachell's, or his almost daily calls at the Low villa. Little did they realize how difficult it was for a Unitarian to grasp the idea of the Trinity, and how much explaining it took Mr. Vachell during long walks to the Campo.

All that year there was turmoil in the Factory. The new chiefs were on cordial terms with the Americans and the Cohong; the trouble sprang from higher sources. News of the opium traffic at Lintin had finally reached the Emperor, who commanded the viceroy and governor to investigate and put an end to it. "Opium is a flowing poison in degree immense," said his edict.

A member of the imperial household had died of this poison, a fact which the Fanqui always managed to use as an argument in defense of the traffic. They also claimed that the drug did less harm than the vile native wine, samshu. However, no moral issue was recognized in the matter except by Zion's Corner and a few eccentrics.

A great deal more dust was raised about a trivial matter. The British took much pride in the improvements they had made in front of the Factory, which was now a private front yard with a fence and a stone quay. Strictly speaking, the foreign quarter was owned by the Cohong and leased to foreigners, and the British tenants had overstepped themselves. At least that was the excuse for the governor's visit to the Factory on May 12. He arrived with the Hoppo and a body of armed attendants and proceeded upstairs to the dining room where the portrait of George IV still hung, though young Victoria had now succeeded to the throne. He ordered the portrait uncovered, and then rudely turned his back to it, sat down, and proceeded to hold an inquisition.

He summoned Houqua, Jr., who had assumed many of his father's unwelcome duties as security merchant for the Factory, and also its linguists, who played the role of custodians of morals. Atam the linguist appeared first. He was arrested and threatened with beheading if the Factory grounds were not promptly reduced to their former state. The same threat was made to young Houqua, and he was humiliated by having to remain an hour on his knees before the Hoppo intervened and gained him time.

"He came upon us like thunder," Houqua, Jr., said later, "and would not listen to a word of reason, but treated us like slaves."

The next day workmen appeared in the Square, uprooted the trees, tore down the fence and the stone quay. The viceroy backed up Governor Le's actions and condemned the linguist and Houqua, Jr., to be beaten, but then remitted this disgrace because it was the Emperor's birthday. He had made his point.

The Factory threatened to cease all trade, and actually handed over the keys of the hong to the governor. The British Navy again hovered, there were endless pourparlers, and by the end of the year things had reached an uneasy truce. But both sides realized that the situation was impossible.

The insulting treatment of Houqua, Jr., was especially sad because in September the brilliant young man was killed by lightning. Wu Show-chang had been the pride of his father's heart, honored by rank as a mandarin of letters and presented with the Peacock Plume by the Emperor. His body was placed in a funeral house until the astrologers determined the auspicious day for his burial beside his grandparents in the family temple at Honam.

When the first issue of Mr. Wood's *Courier* came out late in July, Harriet declared it was a spirited beginning.

"But I am afraid he will make himself enemies," she added.

That was underestimating Mr. Wood's powers. He managed to step on everybody's toes because he didn't quite know where he stood, and stumbled in all directions at once. The issue of the moment was the renewal of the Company's charter, which looked more and more doubtful, though seven of its directors sat in Parliament. He began with that.

In a degree Wood sided with the Factory in foreseeing an era of confusion if trade should be opened up to a swarm of new and inexperienced merchants. But the British did not relish his prediction that the English "will try to Anglicize the Chinese as they have the people of India, treaties will be dictated at the point of a bayonet . . . Old Custom will be annihilated, and the missionaries, whose efforts have always been a dismal failure, will be busy again."

And yet Wood appeared to advocate the mailed-fist policy, insisting that the Chinese must be brought to terms "by force, efficient and well-directed compulsion, to respect the rights of those they have so long trampled on with impunity."

The Americans liked none of this. It was fair enough for Wood to attack the *Register,* but they resented his insulting remarks about the popular Factory chief, Majoribanks, and the missionaries. That first issue cost Wood half his subscribers.

He held his friends, because after all he was an entertaining fellow, keeping his office mates, William Hunter and Mortimer Irving, nephew of Washington Irving, in roars of laughter. One of his quips was at the expense of Dr. James Bradford, who as the resident physician for an assortment of healthy Americans often had to drum up business.

One day he gave Wood a professional jab in the side.

"Ah," he cried when Wood squeaked. "A touch of liver. A little medicine would do you no harm." And he sent over what the colony called "two and one," followed a day or so later by a call.

"Ah well, Wood, you seem all right now. See what it is to follow my prescription."

"Had I followed it, Bradford, I should have broken my neck. I threw it out the window."

Dr. Bradford's face was saved when he pulled young Hunter through a really serious illness, and sent him down to Macao to convalesce under the nursing of the Low ladies. By now their house had become the American center in China, the first port of call for sea captains, a sort of club during the vacation season where all the Yankees had a standing invitation to tea—which meant supper—and where they would find the dignified Mrs. Low and the effervescing Harriet at their prettiest in sheer summer ruffles.

William Hunter's visit was a godsend to Harriet, because he

was always connected in her thoughts with Abbot. They were the same age and had something of the same gentle humor. At any rate he was a young brother to care for, the very thing she needed now. For her long confidential talks with Mr. Vachell were no longer about intangibles; mighty things had occurred.

Could she see herself as the wife of this charming young chaplain, in the very heart of the Macao colony? She fluttered and debated and wept in the privacy of her immense bedroom. No, she could not. Neither could she bear to lose her dearest friend.

Accordingly Mr. Vachell dangled, and hoped. He continued to call and join the afternoon walks to the Campo or the Peña, tagging along behind the bodyguard of half a dozen Yankees. Harriet continued to see him at Company dinners, but no longer allowed him to monopolize her—which only made him look tragic and fanned the gossip about them, causing her sleepless nights.

There would be soothing interludes of fussing over William Hunter, evenings of merriment when the facetious Mr. Wood dropped in, and there was the constant challenge of keeping the American colony amused. Mr. Vachell was conspicuously jealous when he came upon her walking with somebody else. Finally Uncle William realized the state of affairs. She was walking with him and a young American when the chaplain came up and had the effrontery to offer his arm to Harriet.

Uncle shook his head when they were alone again. "It won't do, my dear Harriet."

"No, Uncle, it won't do. There must be an end."

The end dragged on, through long painful conversations with the suitor, servants scurrying back and forth with notes, morning consultations with her intimates among the Company ladies. Finally, when the men left in October, the affair went to Canton with them. Harriet knew what Uncle would say to Mr. Vachell: "I cannot allow you, my dear sir, to pay your addresses to my niece." But when Uncle's letter came there were more tears, and more visits to her confidantes, and a haunting suspicion that Mr. Vachell had not yet given up.

Young Hunter was going home for a holiday, and she loaded him with messages for Abbot.

"Tell him he must come out to China," she directed him. "If he's not tempted by the fortune he can make here, tell him that his sister is going into a decline, and only the sight of her dearest brother can save her."

Examining her face in the mirror later, she decided that now, before her twenty-second birthday, she was as old and broken-down and yellow as a tallow candle. Her color had always been so high that the gentlemen teased her: "Really, Miss Low, you are positively in rude health."

When she asked Dr. Colledge to prescribe Peruvian bark for her, he looked at her thoughtfully.

"No, you don't look as beautiful as you used to, Miss Low."

"If you don't restore the roses," she cried, "I'll never forgive such an ungallant speech."

Dear Dr. Colledge! In the rush of things she had overlooked his sterling qualities. It was a good thing she had thought about Peruvian bark.

5

Romance

with

Gestures

It was a happy spring. Caroline
Shillaber, an old friend from Salem who had come out with her
brother, was making a long stay at the Low villa. Caro was a little
younger than Harriet, a girl with flashing black eyes, quick per-
ceptions, and no small talents as confidante. There was a good
deal of merriment in the house, especially during hair-brushing
sessions at bedtime, when the girls reviewed their combined flirta-
tion with Dr. Colledge, the darling, the *parfait amour*.

He was in and out of the house a good deal, socially and pro-
fessionally. The three ladies had slight indispositions, and as for
the chambermaid, Nancy, it was no longer possible for Dr.
Colledge to call her trouble "a touch of liver." It was a touch of
Nature, for Nancy had been betrayed by some villain and was
about to have a child. The kind doctor helped them through the

ordeal; Nancy was sent off to India with some Britishers, leaving her baby for adoption.

Harriet shared Caro's rhapsodies about Dr. Colledge, but sometimes thought him a bit too much the British aristocrat, and almost as merciless as Uncle in pricking bubbles. One morning the two men were discussing the romantic American versus the European system of marriage, perhaps drawing things out because the girls were listening. They agreed perfectly that parents should choose their daughters' husbands, with money as a first consideration.

"Uncle," Harriet wailed, "you're the death of romance. If we admire the dashing of the billows, you say it looks like soapsuds."

There was nothing prosaic about Mr. Wood. He could keep her laughing from one in the afternoon until ten at night. The drawing lessons now proceeded in a quartet, with some youth sharpening the pencils for Caro. There was always a droll twist in Mr. Wood's talk or his notes. One morning the old Portuguese ayah who had replaced Nancy lumbered up the stairs with a formal legal document.

"Oh, Caro, listen to this: 'The petitioner humbly solicits the pleasure of carrying *arms* with Miss L. this afternoon——' Isn't he an original! Carrying *arms!*"

Mr. Vachell was still offering his, when she met him out walking; he was still doggedly attentive. She snubbed him; she walked with Mr. Wood, with her Yankee "brothers." She hardly had time for her Spanish lessons, for the sea captains were coming in: Charles Roundy, delivering a precious miniature of Mary Ann; Captain Little fresh from the Sandwich Islands with a bad report of the American missionaries debauching the innocent natives with Mother Hubbards and hymns and hell-fire; Captain Whitney with tales of Lima and Valparaiso, Java and Bengal; and the dashing officers of the USS *Potomac*, making a friendly visit in Chinese waters.

"I wish I were a man," she sighed, brushing her brown curls in the doorway of Caro's room. "Then I could take up my bundle and go where I pleased."

"You mean," Caro protested, "*walk*, like a tramp?"

67

"Of course not, dearest. I'd sail to every port on the seven seas." She pondered, her lower lip caught in small white teeth. "I'd like to fall in love with a supercargo. I'd put it in the marriage agreement that I could go wherever I pleased, and do whatever my husband did."

"Harriet!"

"Well, I do hate this dependent system, being a woman."

"Let's talk about the ball," Caro suggested hurriedly.

The Lows' ball early in April was the result of a systematic campaign by all the gentlemen, including Mr. Vachell. They cleared out Harriet's elegant bedroom as a supper room, had her Spanish teacher as master of ceremonies, borrowed a piano and hired a guitarist and four Portuguese fiddlers. Aunt wore a China gauze, Caro pink aerophane, and Harriet blue crape, all with white satin underskirts. Their fresh flowers were sent by "the youths." The forty guests had an enchanting time. In the flurry Harriet managed to keep a present Mr. Wood sent downriver with compliments so ceremonious she was rather alarmed. But not so alarmed as to return the present.

Mr. Wood's *Courier* was a nightmare to the British and to most of the Americans. Dancing on his editorial tightrope, he had dropped his *pas seul* in favor of the Company retaining its charter, and was now doing handsprings. The monopoly, he said, worked for order in China, but it was, after all, undemocratic. Wood abused the Cohong, excoriated the Factory, and insulted his rival, the *Register*. He received many letters of protest signed Vindicator, Punkah, Tit-for-Tat, and Bagpipes, which he cheerfully printed.

The exchanges with the *Register* became increasingly vivid.

"The Canton *Register*," said one of Wood's editorials, "a paper which has hitherto been principally distinguished for its disgusting details of Chinese depravity, and a servility which has rendered it a proverb among us, has now descended still lower . . . to become a vehicle of the most brutal specimen of anonymous abuse which has ever disgusted the Foreign Community."

Mr. Keating, editor of the *Register*, decided to take this personally. He called on Wood and demanded an unconditional apology.

"I'll apologize," said Wood, "if you will make one equally strong to me, in print."

"No," said Keating, "the apology must come from you, and it must be unqualified."

"I refuse, naturally," said Wood.

"Very well." Keating stalked out.

Wood prepared for the worst. Since Mr. Russell was away, his partners, Low and Heard, were in charge. Mr. Low? Perish the thought! Wood appealed to Augustine Heard, who was agreeably roused by this affair of honor.

The challenge was delivered by Mr. James Innes, an independent Scots merchant who had more than once made Canton ring with the cries of the old border chivalry. The Laird was sixty, with never a peaceful year behind him, gaunt, erect, with a dueling scar across his face. Once, when a Britisher had offended him, Innes went to his house at dinnertime and horsewhipped him at the head of his own table. Of late his long feud with the British had been halted because he was very busy in the opium trade and the Factory could profit by his defiance of the authorities and still keep its own skirts clean, since the Laird was not credited to the Company. At any rate he now delivered the challenge.

Mr. Heard then arranged for a duel with pistols at five the next morning on the bank of the Inside Passage to Macao. For all his experience, the Laird was nonplused. Evidently his principal had not expected more than an apology.

"But, my dear sir," the Laird protested, "how can you and I answer to our God for risking the lives of these young men and breaking the Chinese laws against homicide?"

"Oh," said Heard, "that is your affair in demanding such an apology. Life's not a very important matter, compared to honor. We shall expect you at five in the morning."

Heard went to his room and oiled up an old pair of dueling pistols. He told Wood to put his affairs in order and get a good night's sleep. But before bedtime there was a letter from the Laird. He could not risk breaking the Chinese laws. He and Mr.

Keating would take a sailboat down to Lintin Island and await their opponents there.

Chuckling, Wood and Heard concocted a reply. Their challengers might go to Manila or Ballyhack if they chose, but Mr. Wood could not leave his business to follow them.

Mr. Keating tried to save face by actually going to Lintin and suspending his paper for five weeks. But there was laughter all down the row from the Factory to Houqua's hong, especially after Wood explained the real reason for calling off the duel.

"There was no abbey," he said plaintively, "in which to bury the body."

In July Mr. Vachell gave up his long campaign and took to his bed, gravely ill with melancholia. Harriet was dreadfully worried, and yet she could not blame herself for his breakdown. "I hear," she wrote Mary Ann, "he makes a great many good resolves, which I hope he will keep. I fear there is great need for reformation in him as well as others."

Her friends were not blaming her. Dr. Colledge told her that he had never heard anyone speak ill of her. He promised her and Caro each a cashmere shawl and lace veil when they married.

But she was restless, at a stalemate. What roused her was Mr. James Sturgis, who suddenly emerged from his shell and began making daily calls. She put him down as a "harmless good creature, perfectly well disposed," but of course too old to be taken seriously. He invited the ladies to his birthday party and admitted to being forty! But his house was magnificent, and "Uncle Jem" most agreeable.

A night or so later Harriet cut short the hair-brushing chat with Caro. "Uncle Jem says I must keep better hours," she said, moving toward her bed.

But after she had blown out the candle Caro called from the next room, "Darling, he doesn't seem much of an uncle."

There was an interval of giggling, then Harriet lit the candle again and puzzled in her journal:

"Wonder if he is as good as he seems. Oh, dear! I am dreadfully suspicious, unhappily so for my own comfort; but oh, this heartless, deceitful world! People laugh and look quizzical at the old man. Not that his age is at all objectionable to me. I believe I am a great hypocrite, for I treat people delightfully when I ought to frown upon them, and all for why? Because I am a girl, and must not put on airs. Oh, ye married ones! The privileges that are yours for having taken to yourselves helpmates. . . . Well, unhappy spinsters! I say throw off all this unfeeling general attention, centre it all on one, and then there will be some chance for your happiness!"

Somehow she knew this summer would decide everything. Her suspicions of Uncle Jem were soon confirmed; he declared himself. What should she do?

Without warning, the next day when they came in from the terrace Caro was taken with fever and ague. Dr. Colledge hurried over and gave her quinine, but during the week that Harriet was nursing Caro the nightmare of indecision made her rush sometimes to the terrace to weep alone. No, she could not marry Uncle Jem. She told him so, she had to appear selfish and hard-hearted—but how could she marry this old man of forty? He continued to come in every day, giving her time to change her mind.

But Mr. Wood was now down from Canton, hero of an affair of honor, ready to talk brilliantly about every subject, even serious ones like metaphysics. He could fetch her out of moods of despondency, just as Mr. Vachell used to do.

The next day she met the chaplain as she took a farewell walk with Uncle Jem, who was leaving for Manila. Mr. Vachell was just out of bed, looking desperately ill.

Why was it? Why must she make them so miserable, wreck their lives perhaps? Why couldn't she care for anybody? She was dying almost for someone to love, and yet the right one would not come along. . . .

Three days later William Wood proposed.

Yes, he was a friend to be proud of, a man of high and noble feelings. She could almost be sure. But he was going to Canton the next day.

"I must think. I must have time."

71

The typhoon struck just after Wood and Uncle and several other Americans had left for Canton. The house rocked with it, it scooped up every shrub in the garden and dismasted the trees. Captain Philip Dumaresq fought his way ashore from the *Martha*, her mainmast gone. The *Don Quixote* was shorn clean to the decks. The *Spartan* went out to sea in the thick of the gale and picked up the survivors of the *Fair American*, sunk off the Great Ladrones.

Uncle—and Wood—in the little river boat. She had begged for time to think, and sent him out into the typhoon.

Two days later a letter came from Uncle, saying that they had managed to get inside the river safely before the storm struck.

Harriet tried to settle down and read, but she had already read the novel Mr. Vachell had just sent her, she was bored with Cooper's *Bravo*, and found Walter Scott's last novel dry and uninteresting. The letters from home were better reading—one from Josiah, as comical as ever, news of dear little Ellen, and the great tidings that Mary Ann and George Archer would marry soon.

As always the sea captains and supercargoes came to tea, and soon there was an anonymous letter for Harriet, which she discovered came from Mr. Ward of the *Don Quixote*. It was an acrostic, spelling out "To Miss Low."

> There is a winning charm of gentle nature
> O'er all thy being like a perfume thrown,
> Making each beauty, both of mind and feature,
> Inseparable—not to be singly known.
> Something there is that as an unseen power
> Subdues the wonted current of our thought,
> Leaving the heart all passive. But one hour
> Of thy sweet converse, and the soul is fraught
> With feelings of a cast, oh, too, too deeply wrought!

She quite forgot the graceful tribute because just then William Wood's letter arrived from Canton. She was sure now. For nearly two months the love letters sped between Macao and Canton without Aunt suspecting the engagement. Harriet was in high spirits, enjoying her bevy of beaux, getting indignant over Mrs.

Trollope's unkind remarks about America, fluttering over the beautiful dress materials Uncle had ordered her from France, making a new bonnet with a splendid ribbon and wearing it to church—which prevented at least one of her admirers from hearing the sermon.

Poor Mr. Vachell! He was going home to England, he was juwabed, jilted, finished. It was hard, even now, losing such a faithful friend. And Macao was still gossiping about her. The rumors now had it that she was engaged to Captain Dumaresq, because she had gone walking with him a few evenings. If they only knew the truth!

In mid-October Harriet was called to her aunt's room. Mr. Wood had at last spoken to Uncle, as Harriet's father pro tem. Uncle had refused his consent to an engagement, and sent his wife a long letter explaining his reasons.

They spent the morning in a tug of war. Harriet had the greatest admiration for Aunt Low, a sterling character straight and true in everything. But of course she was influenced by Uncle, and neither of them understood her William.

"Mr. Wood is not our sort, dear. Both parents on the stage!"

"But they're famous. They're brilliant, respected——"

"Never mind that. But Mr. Wood's not liked in Canton. He's always getting into quarrels."

"But, dearest Aunt, he's right about everything. Let me explain."

She tried to explain the convolutions of Mr. Wood's ideas. Then her aunt read bits from her husband's letter about Wood's instability, his complete lack of business sense.

"Harriet, I couldn't conceive of you as a poor man's wife."

"Money! Can't people think of anything but filthy lucre?"

She went off finally to carry on the argument in a long letter to her uncle. He replied with a downright refusal to give her his blessing. She spent another morning in Aunt's room, tearful this time, and a letter from her lover only made her more wretched.

"Oh, romance, where dost thou dwell?" she stormed in her journal, in a style that lately had taken on the Woodsian flavor.

73

"Our dearest and fondest hopes are often dashed for want of the filthy lucre, our fairest schemes defeated, our plans broken . . ."

Then she washed her face and went out to dinner, laughing inwardly at one of the other guests, a conceited young puppy who was growing a ferocious pair of mustachios in defiance of the approved clean-shaven style. She grew hysterical at bedtime laughing at "Don Whiskerando."

Mrs. Low moved quickly. Their friend Captain F. W. Macondray was now in charge of the storeship at Lintin, and Harriet was sent with his wife for a few days' visit on the *Lintin*. Phil Dumaresq took them down the bay in his vessel, and by evening they were aboard the luxurious storeship, with a flotilla anchored around them.

It was a gay life there on the water. They took moonlight rows in the longboat, visiting the ships in turn. The British opium clipper *Red Rover* was there, the most beautiful vessel in the East, and prophetic of an era yet unguessed. The ship was named for the hero of Fenimore Cooper's romance, and her design was also American, for her lines had been taken from a swift Baltimore clipper captured and sent to England in the War of 1812. Their friend Captain Clifton and his officers wore elegant blue jackets, red waistcoats, and white trousers. They danced a quadrille on deck with the ladies while the little band played.

Their visit to the great Indiaman *Orwell* was more impressive than the stiffest Company dinner. Potbellied, cumbersome, in design and rigging hardly changed from the days of Queen Elizabeth, the Indiamen still had a stately air. They were full-bottomed cargo carriers that felt themselves frigates, and indeed they were heavily armed and flew the coach-whip pennant of the Royal Navy. But their voyages were phenomenally slow because of their build and their quaint tradition of "making snug" for the night, taking in so much sail that they barely moved.

The captain had the ladies piped aboard, and allowed them to take in the splendor of his waistcoat and breeches of deep buff topped by a blue coat stiff with gold braid and gilt buttons engraved with the Company's crest. Then he led them below to a ceremonious tiffin.

They climbed the peak of the island, they exchanged many visits with the American ships. But the letters followed Harriet, from Wood, and from her aunt and uncle, so she could not quite forget her troubles. She read and reread her lover's words: "We look upon the stars, flashing and sparkling like jewels in an Ethiop's ear, and sigh to think how much happier may be the tenants of those distant spheres; we long to leave this earth to revel in the happiness of another."

Harriet did not precisely long to leave this earth; after a row she would sit down to a huge bowl of bread and milk, and then watch in fascination the little smug-boat alongside, its hundred dirty rowers catching chowchow or gambling while they waited for the opium chests.

She came home to Macao in a gay mood, smelling, her aunt complained, of cockroaches. She tumbled everything into the wash, and suddenly her thoughts were all of Wood again. She hoped he would have something more tangible to suggest than moving to a distant star.

But the weeks went on through a cold gloomy Christmas, and she saw nothing of Wood but his portrait at Mr. Chinnery's. In his letters he had begun to analyze her good points, also the bad. The whole romance slowly faded in her mind, like a dream.

Badminton was the new rage in Macao, and she was chagrined to find that her brothers and sister at home could keep the shuttle-cock in the air for two thousand strokes, "which beats us all hollow." Probably it was the Chinese construction of her sets, "and the bird goes any way but the right."

Caro and Dr. Colledge were engaged in February. During all the months Harriet had been playing battledore, keeping hearts in the air as long as she could, they had calmly been falling in love, and planned to marry in a few weeks. She set to work on Caro's wedding dress, boldly cutting into costly lengths of satin and lace. As she sewed with expert fingers she worried about Uncle's constant cough and his pallor. She thought about the new chaplain, Mr. Wimberly, who was far superior to his predecessor . . . what was poor Mr. Vachell doing now? Mr. Wood was going down to the Philippines to raise coffee and sugar. Uncle Jem was there, too, at Russell & Sturgis.

Caro's brother was coming for the wedding. For Harriet, no wedding, no beloved Abbot. She was quite resigned now about never marrying, but she longed with all her heart for her brother.

In Canton that March young Minqua of the Cohong took a wife, and to the general astonishment the factory chiefs were invited to see the bride in her wedding finery. The Fanqui were seated in a semicircle, and warned not to rise when the lady entered.

The bride was of course a lily-foot girl, and toddled into the room supported by two bridesmaids. She made her painful circuit, curtsying to the Fanqui, who were purple with embarrassment because they could not rise and bow. She was a pretty creature, painted like a doll and wearing a robe of priceless embroidery, her hair piled high, and from the comb which held it loops of pearls made a frame around her face.

Finally she backed out of the room, looking relieved, and then the Fanqui were shown the wedding presents, fabulously rich, some of them large cakes of pure sycee silver. The bridegroom took a bumper of wine with each guest, and they left him in a most festive mood.

In Brooklyn on March 14 Mary Ann Low married George Archer, long her father's apprentice and now his partner, and then the happy pair settled down to live in the Low house until they could afford one of their own.

In Macao four days later Harriet dressed the bride in her white satin and lace veil and stood beside her in the English chapel, approving the chaplain, but shocked at the blunt words of the Church of England marriage service. At the villa there were seventy guests to breakfast, with a band of music, and half a dozen Italian opera singers who had happened to stop en route from South America to Calcutta. After the Colledges had gone to their house there was supper for the bridesmaids and groomsmen. It all went off perfectly, the most splendid wedding Macao had ever seen.

At last the villa was dark and Harriet lay in her great bed

thinking that on this very day Mary Ann might have had her wedding too. Her two sisters—for Caro had been her sister for months—were now resigned to splendid husbands.

Harriet slipped out of bed and looked down into the dark garden, thinking, How is it that I have come halfway around the world, only to be so lost?

In the deep quiet she heard her uncle's racking cough.

6

Young Man

on a

Skyrocket

The gale late in August went on
day after day, keeping the villa dark as Erebus. Harriet put herself through her routine to keep from flying to pieces: after
breakfast French exercises and reading, then Spanish and drawing
until dinner at three. It had been an amazingly dull summer;
socially Macao was feast or famine.

After dinner she and Aunt tilted the venetian blinds so they
could see to read. Uncle was resting; he was very thin and ill
now, and Tom Colledge hinted that they had better plan to
take him home. They sat in a corner of the drawing room
with Harriet's little bird for company, until finally she threw
down the life of Peter the Great she had been pretending to
read.

She went to the french windows and looked out at the Roads,

whipped frantic under the gale. "I can't see anything in that murk," she sighed. "Five months out."

"Don't worry," said her worried aunt. "The *Cabot* will be in before we know it."

The *Cabot* was Uncle James Low's ship, and it was bringing Abbot for a career in the China trade. They had been on tenterhooks for weeks, telling each other that the delay meant nothing worse than slow sailing. But that day Harriet was nearly out of her mind with anxiety, when suddenly Uncle James came in from the Roads, promising that Abbot would be along by bedtime.

He arrived very late, burned dark by the summer passage. When Harriet flew into his arms four years of separation melted, and this young man of twenty-two was still the little brother she loved best of all.

"Oh, Botus, my darling! How like a pirate you look! What a thicket of hair! We'll have the barber in, first thing in the morning."

He laughed. "You haven't changed, after all. Except"—he held her off to look at her—"to grow prettier than ever. The way you've been talking in your letters, Harriet, I'd expected to find a toothless old crone muttering over her sins."

"I am old, terribly old and sedate, Botus. As for the sins—does Father really think I've caught the immoral contagion of China, as he calls it? How that lecture made me weep!"

"No, my dear. Only, why come out here to get mixed up with an English parson and an actor from Philadelphia, et cetera? Every time a ship lands in New York we hear you're engaged to half a dozen new pretenders."

"Dearest, if only you'd been here, I shouldn't have gotten into such hobbles. You have so much prudence, Botus, and I have so little caution. I've been sailing among shoals and quicksands without you."

Abbot did not go up to Canton for almost a month, and Harriet, blissfully mending for him, got the details of Mary Ann's wedding along with slices of her wedding cake. She heard about her young brothers cutting a swath in the best society of Brooklyn, and Grandmother Porter's fidelity to Salem.

79

"She always insists," Abbot said, "that she can never find anything in the New York shops to compare with Mr. Batchelder's store at home. Every week she reads the Salem *Gazette* from end to end, including the advertisements."

It was settled now that the William Lows and Harriet would go home. Dr. Colledge, with all his blisters and leeches, could not arrest the disease he was too kind to identify as lung fever. October was a month of packing their accumulation of treasures, the best of them Chinnery's portraits of Abigail and William Low and Harriet, hers looking, everybody said, as if she had walked smack into the canvas. In November there was the last declaration of love from some bore in Canton, the last "shooting of pasteboard" by the Company gentlemen going upriver, the last visits to Caro, happily domestic with her catties of oil and taels of fish, the tearing up of old love letters, which still could hurt.

Abbot came down for ten days before they sailed in the giant Indiaman *Waterloo*. The tea fleet was in, and Captains Roundy, Macondray, and Dumaresq escorted them down the bay to the Roads. All their Chinese servants had offered to come with them, and they took one devoted boy to look after Uncle. Harriet had forgotten that the household had once seemed to her a band of uncouth heathen.

Surely they would be home, even against the monsoon, before Uncle was worse. They expected the sea voyage would benefit him. But they had to leave the *Waterloo* at Capetown, and months later Mrs. Low and Harriet sailed home on another ship. Behind them, under Table Rock, was William Low's grave.

Abbot Low was one of those rare people with perfect timing. More than once in his personal life the right door swung open for him at the right moment; in his career as merchant he deserved the name of Benvenuto. As an economic creature he rode the crest of three waves. The first had carried him down to New York with the migration of business brains; the second brought him to China in the era of Yankee expansion; the third, a dozen years ahead, was to bind New York and China with the miracle of the clipper ships.

He arrived in Canton a few months before Parliament, in angry sessions, dissolved the Company monopoly. The passing of the Factory was expected to release and stimulate British commerce. Instead, it shook loose a great volume of business for Russell & Co.

To Abbot Low the most important effect of the Factory's loss of supreme power was Houqua's release as its chief security merchant. For many years he had been forced, despite his almost yearly petitions, to be the buffer between China and England. In the process he had worn down his health and sacrificed the dignity of his oldest son. Now at last he was free, and what he did was significant: he threw all his business to Russell & Co. This gave the house a very large volume of new trade, to say nothing of the guidance and friendship of the most brilliant merchant in China.

Moreover, Abbot was now to inherit the filial position young John Forbes had enjoyed with Houqua during the last three years. John was soon to follow his older brother, Robert, back to Boston, leaving the old hong merchant in the market for another American "son." John Forbes, besides his work for Russell, had acted as Houqua's private secretary and confidential agent. He had a tremendous private business with India, England, and the United States, disposing of surplus teas and silks. Since he could not read English nor write more than his signature in English characters, he needed a trustworthy assistant to read and answer his letters and keep him posted on foreign affairs.

It was on the cards that Abbot should be the third American to be adopted by the paternal Houqua. He had loved John Cushing, and partly for his sake had befriended his cousin John Forbes, though in his own right Forbes was one of the bewitching personalities of his time. Now Houqua found a peculiar affinity with Abbot Low. Their temperaments agreed; they were keenly observant, hard-working, shrewd, cautious and fair in bargaining, moderate and kindly in their general view of things, and intensely loyal and generous to those they loved.

At the moment Houqua had no son to help carry on his hong; his oldest surviving son was in Peking and the next in line was a boy of ten. He hoped that by the time they inherited the family business Canton would "enjoy the repose of gladness and of gain," as the Chinese put it. To that end he was deliberately building up Russell & Co.; Americans had never given him the slightest trouble.

On the whole the freeing of English commerce did not produce the expected chaos. The Factory remained, only now it had competitors. The Cohong did not dissolve as predicted, though its tight control gradually relaxed. The opium traffic went merrily on. However, the most conspicuous symbol of the Company's might, the Indiaman, was scuttled. Now that the Company must compete with the field it could no longer afford the big lazy behemoths that made snug at night and kept exaggerated crews fat on beef and rum. Forty-six of the vessels were sold at a good figure, and sixteen others were broken up for their copper. A fantastic era had indeed passed.

In the China trade a young man was supposed to stay in Canton seven years, beginning as clerk and ending, if he was exceptional, as a partner. There was a great gulf between the grub state of clerk at an annual salary of five hundred dollars, all found, and the glorified status as a Russell partner, which during Abbot's last years brought him annual company profits of twenty-five thousand dollars, besides his private ventures.

The gulf was not social in Suy Hong as it was in the British firms. The clerks had their desks in one room on the first floor, the partners in another, but all had bells on their desks to summon their personal servants if they wanted a glass of water or an errand run. And all dined together on the second floor, and dined extremely well. Abbot in particular profited by the fact that the older men took pains to groom promising juniors for partnerships.

But his skyrocket success was really due to the fact that he had a father on either side of the globe throwing business his way. The young factors were allowed to carry on as much private trade as they could manage along with their company duties, and Abbot, who was a prodigious worker with calm nerves, managed a network of ventures.

Through the efforts of Father Seth Low he expanded the

market in New York for Houqua's silks and teas, to be rewarded by more and more purchases of his Yankee goods by Father Houqua. Abbot and Seth Low had a continual exchange on joint account, and between them they began setting up the younger brothers in small ventures, and reinvesting the returns. Mr. Low drummed up a good deal of commission business for his son from New York merchants and from his prosperous brother, Daniel Low, who had a trading house in Paris.

Abbot particularly enjoyed his business relations with the good Josiah Dow. The Dows were Brooklyn neighbors and close friends of the family; Ellen Dow was an intimate of Harriet's and at one time or another most of the Low boys were in love with her.

Abbot drummed up business for his father, who acted as agent for many of his son's Canton friends. There was such profit in China trade, if shrewdly handled, that a small investment snow-balled within a few years into a competence, the slowness of communications alone making the process less than spectacular. Houqua could always be counted on for a masterly forecast of the Canton market, so that Abbot could tell his father what to send in the next shipment. The New York market was far more ticklish because of sharp competition and sudden shifts in popular demand. Just now, for instance, French and English tableware was the rage, and the porcelains which gave china its name out of demand. Ladies were affecting silver combs in their hair, and Chinese tortoise shell must be sent to inferior markets in the back country or South America. Seth Low's frequent letters were complete and shrewd market reports. He told Abbot what varieties of silks would please the world of fashion, and advised "quaker colors."

As a drug specialist he knew the supply-and-demand picture down to the last chest of camphor. Musk was in good demand; Abbot would do well to send on joint account 1200 ounces of the common quality. "Better ship good handsome rhubarb, best quality now sells at eighty cents and supply short. Plenty of cheap stuff on the market." Teas and gamboge had a fair prospect, and the Chinese wine Abbot sent was bottled and selling.

83

The news was not always encouraging. In 1835 a great fire destroyed most of the business section of New York, with a loss of twenty millions. Abbot had his own loss in that disaster, for his first shipment of rhubarb parings, only partly insured, burned in the warehouse. More serious was the "absquatulating" of the *Margaret Oakley's* captain, who left China with a consignment of silks from Abbot Low and decamped with the entire cargo.

"How could the Russells be so in the mist about that man's character?" Seth Low wrote his son. "But these things must be encountered, and you may comfort yourself that you are not doing business in New York." Money was very scarce, he said, and notes of the best sort went begging on Wall Street. He blamed President Jackson's "unprincipled administration and experimentation in currency."

However, the Low segment of the China trade was building up. Since Seth Low regarded opium merely as a drug like rhubarb he sometimes included it in his shipments. "This article," he wrote of a consignment of Turkish opium, "we have had a handsome time, and it cost $450. It may be a little drier than desirable for your market, but the quality is good. We have to remark upon opium that the product of the present season is unusually small and the stock in our markets is much reduced and the price advancing. . . . We hope therefore that you will be able to bring us out well on this article."

The faithful George Archer, Mary Ann's husband, made out the complicated invoices and accounts, sent in duplicate or triplicate by different ships to forestall loss in a ship caught by the Malay pirates or an even more savage typhoon. One annoying snag that gave Abbot matter for thought in these years was the fact that Russell's competitors sometimes held up crucial mail. Their ships would leave New York on an unannounced day, so that Mr. Low could not get his letters aboard, or if they carried mail for competing houses they would hold up delivery in Canton until their own consignees had a chance at the market.

The Lows on both sides of the globe noted the length of voyages, and always sent goods and letters on vessels with good sailing records. A slow passage of 130 days or more might mean

84

that a shipment of fresh teas missed the spring market in New York.

Brooklyn Heights was a vantage point for watching ships pass in and out of the Narrows, which was one reason so many shipping merchants were becoming neighbors of the Lows. However, there was a fairly complete signal service from Sandy Hook to downtown New York. A lookout station in the Narrows caught the name of an incoming ship, painted on her foretopsail, and by flag signals flashed it to Staten Island, which relayed the news to a signal house on the roof of Holt's Hotel at Fulton and Water streets.

Abbot was considered a little fanciful in believing that something would come of Samuel F. B. Morse's experiments with an electric telegraph. He stuck to his faith and his intense interest in the electromagnetic telegraph even when, years later, it became so successful as to alter the whole pattern of the China trade.

There was a continual exchange of presents between Brooklyn and Canton. Seth Low sent his son the latest books, and Mary Low tucked in cranberries and sweetmeats and her special gingerbread, thin spicy sheets that arrived fresh and crisp after the longest voyage. Abbot Low showered lengths of silk on the womenfolk, Houqua's exquisite Padre souchong on his father, hand-painted wallpaper, sewing kits of carved ivory, bits of jade and boxes of lacquer and cinnabar, on all the Tribe of Seth. He presented the East India Museum in Salem with a suit of mandarin clothes, complete with fan bag, chopsticks, and sheath knife, whereupon his father reminded him that Brooklyn, too, had "a noble institution in our Lyceum." The Lyceum, which Seth Low helped provide with lecturers, was one of his many public interests in Brooklyn.

The gift that most delighted the family was Chinnery's portrait of Abbot.

"Your portrait," his father wrote, "is suspended in our front parlor—that of Harriet and your Uncle Daniel Low are the only other pictures promoted to that high dignity. Those persons who have seen you lately pronounce the likeness excellent. Some think it is a likeness of a much older man than yourself. I notice that you have more flesh on your face than when you left us, but had no hesitation in recognizing your face. Your mother did not rapidly perceive the likeness but it comes out more and more the oftener she sees it."

A true portraitest, Chinnery caught the lines maturing in the young face, the suggestion of a gentle lion in its round contours, and the serenity which in that day marked the successful merchant or the prince of the quarterdeck.

The family was losing Harriet again, a radiantly happy girl who quickly dropped all idea of eternal spinsterhood when she met John Hillard. He was a young banker bound for London as a partner of Messrs. Coates & Co.; Harriet seemed fated to live among the English. John's mother was English, his father was a Virginian and member of the famous Black Horse Cavalry in Richmond, where John had grown up. The Lows, who were not overly fond of Southerners, were glad that John had been stamped by Boston, where he was educated, and where his older brother, George Hillard, was making his mark. The law partner of the great Charles Sumner, George was a Massachusetts senator, lecturer, and author of popular school readers. He was a lifelong friend of Nathaniel Hawthorne, who lived with him while he, Hawthorne, was in the customs service.

Harriet had been excessively happy at home, especially because Mary Ann was still part of the parental household with her two George Archers, husband and small son. She shed a few tears because Abbot was not at her wedding late in 1836, and many more when she and John sailed away. But London was only two or three weeks from home, and she was deeply in love with her charming John.

It was fortunate that the sad news about her young brother Francis came long after the wedding. Seth Low had sent him out to Canton in the forlorn hope that the sea voyage would cure his tuberculosis, but the boy died at sea.

The next spring, when Abbot was enjoying his new dignity as a Russell partner, all his father's dire prophecies about President Jackson's currency policies came true.

"It is with no small degree of pain," Seth Low wrote, "that I sit down to record the disasters which have overwhelmed the mercantile community throughout this country with almost indiscriminate ruin. You have no doubt in recollection that General Jackson and a few unprincipled parties have indulged the preposterous idea that a metallic currency was highly desirable in this country, and in order to secure the support of the democracy, that is, of the mechanics, laborers, etc. they have been constantly belaboring the United States Bank and the merchants until they have prostrated both.

"The removal of the deposits from the United States Bank to the State Bank has afforded to speculators an opportunity of using immense amounts by way of side loans, so called, in the purchase of lands in the Western country and elsewhere. This proceeding has filled the Western country with money and induced immense speculations in lands both by Negroes, planters and traders.

"In the meantime everybody in New York, supposing that the Western country was immensely rich, have been sending goods to the merchants on long credits, without even making, apparently, any calculation how the money was to be brought to New York to meet agreements."

As a result, money became scarce, interest rates soared, and brokers went to their utmost strength. By the middle of March one house after the other had stopped payment, until finally no draft could be sold anywhere, and no note could be discounted on Wall Street at any price. Seth Low suspended payment on the first of May, his friend Josiah Dow a few days later. Soon the New York banks froze their specie, followed by all the Eastern and Canadian banks. The government was bankrupt, and New York business paralyzed.

This blow fell after the best spring season Mr. Low had ever enjoyed, though he had felt trouble coming and had not overextended. However, he could not collect money due him from Southern customers, which meant he could not send Abbot any remittances at the moment. He expected that John Hillard would write Abbot about the state of affairs in England (Russell & Co.

87

cleared its paper through Baring Bros. in London), "as he is intelligent and clear-headed and in a position to acquire correct information."

It was a proud moment for both of them when Abbot Low was able to advance his father enough money and credit to help pull him through. Merchants were failing all over the country, among them Mr. Dow and Robert Forbes, who was wiped out clean in Boston. His friends subscribed enough to get him back to China and in the trade again.

One effect of the business collapse was to prevent Abbot's young brother, William Henry Low II, from coming out to China. He had been promised a Canton connection with a New York house, but the world-wide panic which followed the American debacle froze all plans. Abbot, writing to William late in 1837, said, "I should not be surprised if a few months hence, two thirds of the houses in India, China, Java and Manila were to be bankrupt. Not long ago I thought myself pretty well off, but fortune is more than fickle nowadays and ere long I may find myself in a worse box than when I began. . . . The times are indeed bad; will probably be worse, but must be better by and by."

Still, he wanted to have William with him, and urged him to come if he could get commissions enough to cover the cost of his outfit, the round-trip fare of six hundred dollars, plus incidental expenses of another hundred or two. Having brought the effervescent William up from babyhood, Abbot, with five years' seniority but unfailing tact, gave him some advice in case he might find a way to get himself East.

"Do not fail," he wrote, "to apply yourself on the voyage to Navigation, Bookkeeping, and books generally. Unless you have made better use of your time than I did at home, the chance is that you will find yourself on going abroad, behind 9/10ths of those you meet in general reading! I find it impossible to acquire studious habits. You take care to do better, while you are younger. *I mean to improve.*"

He then read William a lecture which he knew would be relayed to the whole family, about writing more letters, and making sure they caught ships ready to sail for China. "I have begged you

88

to write me by every conveyance & so have I begged of all—but there is no one who will take the least pains to meet my wishes, unless a vessel is publicly advertised to sail from before your doors. . . . You may think me warm on this subject, but I have not spoken one hundredth part of what I have felt."

Abbot was frantic for news during the crisis, worried about the family at home, about Harriet, whose husband, too, was feeling the effects of the bank failures. The letters never came soon enough, but they bore increasingly hopeful news. By the next year Seth Low had settled most of his debts at seventy cents on the dollar, though he had collected nothing of the twenty-five thousand dollars due him from various parts of the country, and had done only enough business to pay store rent. Abbot's help had made it possible for him to hold on to the Brooklyn properties. Slowly business pulled up out of the slough, and father and son were again writing of pongees and rhubarb.

By the fall of 1838 it was plain that Russell & Co., far from being caught in the money panic, was more flourishing than ever, and Abbot felt safe in encouraging William to come out, if he wished. But William was then working with his uncle Daniel Low, and might be given a post in the Paris branch of his house. "In fine," Abbot wrote him, "I think you will make a better Frenchman than Chinese, but take your choice."

He reminded William that the only amusement in Canton was hard work. "Paris holds out a thousand enjoyments of a higher order whilst in China there are none. There are, too, a thousand dangers and temptations in the most alluring forms, against which you must be constantly on your guard."

William found the warning itself rather alluring.

7

Siege

of the

Hongs

Late in 1838 James Innes, the
Laird who had acted in Wood's affair of honor, stupidly set a
match to the Canton powder mine. He was caught red-handed
bringing opium into the city in broad daylight and packed in
dollar boxes. His carriers, put to the torture, declared that the
opium came from a Russell ship. This was patently a lie, but Puankeiqua, the hong merchant who was security for this ship, was
arrested along with Russell & Co.'s comprador. A general embargo was laid on trade, at the height of the season.

Abbot Low was alarmed enough to write his father a statement
of his company interests "to serve in case of accident to myself."
It was written just after the annual New Year's meeting of 1839;
by the next year Abbot was determined to leave Canton. "It will
probably require some resolution," he confessed, "to break off a

connection just at a moment when it bids fair to be most valuable, but I do not think that ambition or a desire for great wealth will keep me here."

He was doing well enough. Starting two years before with one sixteenth of the house profits, he had now nearly trebled his share, and was making twenty-five thousand dollars a year from his Russell dealings alone. But this was China, trade was paralyzed, and anything might happen.

The mistake about the Russell ship was soon cleared up after the Yankees presented a formal petition to the mandarins at the city gates. But trade continued frozen until Innes, sentenced to perpetual exile, finally left Canton. By that time it was clear that the Emperor had determined to end the opium traffic. News filtered from Peking that he had appointed a special commissioner, Lin Tse-hsu, to come down to Canton and stop the drug trade forever.

The Company still kept its hold on opium running, which now amounted to about thirty thousand chests a year, worth twenty million dollars. American dealings were much lighter; at the moment Russell & Co. had about eight hundred thousand dollars' worth on consignment to English buyers. Aside from the fact that opium was murdering and enslaving countless Chinese, the government objected to the traffic as taking too much specie out of the empire, and it was true that China had an unfavorable balance of trade with England. With the Americans the balance was decidedly in China's favor.

The local mandarins, alarmed by Commissioner Lin's imminent arrival, decided to clean their own house by pouncing on Chinese dealers in such a way as to frighten the Fanqui. One February noon they staged the public execution of a native opium dealer in the Square directly under the American flag. The most painful and ignominious form of execution was chosen—a combined crucifixion and slow strangulation.

The chief mandarin arrived in full regalia, with a cloud of servants carrying a tent, tables and chairs, and the usual equipment for making tea. After the stage was set the opium dealer was dragged to the spot, and a wooden cross was driven into the ground. Before the victim could be chained to the cross the

British and Americans rushed out into the Square. As usual, Hunter was spokesman.

"We forbid this execution," he said.

The mandarin accepted a fresh bowl of tea from his servants and stated that the Square was part of His Celestial Majesty's empire, and the sentence would be carried out.

"This ground," said Hunter, "is leased to the Fanqui. We will not allow it to be desecrated."

The mandarin ignored him while he drank his tea and smoked his pipe. The Chinese soldiers and chair-bearers stood by, highly amused at this comedy. The victim stood there with a chain around his neck, held by two guards. For a few minutes the ghastly scene was frozen, while the mandarin smoked pipe after pipe.

Suddenly a boat's crew from the Indiaman *Orwell*, which Harriet had visited years before, landed from Whampoa. They had come to spend liberty day on Hog Lane; now they found better sport offering. They tore the cross from the ground, smashed it, and used the pieces to beat the gathering mob. They ripped down the mandarin's tent, overturned his tables and chairs, and would have made lobscouse of him if the Fanqui had not intervened. The mandarin finally retreated as the tars cheered.

That did not bring peace to the Square. The mandarin had given the nod, and a mob of about ten thousand Cantonese, yelling like banshees, poured in and attacked the factories with stones and brickbats. The Fanqui ran indoors and barred their gates, but the rioters kept up their fusillade. They routed the guards at the corner of the American hong, tore down the heavy posts before the factories, and used them as battering rams. The streets at the rear were full of mobsters, no Chinese soldiers were in sight, and it was plain that the officials had left the Fanqui at the mercy of the mob.

There was little the Americans could do. They threw broken glass down from the windows to discourage the barefooted Chinese from getting too close, and barricaded the rear entrance with casks of coal. There was a hurried council of war. If only they could get word to Houqua he would save them from butchery.

But they were surrounded on all sides. Finally Hunter and another volunteer scrambled out on the roof of the rear hong, ran across it to the roof of a shop on Hog Lane, got down to the street, and ran pell-mell to Houqua's hong. They found that Houqua had not heard the pandemonium from his end of the row. He immediately sent a messenger to the chief magistrate, and the Yankees went back to Suy Hong the way they had come.

Soon there was the welcome sound of a police gong, and a body of Chinese soldiers marched into the Square and whipped the mob away. Some of the rioters stampeded through the streets, others took to the river and were drowned, as none of the boats dared take them aboard. The factory gates flew open and the Fanqui emerged with sighs of thanksgiving.

That night the Square was guarded by a group of mandarins who sat and smoked, with their all-powerful lanterns lighted to keep prowlers away. When the Chinese wanted peace and order they knew how to get it. The next morning the Fanqui organized a ceremony of thanking the mandarins, and things quieted down again. But the foreign colony met and agreed not to hoist their flags in the Square.

And Lin was on his way.

He arrived March 10 in an official junk, attended by red- and blue-button mandarins. Commissioner Lin was a fat old fellow with a heavy black mustache and long beard, a stern and dignified man, and, as they were to discover, honest and determined. He was received by the local bigwigs with a great official and military reception. For several days nothing alarming happened.

Lin began his campaign with a message to Queen Victoria. She strictly forbade opium to her own subjects as harmful. Why then send it to China? "Suppose those of another nation should go to England and induce its people to buy and smoke the drug—it would be right that you, Honored Sovereign, should hate and abhor them."

On March 18 he pounced like a tiger. The Fanqui were to surrender all the opium in the receiving ships at Lintin, and give their bond to cease the traffic. If the order was not obeyed within three days the Cohong was to suffer dire punishment.

93

The Fanqui played the game of "putty off a little" and on the third day asked for more time, but said they were willing to pledge themselves to stop dealing in opium. Lin gave them one more day, announcing that at ten the next morning he would go to Consoo House to sit in judgment on the Cohong. Thereupon the hong merchants called the Fanqui to meet them at the newly organized Chamber of Commerce, a safer rendezvous now than Consoo House. There Abbot's suffering began, for Houqua confided that unless Lin got his opium the lives of two of the Cohong would be forfeit. After much discussion the foreign merchants agreed to give up a thousand chests, about a twentieth of the drug actually on hand, and the meeting broke up at two in the morning.

Very early Houqua and others of the Cohong went into the walled city with their offer of a thousand chests. It was impatiently brushed aside—but Lin after all did not sentence the Cohong, and this "putty off" lulled most of the Fanqui into thinking Lin was going to follow the fine old Chinese custom of accommodation. Not Abbot, who had spent a sleepless night worrying about Houqua.

Lin that morning made a surprise move. He demanded that Lancelot Dent, one of the chief opium dealers among the British, come into the walled city for a conference. That set the English in an uproar, for in times past Britishers had been enticed into the city and kept imprisoned for years. They would not allow Dent to venture inside the gates.

The next day, March 23, the Cohong suddenly called the Fanqui to a meeting. There was a gasp when the hong merchants came in, all without their buttons, and Houqua and Mouqua wearing chains around their necks, as if they were about to be strangled on crosses. Goqua and two others of the Cohong were imprisoned in the city.

Very soberly Houqua explained the crisis affairs had now reached. Lin must have Mr. Dent as hostage, or before night two of the Cohong would be strangled. Plainly that meant old Houqua himself, and Mouqua. He asked if it was reasonable that Dent should refuse to go into the city under Lin's safeguard, and subject innocent men to a horrible death.

The British refused to consider the safety of anybody but Dent. The arguments went on and on, and finally everybody adjourned to Dent's hong for more debate. Meanwhile the mandarins were impatiently waiting at Consoo House, while English interpreters ran back and forth trying to keep them appeased. Finally the mandarins came in a body to Dent's hong, but even then he refused to give himself up.

The meeting had gone on from ten in the morning until five; Lin had vowed to put two of the Cohong on crosses by nightfall.

"I suffered greatly," Abbot wrote Harriet, "to see old Houqua —so long and so good a friend of our house, deprived of his honour without cause—degraded with a chain upon his neck, and then exposed to a most ignominious death. I fully believed then that his fears were but too well grounded and could not satisfy myself that Dent's were so reasonable."

And yet, as so often happened in an impasse, it was the Chinese who gave way. The mandarins did not seize Dent, they did not take Houqua and Mouqua before Lin for execution.

Refused Dent as hostage, Lin made the whole foreign colony hostage, under house arrest. They were already sealed off from the back streets, now Lin prevented their escaping down the river by putting a triple cordon of armed boats across it. He sent four hundred fully armed soldiers into the Square. And, as a new twist in the ancient arts of torture, he ordered every Chinese to leave the factories, on pain of death. Hundreds of competent servants and coolies, all those quiet men who had cared for the Fanqui by processes mysterious and intricate, now vanished. The Siege of the Hongs had begun.

Lin evidently intended to starve the Fanqui into submission. But the faithful Cohong had not learned smuggling techniques for nothing. They sent in fowls, pigs, sheep, all alive and penned together, producing unpleasant noises and smells, but nevertheless welcome. Houqua's coolies spirited in hot meals to Suy Hong after dark.

The Fanqui weren't to starve, but they did have to perform duties which were not only distasteful but were completely outside their experience. Robert Forbes organized the household. He

95

began by making every man responsible for his own rooms. "I have played cook and coolie," Abbot wrote Harriet, "sometimes making mush, at others carrying water into our third storey to replenish my bathing tub!"

It was a chore getting water upstairs from the casks below. They got so tired of this that they tried hoisting up pails of water by a pulley arrangement. But the ropes got twisted and the pails hung suspended in mid-air. Thereafter the gentlemen left the state of their skins, along with the wrinkles on their beds, to their private consciences.

Communal duties were drawn by lot. Abbot Low drew the chit as head cook, and before the first meal, which was Sunday breakfast, he and Forbes went into the kitchen, which no white man had ever entered. They spent a grim hour cleaning it up, and then produced ham and eggs like something dug from a petrified forest, and toast charred black. Abbot was deposed with hisses, and Warren Delano voted in his place. The rest of the duties were posted:

> J. C. Green sweeps the dining room and makes tea.
> R. B. Forbes attends to the glass and silver.
> A. A. Low sets the table.
> W. C. Hunter fills and trims the lamps.
> Joseph Gilman attends to the wine, beer, and cheese.
> Miranda and Silva wash the dishes, clear the table, and clean knives.

(These last two were minor Portuguese employees of the hong.)

Forbes, at least, was vigorous about looking after the glass and silver. He got from the stores a great piece of sheeting which he kept on the sideboard. Every now and then he would tear off a length for a towel, and when it was soiled he would cheerfully throw it in a corner, which erased the laundry problem.

The venerable P. W. Snow, acting consul, was spared communal duties. Being his own chambermaid almost overcame him, and he especially hated emptying the slops. Meeting Forbes on the stairs during one of these horrid errands, he sighed, "Is it not too bad, Mr. Forbes, that a public official at my time of life, not

The Gardens of Houqua. By a Chinese artist. *Courtesy of the Nantucket Atheneum.* Photograph by The Metropolitan Museum of Art.

William Henry Low II. From a miniature. *Courtesy of Mrs. Benjamin R. C. Low.* Photograph by William Leftwich.

owning a pound of opium, should be imprisoned, and compelled to do a chambermaid's work?"

But the hand of Victoria Regina stretched everywhere. That Sunday afternoon as the Yankees were promenading the Square, trying to forget Delano's dinner, a ship's boat wriggled through the triple blockade. It came from the British war sloop *Larne* down the river. Aboard was the British Empire embodied in Captain Charles Elliot, the new Superintendent of British Trade.

His entrance on the crowded stage where he was to play a star role was in the best British style. He leaped ashore sword in hand.

"Hoist the British flag," was his first command.

When the Union Jack streamed from its pole he announced, "I will call for volunteers to bring Mr. Dent under my protection."

Since Mr. Dent was in his usual quarters instead of, as Elliot supposed, in Chinese hands, it was a simple matter to fetch him, but the whole foreign colony formed an escort of honor. There was something about Elliot that evoked demonstrations of this sort.

He now addressed the colony, promising to protect them. But —and now his errand was explained—the opium must be surrendered. As he put the matter, it didn't quite sound as if it were to be surrendered to Lin. Every man with British-owned opium must give it up to Elliot in the name of Queen Victoria and for the service of Her Majesty's Government, for delivery to the Chinese authorities. He gave his personal pledge that the British merchants would receive compensation for every ounce delivered.

There was now a scramble to yield up the opium to Lin. Schedules were made out, certificates issued against the chests. Often they were cleverly repacked with substitutes at the bottom, and a certain amount of the drug was thus held out for smuggling. By March 27 Elliot had twenty thousand chests in his hands, with a nominal value of twelve million dollars. Of this amount Russell & Co. surrendered 1407 chests, losing only their commission. The house had already announced that it would no longer handle opium.

"I am glad," Abbot wrote his sister, "we are done irrevocably with a branch of business that of late has seemed actually disreputable, a trade that has brought us into contact with the most degraded Chinese, and consequently served to sink us in the estimation of the better classes."

Until the opium was delivered to Lin for destruction the Fanqui remained prisoners, and the Cohong stood guard day and night before the Factory to prevent Dent's escape. The sight of old Houqua, who spent most of the day running back and forth to the city to confer with Lin, keeping vigil under the Factory veranda all night, filled Abbot with concern. Houqua's feet and legs were much swollen, but at least he was still alive.

Nobody believed that Lin would really destroy twenty thousand chests of opium, but Lin was always surprising the foreigners. His men built three great vats on Chunpee Heights near the river, the opium was dumped in and mixed with unslacked lime and rock salt, then the sluices were opened and the horrid mixture was flushed out into the river.

Then Lin made a demand that Abbot called monstrous. He ordered the taipan of each nation and each individual merchant to give him a signed bond agreeing to stop trade in opium himself, and to prevent every other member of the foreign colony from dealing in the drug. Elliot refused a blanket pledge for the English, and Mr. Snow for the Americans. The most Lin could get was individual pledges.

Therefore he kept the Fanqui prisoners for forty-five days, until May 5. They tried to keep up their spirits in spite of acute creature discomfort. The older men played whist, the younger ones organized foot races, cricket and ball games, and rat hunts with terriers. They had a good supply of both. The Chinese soldiers guarding the Square believed that the Yankees lived on rats and beer. They lived mainly on Houqua's smuggled meals and on hope. It was a glad day when the guard was finally withdrawn and the boats came up from Whampoa with news from home.

In Abbot's pile were letters from his father about the plan to send young William to Canton to join his brother.

Seth Low now had taken fifteen-year-old Charles as apprentice, where he could keep an eye on him. The boy had already had a hard year with Gideon Frost, a wholesale dry-goods jobber whose Maiden Lane shop was just behind Mr. Low's. Frost had failed in business, and Charles was now deep in cases of bird peppers and asafetida, urging the Negroes who hoisted the boxes to sing, as sailors did when they shifted sail.

One compensation was the sailor's boardinghouse across the street, where Charles learned to splice rope, make knots, and box the compass. Sometimes he escaped to go down to the wharves and board the ships to climb over the rigging.

South Street, running along the East River, was his paradise. Square-riggers from every port stretched their jib booms far over the pavement, and the forest of masts reached from below Wall Street up above Market. At the foot of Maiden Lane and Pine Street the Savannah packets docked, and Grinnell, Minturn's liners to England. Near them were the "Down Easters" with Maine lumber and the cotton droghers from New Orleans; at Burling Slip the West Indies boats, redolent of fruit and rum, and the canawlers from upstate with their grain. Charles loved them one and all.

At twelve he had nearly succeeded in running away to sea. He and a chum had sneaked over from Brooklyn and got berths on a brig for Savannah. The family had caught them just in time. Now, unfortunately, Seth Low's brother, Captain James, was encouraging the boy, and letting his Dutch mate teach him all the running rigging and how to send down a royal yard.

Mr. Low was ignorant of Charles's secondary passion—running to fires. He and his wife worried dreadfully because William and Edward were members of Live Oak Engine Eight, much as the volunteer companies were needed; they would have worried more if they had dreamed that Charles was torch boy for the company.

There were so many fires that his brothers were called out almost every night. They left by the front door, and Charles left sailor fashion. He kept a long rope hidden in his room, and when his brothers were alerted for duty he tied it to a trunk in the back entry of the third floor and slid down to the veranda roof, where a stout grapevine got him to the ground.

Charles was determined to go to sea, but as an unpaid apprentice

99

he had no way of buying a sailor's outfit. Finally he got the quaint notion that if he learned farming he could earn his kit. He subscribed to Judd's *Agriculturist*, and for a season the family thought Charles was at last getting interested in the solid earth; his oblique approach lulled their suspicions.

The invaluable Josiah was working with his father, and Mr. Low's second son, Haskell, who always set the Salem girls in a flutter, was now marrying one of them, Rebecca Ann Cutler, and would presumably settle down. As for William and Edward, Seth Low wrote, "they are spending money and doing nothing." Edward had gone down to Florida to stay with cousins and look for work, still hard to find since the business crash. But he reported that things in that "bloody murder country" were hopeless, and asked his father to find him something in New York.

William was no longer working for his uncle, and had rolled up debts of two thousand dollars that Seth Low could not pay. "He is too popular with the young men here to live prudently," he wrote. Abbot's offer to get his brother started as a Russell clerk was thus a godsend, and the family was only waiting to get Harriet's opinion. She was still consulted on every important problem in the Tribe of Seth.

Harriet approved, and William sailed for China the middle of June, writing back warnings to Charles about the horrible life ship's boys lived, getting seasick, doing all the menial work. "If Charles wants to," he wrote his parents, "let him go one voyage, I think it will cure him."

William missed the visit home of Harriet and her baby Katherine, an event of the first water. Naturally there was a to-do about the first granddaughter in the family, but even in her first infancy Kate was an extraordinary person, born with brains and charm.

It was well into September before the family in Brooklyn got news that the Siege of the Hongs was over, and foreigners would now, they thought, be safe in Canton. Seth Low was shrewd enough to disagree; he knew the English would still try to smuggle opium.

The opium trade went on apace, with more circumspection. The British now landed shipments at Singapore or Manila to be picked up by their clippers and taken to depots along the coast, where they sold at sometimes ten times the normal cost. Inside Canton, where there was supposedly no opium whatever, chests were bringing as much as three thousand dollars. Lin had imposed a death penalty for anyone caught with an opium pipe.

In June Robert Forbes became chief of Russell & Co. Abbot Low was ready to leave as soon as William had been trained in; meanwhile he had given up all thoughts of a summer vacation in Macao, for the Americans had inherited a tremendous amount of British business. The English, on Captain Elliot's orders, had left en masse for Macao or for Hong Kong, which was a mere anchorage, but which they had decided would be worth developing.

Captain Elliot called on Forbes to urge him to close up Suy Hong. "If Russell & Co. leave," he said, "all the other Americans will follow, and we shall soon bring these rascally Chinese to terms."

What Elliot wanted was to freeze all trade just enough to make the Chinese suffer, but that was not good business.

"No," Forbes said, "I didn't come to China for health or pleasure, and I shall remain here as long as I can sell a yard of goods or buy a pound of tea. We Yankees have no Queen to guarantee our losses."

"Are you willing, Mr. Forbes, to do business with a chain around your neck? I'll soon make Canton too hot for you."

This was not a threat, it was merely Elliot's way of talking, as if he were a sixty-pounder. He was determined to use sixty-pounders if necessary, and the Americans might find themselves in the line of fire. Meanwhile, as both men knew, the Yankees would be useful in keeping up the stream of British trade.

All through the summer the new system worked at top speed. The Yankees increased their merchant fleet by the purchase of several British vessels, and did all the carrying. The British downriver sent their goods up to Canton at the fabulous freightage of thirty or forty dollars a ton, and got their teas down again, all in American bottoms. Soon Forbes went down to the Hong Kong anchorage, where the English assigned him a ship for living quarters, to keep the traffic moving. In Canton Abbot Low and his friends Edward King and William Hunter worked like mad on the Anglo-American shipments. In addition to this, Houqua and Abbot had some stupendous deals going on their joint account, and to their great profit.

Forbes's old storeship *Lintin*, now company property, made several lucrative trips up and down the river in tow, with all her upper spars down to make room for the cotton and tea piled up to her leading blocks. Freightage on cotton was seven dollars a bale for the ninety-mile trip, more than the rate from America.

The British had not done too well on the Queen's guarantee for their surrendered opium. They tried to get five hundred dollars a chest for opium worth half that, but finally cashed in Captain Elliot's receipts for sixty dollars a chest. They suffered, too, from the Yankee freight rates, and finally some of the larger houses like Dent and Jardine sent their agents and tea tasters up to Canton under the Stars and Stripes, and risked some of their own tonnage on the river.

Commissioner Lin was conscious that the Yankees were carrying for the outlawed British, and issued various new orders which required a change in techniques. The Yankee ships now loaded at Hong Kong, then went over to Manila and cleared from that port without breaking bulk. This took a little longer, but the profits were still high. Another device Russell & Co. used was to ship outgoing teas to the Dutch port of Riouw, where the Britishers picked them up. There was risk in this shuttle service to neutral ports, but everybody counted on Queen Victoria's wanting her duty of two shillings sixpence on every pound of tea badly enough to pay for any trouble that might develop.

One night Abbot was delighted to see the good family friend, Phil Dumaresq, leaping off the *Akbar*'s jolly boat. He had just time for dinner and a summary of his water-bug feats.

"We begin with Hong Kong," he said. "There I took on a big cargo of British goods. Then there was the little side trip to Manila for papers, and up I come to Whampoa. Too busy to see you that trip, Abbot. The Britishers were standing by to load me up with teas. Down the river we go, dump off the teas at Hong Kong, then on to Calcutta for a cargo of cotton.

"The British are getting ready for a big war. They're mobilizing fast in India, my boy. Well, I wasn't sure that by the time I
got back here our friend Lin wouldn't have his threatened blockade in force. But I had to risk it. I took on five thousand bales of
cotton at Calcutta, and now we've discharged cargo at Whampoa
and are loaded up with teas again. I think we can get down to
Hong Kong if we sail with the next tide."

"You'll make it," said Abbot. "But I'm afraid this will be your
last round trip. Things are getting too thick."

Not that the summer had been peaceful. In spite of Lin's death
penalty for anybody caught transporting opium, the British clippers sometimes entered the river and got into battles with the
mandarin junks on patrol. In July one of the clippers had fired
into junks on sentry-go and killed fifty Chinese.

Worse, a party of tars from one of the British warships had
made a raid upon a peaceful Chinese village, looking for liquor
and in the end severely wounding a number of villagers, including
children and old people. Lin demanded that the sailors be surrendered to him, and refused Elliot's offer of blood money to the
family of the one Chinese who had been killed. When Elliot
court-martialed the sailors and convicted a few of them merely
of rioting, Lin made the British evacuate Macao, and they went
scurrying to Hong Kong.

Without stopping to think that he had only two warships,
Elliot declared the port of Canton under blockade. With one
voice the British and Americans protested this folly, so he had to
back down. The period of waiting for reinforcements was a torture to Captain Elliot; he was always making large gestures and
then having to lose face.

It was now late September 1839, just ten years after Harriet's
arrival in Macao, and William Low, handsome, mischievous, with
as yet undisclosed reserves of understanding and sympathy, had
arrived in the powder mine of Canton.

8

Thunder

on the

River

In his room at Suy Hong Abbot
was shaken gently awake one morning to find William, who had
arrived in the dead of night, leaning over him. Any reunion between Lows meant a display of warm affection and the uncorking
of a magnum of news, but to an outsider the brothers must have
presented an odd contrast. Abbot was developing a plump, elastic
figure that suited his round jowls and expression of benignity.
Like Harriet, he had their mother's long, almost oriental eyes,
and tended more and more to keep them half shut. He looked as
Chinese as a Yankee could.

William looked like one of the Lake poets. Extremely slight,
almost fragile, he was all eyes and animation. His hair was already
receding from his high forehead, his mouth and cleft chin were
so delicate that his great wide-open eyes monopolized his face.

He had as much vivacity and charm as Harriet in her Macao days, and being a young man of fashion, he seldom admitted to somber moods; cheerful raillery was his style. Enormously responsive to people, he was popular with the young men, on kissing terms with a host of pretty girls, and devoted to every member of the family. He could not write one of them without sending appropriate messages to all, even remote connections. With all this, he was desperately in love with a girl in Brooklyn.

Abbot calmly took him in hand and broke him in as a Russell clerk. Soon William was writing Grandmother Porter, whom he cultivated as one of the best letter writers in the family, "Abbot and myself agree very well, he is a fine fellow but is somewhat particular about the manner of having accounts made out, whether the lines ruled under the figures are in black or red, etc., but all the advice he gives me will never do me any hurt. Please tell Mother, Abbot has learned me to hold my head up straight while walking, after talking to me a few."

He was also showing William how to pay off his debts and store up enough capital to marry. Only the desperate state of his affairs had prevented him from proposing to the lovely Ann Bedell before he left home. Now, with Abbot's help, he was starting small ventures with two other clerks who, like him, did not propose to vegetate very long on their five hundred dollars a year from Russell. One of them, Joseph Gilman, soon became his best friend, and in their afternoon strolls opened up as much of Canton as the Fanqui might investigate.

William was enchanted; he saw Canton with a traveler's eyes, not a merchant's. He loved Old China Street with its genial merchants, the half-naked children calling for cumshaws, the lovely ladies smiling at them from sedan chairs, the Hoppo boats squabbling over a division of spoils, and in the Square Dr. Peter Parker, relaying the latest news to a knot of Yankees.

Dr. Parker was the first Protestant medical missionary in China. Suy Hong had never been devoted to the earnest young men imported by Zion's Corner to spread the gospel and hold an American chapel, but Peter Parker was extremly popular, and became a lifelong friend of the Lows. Both British and Americans helped him open a hospital in Canton for poor Chinese, where, like Dr. Colledge, he specialized in diseases of the eye.

Abbot, who always watched the international trade picture, had been especially interested in Dr. Parker's attempt to broach the tight fortress of Japan. As it happened, Abbot Low himself was to be the first American actually to trade with Nippon, but that was years later. The combined Peter Parker-Zion's Corner visit of friendship to Japan in the ship *Morrison* had resulted only in their being fired on in two ports; but Abbot respected the attempt. Dr. Parker had talents as a diplomat and was soon to be called into the higher councils in Washington.

William worried a good deal about Ann Bedell. What a fool he'd been not to declare himself and have his fate settled before he left for years on the underside of the globe!

The lovely Ann was one of nine sisters who made the Bedell house on Cranberry Street the mecca for aspiring young blades. Their father, Mott Bedell, was a substantial merchant in the coasting trade to Virginia and North Carolina; their mother a monumental matron with a striking resemblance to George Washington, but with the mildest manners. Most of the nine girls had been "finished" in Mrs. Willard's Troy Seminary, and Ann had then gone on to develop her talent for drawing. (Years later, when she was a great lady wintering in Rome, she recognized the gifts of an obscure young American and gave him his first box of paints. That was John Singer Sargent.)

William worried especially because his brother Edward felt much the way he did about Ann, and now had a chance to improve his prospects.

"I suppose," William wrote Josiah, "No. 6 will be watching for a chance at the pride of Brooklyn, and I have no doubt she can have a trial if she wishes. . . . I want to hear about the Miss B's in particular and the young ladies in general. But I must have patience. It does not do to worry in this country. I leave it to you to remember me to all the young ladies of my acquaintance, just to put them in mind of me once in a while so I shall not get out of their books."

That was the debonair William, not yet ready to confide his anxiety, even to Josiah. But before long he was to realize what slow communications meant in affairs of the heart. Soon after he arrived in Canton he had written Ann, hinting at his feelings. When it came to him that he might have to wait a year for her reply, and that meanwhile the Bedell house was full of beaux, he decided to appoint Josiah his suitor by proxy. His younger brother was eighteen, with considerable experience already in charming the young ladies. William could count on his skill, and also on his fidelity. Therefore he sent instructions on the tea boats, one after the other, while he waited for the next year's monsoon to bring him an answer from Ann. Some of his friends had written him of the rivals clustering around her, especially one J.H., constantly at the Bedell house and apparently in her favor.

"Now this is coming upon a poor fellow rather hard," he wrote Josiah, "but I hope and trust she will not form any connection with J.H., for neither he nor his family are people of my fancy, and if Ann knew J.H. as well as I do she would not have anything to do with him. But I have written her pretty fully on the subject."

Some of his letters to Ann went direct to Cranberry Street, others were entrusted to Josiah to be delivered in person, the call giving Josiah a chance to talk up William. This arrangement did not meet with Harriet's approval. She was tender about her brothers' romances, and encouraged Josiah to write her often. "You will only be getting your hand in against you want to write love letters," she explained. When Josiah confided a broken romance of his own, and his brokerage for William, she shook her head.

"I notice all your remarks upon certain young ladies, and am always glad to find my brothers one and all have such a taste for ladies society. There is in my opinion no better test of good dispositions and characters . . . don't be in a hurry dear, there is plenty of time for you yet, and a little further observation will do you no harm.

"I shall write to William I think and give him a bit of my mind as to *courting* by *proxy*. It is very dangerous business for all parties, particularly when the parties are both 'very agreeable and interesting young people' as you say she is and I know you are. Perhaps I was wrong in what I said about Billy's engaging himself —and if it serves as you think it will, as a stimulus to greater exertion and to uprightness and good principles, it will certainly be for his good."

William had other stimulus to exertion. Abbot was showing him the secrets of quick profits, and the news from Seth Low was encouraging. "We find the present value of your goods is now double the invoice," a report not rare in the China trade, but welcome after the grim depression. Mr. Low was now selling drugs to England, and calling for musk, camphor, vermilion, and oil of cassia. Abbot and William busily filled orders in the midst of a war still to be officially announced.

Hostilities began early in November with a clash between British warships and thirty war junks. Five or six of the junks were blown up, killing six hundred Chinese. A little later the Chinese batteries near Hong Kong fired ineffectually on British shipping, and there were frequent collisions between the opium smugglers and the patrol boats, with some loss of life.

As 1840 began the Chinese announced that trade with Britain had ceased to all eternity, and the local officials threatened reprisals against any Fanqui trying to transport goods for the English, which of course meant the Americans. But they continued the profitable ferrying.

Houqua was sad to think that Abbot was going home with the monsoon, but approved the Low family system, so like the Chinese, of having a Number Two son in reserve. Before he left, Abbot Low proved how well he had learned Houqua's art of acting the great gentleman. As always, Houqua had millions of dollars' worth of English goods coming to him on his private account, with Russell & Co. as consignee. He was justifiably afraid that the Chinese officials would confiscate these goods, now that trade had been stopped by the Emperor himself. Abbot arranged for Russell to buy the merchandise outright and handle it for Houqua, turning over to him all the profits, though he had waived them, and taking only their ordinary commission.

The war situation caused many changes along factory row. The British had evacuated to Hong Kong. Two American houses closed altogether; at Zion's Corner old David Washington Cincinnatus Olyphant retired, leaving a revamped firm. Augustine Heard and Joseph Coolidge, Jr., formed a new partnership. At Russell & Co. Robert Forbes remained chief for a few months, to be succeeded by Warren Delano.

Abbot was to sail on the *Zenobia* late in January, and the brothers were too busy to have much time together. The Chinese New Year's was approaching, when the coolies would have a long holiday, and clerks and partners worked almost around the clock dispatching ships. In one week they loaded six vessels, Abbot himself buying, weighing, and invoicing teas.

But he found time to advise William what to do if the war situation got too dangerous, and to give his private affairs a generous lift. He advanced his young brother three thousand dollars in cash, and asked Russell & Co. to advance credit of another eight thousand dollars for teas then being loaded for shipment to Seth Low.

William went down to Whampoa with his brother and "bid him goodbye with as good a heart as I could, but it started the tears," as he confessed in a letter to Harriet. He spent the New Year holidays in a little wing shooting near Whampoa, sleeping on the *Ann McKim*. Then he went back to Canton determined to make money as fast as possible, so that he could follow his brother home.

William had not lost his passion for fire engines, and followed the home news of riots and fracases between the rival teams in New York and Brooklyn. When Mr. Forbes heard that he was an authority on fire apparatus he asked him to set up the engine that had just arrived for the protection of Suy Hong.

"One afternoon when it was good high tide," he wrote Josiah, "we sent down to the hongs and obtained some coolies, took the Engine down to the water in front of the factories, and after I had got on the suction and hose I took the pipe and gave the word for them to work. It threw a very good stream indeed, very nearly touched the top of the liberty pole. When they had got the engine well under way and I had collected a large quantity of Chinamen around, I suddenly lowered the pipe and gave them such a washing as they had not had for many a day. Tell Mother not to worry, as there is no probability of getting up a Fire Department in this country. The weather is too warm and the *gentlemen* here are not over and above fond of such work."

They preferred the new ninepin alley in the back of Suy Hong, where all hands repaired after dinner. They were working hard, too, unloading and loading a dozen ships. One of them was the *Ann McKim,* which had made her first run to China that year, after a shining career in the South America trade. Howland & Aspinwall had bought this beautiful Baltimore clipper from its owner and builder, Isaac McKim, and in the next years were to make history with her.

To William Low and the others at Suy Hong there was a great fascination in this ship-rigged schooner. She looked familiar, own cousin to the opium clippers *Red Rover* and *Sylph* and the rest, which had been inspired by Baltimore clippers of a generation before. She also—and this they almost realized—looked prophetic, for certain of her principles were to be carried into the coming era of true clipper ships, creatures of slender sharp lines and a great spread of canvas in proportion to tonnage. Like most Baltimore clippers, the *Ann McKim* had a marked dead rise midships, long easy convex water lines, a low freeboard, and raking masts. Altogether she was a graceful lady, fastidiously fitted, and her small cargo capacity made her ideal for teas, which required relatively little space and which, it soon proved, were immensely superior in flavor to those kept too long at sea.

Under the influence of John and Robert Forbes, Russell & Co. were becoming interested in ships, and ships able to sail fast. In Boston Samuel Russell and John Forbes had already built and sent out the *Akbar,* a notable improvement over the old China traders. They were also planning some opium clippers to be stationed in the East, and soon Abbot Low was to be involved in this new development. Now that Robert Forbes was going home to Boston, the Russell interest in fast and splendid ships would increase;

before he was through, Black Ben Forbes was to build or own seventy vessels, many of them famous.

Dr. Peter Parker went home with Forbes on the *Niantic;* the medical diplomat was planning to deliver lectures in New York and undoubtedly Seth Low would capture him for the Brooklyn Lyceum. William urged his brothers to attend Dr. Parker's lectures, "and gain a great deal of interesting information in regard to this wonderful country and still more wonderful people."

At that moment, late in June 1840, Queen Victoria's war began in earnest. The warships *Volage* and *Hyacinth* were at the mouth of the river, and Sir Gordon Bremer, commanding a squadron of Navy ships, declared Canton under blockade—the gesture Captain Elliot had been forced to forgo. Several troop transports arrived from the British West Indies. On July 5 the British captured the island of Chusan, with little bloodshed but much plundering and needless destruction.

As the trade season closed and the overworked Americans departed for Macao they were heartened by one of Houqua's gestures of solidarity. Captain Elliot, perhaps for Lin's benefit, warned the Cohong not to buy British goods from the Americans.

"I buy of Amelicans," Houqua said with gentle finality. "How can tell what Blitish, what Amelican? Elliot wanchee stop all trade."

But the blockade meant that American ships were barred from the river, and goods now had to be smuggled.

From Macao William watched the British fleet arrive.

"The frigate *Modeste*," he wrote Josiah, "came in last Tuesday and the *Columbine* on Monday, both in beautiful style with all sail set, studding sails, skysails, and everything in the shape of canvas that they could muster. They kept the fort well employed in answering salutes."

Other ships of the line and steamers were expected to reinforce the fleet, which was then twenty ships of the line, twenty-five transports, and four steamers. Five of the fleet remained to enforce the blockade of Macao, the others moved up to Chusan. The Chinese, said William, were trying to raise a force of six thousand men to drive the ships from the Tiger's Mouth.

"For this last two weeks I have enjoyed myself very much, it has been quite pleasant and the moon shining very bright, and a band of music playing on the Campo almost every night, and lots of ladies walking out without any bonnets on. Raises one's spirits 30 degrees, this suits me to a T. I enjoy myself very much now, plenty of work, plenty of exercise, good appetite, and 'tout les choses comme il faut', and if the girls enquire for me tell them that I am as hearty as a buck and a great deal handsomer than ever."

He was amused to hear that the family in Brooklyn had discovered that he was using Josiah as postman. He was now sending him some paintings to deliver to Ann; what wouldn't he give to be able to take them to her himself, "why, nothing more than *myself, heart, hand*, and all I was worth. I dare say that Mother and others have put me down as a gone goose. Well, if they have I cannot say that they are far out of the way. Now say she is a fine girl, well educated, excellent taste, has a quick discernment. . . . I dare say you might make friends with the father without much trouble. I should like you to try."

Finally the winter fleet was in, with the prayed-for reply from Ann, which made him deliriously happy. As Harriet had hoped, the prospect of an engagement was a steadying influence, and William astonished his young brother by the tone of the next letter, from beleaguered Canton.

"You say that you and Edward have joined the Brooklyn Boat Club. I dare say that it is good amusement, but I fancy it is not a money making pidgeon, and is apt to consume a great deal of valuable time. I do not like to lecture you or Ned, but you are aware that I have been through the mill and savee all such fashion things."

The carefree William was growing up fast.

A big war was on the way, and the Chinese had twenty thousand men posted in the various river forts. Russell & Co. was now keeping most of its staff in Macao, with a skeleton force in Canton to smuggle the teas down the river. On January 7, 1841, William Low and Edward King were relieved, and got down to Macao

British Opium Clippers Anchored at Lintin Island, 1824. At right, a Chinese "Centipede." Painting by W. J. Huggins. *Courtesy of the Peabody Museum.*

Captain Nathaniel Brown Palmer. Portrait by Samuel L. Waldo. *Courtesy of Mrs. Joseph Pearman.* Photograph from the Frick Collection.

just as the British bombarded the Chunpee forts downriver, and captured two of them, slaughtering the seven hundred soldiers guarding them. The mandarins had locked them in the forts.

Captain Elliot had drafted a treaty for ending the war on terms so severe that the Emperor refused to ratify it, so hostilities went on while the British took possession of Hong Kong and started building. Bocca Tigris, called the Bogue, was of course a crucial point, and the Chinese bought the Russell ship *Chesapeake* and turned her into a mandarin warship. With great whoops she sailed down to guard the Bogue, but a few days later the ship, loaded with ammunition, was blown to bits by a Congreve rocket and all on board lost.

On February 24 William Low, with Captains Dumaresq, Hallet, and Endicott, left Macao Roads in a schooner to wait upon Elliot, who was then in the warship *Calliope* in the Bogue. They were bringing him a request from Russell & Co. to allow American ships to enter the river; they were getting tired of smuggling down teas from Canton to Macao.

The next morning they reached the blockade ships and were allowed to pass the lines and proceed to within a mile of the forts. Dumaresq then took a boat and boarded the *Calliope*, where Elliot received him cordially and waved away his apologies for bringing up business when a war was going on.

"I'm rather glad you've brought the matter up, sir," he said affably. "You Americans have been very quiet and patient through this whole business, and have made me not the slightest trouble. I could give Russell an answer at once, but if you gentlemen would like to wait twenty-four hours I think I can promise you more. As a matter of fact I hope to raise the blockade by tomorrow. How would you like to stay and see the fight?"

Dumaresq said he would like nothing better. The four Americans in their schooner now watched the stage being set. During the afternoon the British unloaded their troops on the island of South Wantung, using boats and the steamer *Nemesis*. The Chinese fired on the steamer, with very bad aim.

William said impatiently, "If the Chinese knew one thing about

gunnery, the *Nemesis* would have been sunk on the first trip."
It was dreadful to see the Chinese trying to use modern methods
of warfare.

During the night the British built a breastwork on the island
and set up their mortars and field pieces. The Chinese, who held
North Wantung, fired at them now and then, overshooting so
badly that almost every shot landed in the water.

The firing began at daybreak, with the Americans at the rails
of their schooner. It took only an hour of spirited gunnery to set
fire to some outworks on the Chinese island. Another hour, and
the fort opposite the British battery was silenced. It was a fine
morning with a splendid breeze, and the Yankee captains waited
impatiently for the British men-of-war to get under way. In true
British style the order was delayed until ten, and by then the
breeze had died down, and the warships had to come to anchor
again. The Americans whistled up a breeze for them, and the
ships of the line moved up for their work. The roar of the great
guns made everything shake.

"I swear," William Low yelled, "the hills are rolling down!"

Chinese spectators swarmed on the hills, and others stood on
the fortifications of flimsy earthwork. Soon they understood what
the bombardment meant, and scattered, yelling in terror. In two
hours the British captured the forts.

The four Americans, too excited to think of their own safety,
took a boat and went close to North Wantung before the can-
nonading was over. The tide was stronger than they had reckoned
and it carried them, in spite of frantic rowing, into the line of
fire between a Chinese fort and the *Nemesis*, busily firing at it.
They escaped the shots, only to experience something worse.

"After the English flag was hoisted," William wrote Josiah,
"we obtained permission and went on shore on the island of
Wantung, and I must say that I never saw such a distressing scene.
The dead, dying, and wounded lay in one indiscriminate mass,
many of them with their clothes on fire, and praying for water,
or for an end to be put to their sufferings. The mandarins from
the forts fled before the action was over, having taken all the
boats and fastened the soldiers in the forts. The latter turned their

guns on them, which I am sorry to say did not sink the whole of the vile cowards."

They examined the largest fort, an admirable piece of work, but found that the guns were not properly mounted for quick reloading. If they had been, "nothing could have stood before them, and every ship there must have been sunk." That day William wasn't quite sure which side he was on; certainly his heart was with the Chinese.

The Americans returned to Macao with Elliot's dispatches, while the British fleet sailed up the river. At the first bar they fought some choice Tartar troops that came rolling and tumbling to the attack, only to be mowed down by the great Navy guns. Then, with no loss to themselves, but inflicting heavy Chinese casualties, the British attacked and destroyed all the forts defending Canton. By March 20 there was a truce, and trade was declared open again. The Union Jack was raised on the flagpole in the Square, and the British and American merchantmen left Macao for their old anchorage at Whampoa.

William stayed in Macao to dispatch the teas that had accumulated there, and then in early April went up to Canton, hoping the war was over.

But the Emperor refused to ratify the truce and ordered the war to go on. He was infuriated with the British destruction of lives and property and their many outrages on civilians.

What the Son of Heaven invited for his people was the final horror of the sack of Canton. By May the British got reinforcements from India and under Sir Hugh Gough bombarded the city. The siege was marked by fires, ruined cemeteries and fields, the rape of little girls, robberies, and myriads of people bewailing their five thousand dead and the loss of their homes.

The British and Americans stayed in their hongs until this storm actually burst. William, finding that silks and teas were selling at panic prices, followed the merchant instincts buried in his complex nature and bought up young hyson, sarsenets, and pongees to send down to the *Narragansett* at the anchorage. On May 19 he found a servant posting up a chop from the mandarins urging the Fanqui to remain tranquil and stay in the factories.

"That means a trap," the Americans agreed. The British, too, scented danger and began to evacuate. At Suy Hong all hands worked in a frenzy, sending teas down the river, settling accounts with the hong merchants, and packing up the company books and papers. At two in the morning William Hunter started for Whampoa with the first boatload. At dawn William was ready with the rest of the Russell property and his own baggage, loaded into a sailboat, which had to be towed against the wind. For hours he sat at the tiller under the glaring sun, and when he was finally picked up by the *Narragansett* he was suffering from sunstroke and went to bed.

Toward midnight Captain Lovett woke him.

"Canton's on fire," he said. "They're burning the hongs."

From the deck they could see the glare against the night sky, and then they heard the boom of the British cannon. The next day they learned that mobs had plundered and burned the Factory and the two hongs next to it, and had sent fire rafts upon British shipping. The English were all safely away, but several Americans, including Abbot's friend Joseph Coolidge, had stubbornly stayed behind. They were all captured by the mobs and some of them were tortured, but Captain Elliot managed to rescue all but Coolidge's Portuguese clerk, who had been tossed into the river and drowned.

As the bombardment went on Houqua visited the British men-of-war and offered six million dollars if the British would spare Canton. That precise amount was soon exacted as a ransom, but meanwhile Victoria's troops penetrated sixty miles into the interior, while the Navy continued its savage destruction northward to Shanghai and Nanking.

The Cohong ransomed their city, with some help from the mandarins. Houqua contributed $1,100,000, Puankeiqua $260,000, and other hong merchants together $640,000. Houqua called his gift a thank offering to Fung Shuy (Wind and Water) for his prosperity and the birth of a grandson on his sixtieth birthday a dozen years before, thus completing a cycle of life.

William had suddenly decided to sail home with the *Narragansett*. In less than two years he had paid off his debts and cleared fifteen thousand dollars, enough surely to make his marriage possible. The December before he had felt confident enough to make a formal proposal to Ann, and to write Captain Bedell a detailed statement of his business situation. By the time the ship was in the Indian Ocean William was writing a twenty-page letter to Harriet, not quite in his usual careless vein, but full of confidence. Surely Ann would accept him, especially as he was coming home instead of staying another three years in Canton. How surprised she would be to see him. . . .

But he wrote his sister, too, of those last days on the Pearl River, the haste, the fear, the horrors of fire and cannon that had turned the most delightful land on earth into a "cursed country." He was never able to drop it from his mind; sometimes the horror would surge up and possess him. There would come times when William needed watching.

9

Charles

Goes

to Sea

Abbot Low came home with the
notion that he had finished with the China trade. At twenty-nine
he was a rich bachelor who could, if he chose, follow the Cushing
pattern at home as he had in Canton. John Cushing had married
a Boston girl and settled her in his exotic mansion kept by a staff
of Chinese servants and surrounded by a wall of Chinese porce-
lain; he had a country estate, a racing yacht, and no worries.

Abbot was younger than Cushing and not so rich. He needed
time to get acquainted with his country, now in the paroxysm
of the Whig-Locofoco campaign, and with his family, who had
been growing up so fast that he hadn't recognized Josiah, ten
years his junior.

The Archers had now left the parental roof, making room for
the Haskell Lows and their baby son. Ned was home from the

118

South, still rather rootless as to a career, Charles was a strapping boy of sixteen, and "baby Ellen" was entering her teens. Aunt Abigail Low, whom Abbot had last seen boarding the Indiaman at Macao, had settled in the neighborhood to remarry and be widowed for a second time.

At last Abbot could get acquainted with Harriet's husband, John Hillard, who had come over on a business trip. Sorely missing her "hubby" and heartbroken that she was not home for Abbot's return, Harriet solaced herself by a trip to Scotland with Caro and Tom Colledge. They had returned to England to stay, but the good doctor continued to save Chinese lives by founding the China Medical Society.

Abbot missed his favorite sister, but Sarah slipped into a new place in his affections. She was eighteen, the image of her tall, slender mother at her age, with Harriet's vivacity and her artless way of attracting admirers.

"I must have a girl of my own this summer," he told her. "Will you make the rounds with me, Sarah?"

Every summer the Lows, in relays, visited their Porter cousins in Salem, in return for making their Brooklyn house a "parochial board" for all Salemites during the winter. This arrangement had now been extended by a similiar one with the Dow family. When Josiah Dow had been forced out of business by the 1837 crash he had gone up to Wakefield, New Hampshire, to open an academy with some of his daughters as teachers. During the summer vacation the Dow Academy was thrown open to the family friends, and Abbot and his effervescing young sister started their visits in Wakefield.

Abbot received an electromagnetic shock. Ellen Almira Dow, whom he remembered as a child, had flowered into a beauty. There was a gentle, elegiac quality in her, a repose that assured him he had indeed come home. Being almost as skilled as Houqua himself in screening emotions behind a genial courtesy, Abbot succeeded in keeping everybody guessing but himself, and perhaps Ellen. The family was watching, from Brooklyn, from Salem, from London and Canton, puzzling at Botus' singular procrastination about taking a wife. It all rolled over his head, just as did the imprecations against Martin Van Buren and the Locofocos.

Salem was vociferously Whig, all for William Henry Harrison and his Log Cabin principles. Down in New York Horace Greeley, who had arrived a few years before with ten dollars in his pocket, started his campaign paper, *Log Cabin*, and changed the face of journalism.

Harrison was elected, the Lows and their friends and cousins rejoiced—and Abbot Low was back in the China trade. He had never left it, actually, having many irons in the fire. But he took a New York office to answer his letters, and hung one of Chinnery's portraits of Houqua over the mantel. The benign old gentleman looked at him with brows arched inquiringly over his somber eyes.

"Wellywell, olo flen," Abbot assured him. "Makee tousand per cent plofit. I chin-chin you, Houqua."

William was on his way home, Ned would go out to take his place. As for Josiah, he had a good head for business and the art of keeping in harmony with every member of the family. Abbot took him as his assistant and then as partner, an arrangement that lasted as long as they remained in business.

Prophetically, it was shipping that lured Abbot back to his desk. He watched the building of the little topsail schooner *Angola* which Russell & Co. had commissioned to the famous yard of David Brown and Jacob Bell. As the reports came through of the profits Russell's *Akbar* was making by dint of speed, as the war news from Canton worsened, Abbot could only decide that the race was to the swift smugglers which could evade war junks on patrol, beat against the strong tides and currents on the China coast, and evade the heavily manned pirate boats which could move in dead calms with half a hundred men at the oars.

Presently he had Brown & Bell lay down a larger topsail schooner, the *Mazeppa*, which he planned to send to China as his part of the Russell smug fleet. In Boston Russell and the Forbes brothers added to the China fleet the beautiful *Zephyr*, *Ariel*, and finally the *Antelope*, exquisitely modeled like racing yachts, with long raking masts to carry a spread of canvas.

Now and then Abbot would find Charles at Brown & Bell's, watching the *Mazeppa* grow in the stocks, talking to the shipwrights and riggers and sailmakers. The boy was pale with excitement, and when he saw Abbot coming he rushed back to his father's warehouse, where he made the Negroes sing as they unloaded musk and camphor.

When the *Mazeppa* sailed for China all the Low brothers went along to Sandy Hook. Finally the schooner was ready to drop the pilot and Abbot marshaled his brothers.

"Where's Charles?"

They began calling for him, but Josiah quietly got the captain to order a search.

"Trying to stow away," Haskell said. "No, you don't, dickey ricker."

They found Charles in the bread locker. He jumped down into the pilot boat, posted himself in the stern sheets, and nobody said a word to him.

That evening the stowaway faced the family council. Seth Low and Abbot were stern; the Lows were merchants, not sailors, and Charles would never make anything of himself at sea. It was the sympathetic Josiah who understood the depth of his younger brother's passion for blue water. Patiently Josiah wore ship until the others yielded and agreed to give Charles his chance. His father allowed him extra time to learn the ropes from the sailors along South Street, and finally he went to a navigation school and studied under an old captain.

His mother was relieved to see the transformation in her youngest son; he was merry and overflowing with energy, and went about singing:

> "Old Low, old Low's son,
>   Never saw so many Lows
>   Since the world begun."

William Low was home late in 1841, to find that Abbot and Ellen Dow had married in mid-March and were happily settled in a house on Washington Street with yards and gardens spread over two city lots. He started a more modest house for himself and Ann, whom he was to marry the following May; like Abbot, he had come home thinking he was done with the China trade. He wanted to settle down and forget the nightmares of the war and the throat trouble that was pulling down his health.

The United States Government was watching the crisis in China, gradually arriving at the conclusion that the Opium War was battering open the Flowery Kingdom for freer conditions of trade. Dr. Peter Parker had done a great deal of work in Washington, explaining his views and making, he thought, no effect whatever. But the State Department caught up with him eventually and made him Caleb Cushing's secretary in negotiating the first treaty between the United States and China. Meanwhile Dr. Parker had married a niece of Daniel Webster and gone back to his Canton hospital. His lectures in New York and Brooklyn had made a sensation during a general epidemic of lecture-going that had put the theaters flat on their backs. The Lyceum series on which Seth Low lavished much pains drew crowds that filled the huge Tabernacle and overflowed into Clinton Hall. It took the great danseuse Fanny Elssler to revive the Park Theater.

The next great sensation, early in 1842, was young Charles Dickens, whose visit aroused public demonstrations not matched since the triumphal journey of Lafayette when the Lows were children in Salem. The Boz Ball at the Park Theater presented tableaux vivants with scenes from his books; he was banqueted at City Hall, with Washington Irving as master of ceremonies; and President Tyler, who had come into office after the tragic death of Harrison, gave a White House levee for him. Thereupon Dickens went home to make insulting remarks about the Americans in his *Martin Chuzzlewit*.

The honeymooners, Ann and William Low, were close on his heels, visiting friends on a handsome estate near Baltimore and going to Washington to call on President Tyler. Their tour stretched through the summer, as both were recovering from a stretch of indifferent health, and both loved to travel. Before their marriage early in May, William was so thin that John Hillard declared two people couldn't see him at once. They were overwhelmed by the wonders of Niagara Falls, and wrote Josiah that he must not fail to make the pilgrimage the next season. At the elegant Cataract House they dined with travelers from every part of the world.

"Annie is gaining very rapidly and looks finely," William wrote. "I do not gain quite as fast, but am decidedly better than when I left. I cough but seldom and my mouth is rather better."

After a visit to the Dows in Wakefield and an excursion to Montreal they came back to find that Abbot had a longer trip planned for them. They were to go out to Canton to join Ned. The small house of A. A. Low & Bro. was growing apace, and in China hostilities had now ceased.

The British Treaty of Nanking, signed late in August, gave the victors what they demanded: an indemnity of twenty-one million dollars, the opening to trade of Canton, Amoy, Foochow, Ningpo, and Shanghai, the abolition of the Cohong and the Hoppo system, and the ceding to Britain of Hong Kong. The opium trade was not mentioned. This treaty was followed in 1844 by one with the United States which, having a happier background, gave Americans more concessions and prestige than the British.

The William Lows were going out to China on the *Horatio*, Captain Howland, a Grinnell, Minturn vessel with a good record for speed. Abbot made arrangements for a third member of the family; Charles was to go as boy, without wages. It was hard to understand his jubilation.

"What will you do without money?" Abbot asked him.

Charles waved this detail away. "I'll stick with the ship, and when this voyage is over I'll ship out again."

"I'll see that he doesn't starve," said William.

But no Low started his career penniless. Mr. Low gave his youngest son fifty dollars in cash, his sailor's outfit, and his freedom from the uncompleted apprenticeship. At eighteen Charles started his independent life with money to invest in China goods.

Before they sailed Abbot's first child was born and named Harriet for his loved sister, who now had a second daughter of her own. Early in November, on a fine sunny day, the *Horatio* cleared for China, escorted by a tugful of Lows and lovely Bedell girls. Charles pretended indifference to the farewells at Sandy Hook; he was starting his sea career through the hawsehole, and did not want his crew mates to get any other idea.

They were a villainous lot, put aboard by runners who had robbed them of three months' advance pay and most of their clothes. But drunk as they were, they responded when a chanteyman "struck a light" and the anchors came up and the sails were set to the melodious lament:

> "Then up aloft that yard must go,
> Whisky for my Johnny.
> Oh, whisky is the life of man,
> Whisky, Johnny."

They would get no more whisky till they reached Canton, but there would be plenty of songs. Even prim Captain Howland knew that "a good chanteyman is worth four men in a watch." Charles, who had a passion for singing, felt that rule was the secret of a happy ship.

No doubt his brothers had made sure that he would escape the bugaboos of the forecastle, of which vile smells and language were the mildest; the *Horatio's* four boys bunked 'tween decks just forward of the cabin with the carpenter and sailmaker, who could by tradition be trusted with boys. Charles longed for the day when he could show his mettle; by the gale on the third day he at least proved that his stomach stayed put, but he wanted to prove that his head was steady too.

The gale mounted, and the mate bawled, "Send down the royal yard."

Charles officiously jumped for the main rigging.

"Where in hell are you going to?" the mate yelled.

"I'm going to send down the royal yard," said Charles.

"What do you know about it, boy?"

Charles kept on climbing. "I can send it down," he said, and he did. A seamen was sent along to watch, but Charles handily secured lifts and braces, and got the yard down. When all was snug the mate called him and asked if he'd ever been to sea before. That was a tribute, and before they were done the mate promised to give Charles a lesson in steering ship when they got calmer weather.

After that Charles was treated as a likely lad, escaping some of the boys' work of feeding the pigs and fowls and acting as general scavenger. He was not released from the horrid task of slushing the masts with grease so that the yards would slide up and down easily. It was dirty business, especially in a wind, and he was glad when it came on Saturdays before the crews' washing, when all hands ranged along the lee gangway, scrubbing themselves and their clothes. Sailor's comfort followed, and he learned the code that allowed a patch next a patch as neighborly, but never a patch on a patch, as beggarly. Having a new outfit, Charles could ignore the sewing ditty that his mother, with much supervision, had prepared for him.

He was utterly happy, with a huge appetite for lobscouse and salt pork and plum duff. Sometimes when he took his watch at ten in the evening, walking the deck with a slab of raw salt pork from the harness cask in his hand, William would come forward to ask how he was getting on. But he didn't see Sister Ann until he had progressed to taking a two-hour trick at the weather wheel. She came tripping lightly over the coils of rope—and the rules—to speak to the man at the wheel. Thank heaven Captain Howland was below. Charles, his round jaw set firmly, steered ship and answered questions about his diet, his mates, his duties. He was fond of Ann, and pitied her ignorance.

The master, for instance, was not his idea of a captain. He never came forward of the mainmast, and relayed his orders through the mate. He never appeared on the quarterdeck without kid gloves.

"Captain Howland," Ann sighed lightly. "He's such a gentleman, Charlie, never without his gloves. I'm sure that you must enjoy learning from such a captain."

He gulped. "I've never exchanged a word with him, Ann."

"But, my dear, he's your *captain!*"

"So I'm told. But he's not interested in what goes on in his own ship, Ann. Just wait till I'm a shipmaster, I'll be all over it, and keep every watch in a storm. And never, never will I wear gloves on the quarterdeck."

125

Ann finally retreated, in a dainty flutter of skirts, and Charles hugged the wheel in relief. Still, it was useful, having a family. How else would he have known what the mate, who was always taking him down, really thought of him?

"The smartest boy I ever saw on a ship," the mate told William.

The *Horatio*, one of the fastest ships in the trade, made Anjer in eighty days, and the East enveloped Charles. He saw it mainly in terms of food, the natives bringing out chickens and ducks, boatloads of oranges and bananas, mangosteens, coconuts, and pineapples. They made Hong Kong in a hundred days, a record passage, and found it in a raw demoralized state, as the British had just taken it over formally.

Soon they went across to Macao, where Charles remembered the tales Harriet had told him, and where he met William Hunter, who had settled there permanently in the business of keeping a fleet of small vessels for local charter. Charles lived aboard ship in Macao Roads, his social life mostly in the forecastles of the opium ships anchored near by. But one night, with his hands quite black from tarring masts and stays, he went ashore for a sumptuous dinner at the Macao branch of Russell's. Ann was horrified, but the Russell residents accepted him genially as the latest youngster in the great nursery of the China trade.

At dinner there was a British naval officer who had seen the thing with his own eyes. The French were that year establishing a protectorate over Tahiti, and several British had been invited to the French flagship for the solemn ceremony which marked the transfer of sovereignty from the house of Pomare, a carefree and luckless dynasty. Within a few years Pomare II had died of drink, and Pomare III had succumbed in turn, leaving the rule to his half sister Aimata, Queen Pomare IV, who hated missionaries and foreigners in general, but whose native chiefs had forced her to accept the French "protection."

Ashore, there had been great preparations. The lovely fat Queen had been coached in protocol, her "cousin" the Queen of France had sent her an elaborate toilette, and she was arrayed and rowed out to the flagship in her gorgeous barge. Escorted up the ladder, she encountered the smart marines in stiff lines from gangway to quarterdeck, the bluejackets standing to their guns, the admiral advancing, plumed hat in hand, as a broadside was fired.

Pomare was truly royal. She stood there, receiving this starched homage with a look of complete boredom on her face. Her eyes swept over the lines of marines, glinted at the sight of the shiny brass guns just fired, and then fixed themselves on a tremendous half-naked French tar swabbing out a smoking gun.

She picked up her Parisian skirts and fairly ran across the deck to him. She embraced him, babbling delight. The royal finger traced the tattooing that ran down the tar's tremendous arms from shoulder to wrist, then the bold design on his hairy chest, then the arabesques on his legs revealed by rolled-up trousers. She fairly cooed. Tahitian work, the very best!

Not, of course, as splendid as her own. Alas, her plump brown arms were covered by tremendous sleeves. But as admiral and staff, British guest officers, marines, and seamen watched in fascinated horror, she hoisted up her skirts and held out one leg after the other to show the tar *her* tattooing. The skirts went higher and higher, until the brown stenciled thighs were revealed in their glory. . . .

"I think that was lovely," said William.

The gentlemen exchanged glances, and somebody suggested that they join the ladies. William decided not to repeat the tale to Ann when they got home.

During the next years Russell & Co. were to establish branches in Hong Kong and the new treaty ports, but the main house remained in Canton. To the Low brothers the China trade meant the friendly city on the Pearl River where Houqua was the presiding spirit, and where they felt at home. The agony and devastation of the war were erased the sooner because the British had retired to Hong Kong.

Charles learned Canton as nobody in the family had known it, from Whampoa, still the anchorage for merchantmen. It was the sailors' city, the streets back of the foreign hongs, that he first knew, convoyed by runners from Hog Lane who took the seamen to shops where they were given tea, pork chops, and boiled eggs, and enough rum to open their pockets. Charles prudently spent his liberty investing his small capital in pongees and silk handkerchiefs, then visiting William and Ned in Suy Hong.

He learned what Harriet, and later his own wife, considered the most horrible thing in the celestial kingdom, worse than fires or pirates or typhoons—the cockroach. They were legion, and they were insatiable, eating the labels from the tea chests, the men's boots and oilskins, nibbling their toenails as they slept. A Whampoa ritual was carried out by Chinese specialists, who caught the roaches in baited rattan baskets, at the rate of thirty bushels a day. Then the ship was smoked with sulphur and charcoal to drive off the rats, and there was a fair chance of arriving in New York with a whole cargo.

Home in mid-August of 1843, Charles found everybody but Josiah and Ellen were making the rounds to Wakefield and Salem. Sarah had gone to London to spend a year with Harriet. At once Charles realized the power of a man before the mast. He could go to London to see his sisters.

Five days later he shipped as an ordinary seaman on the big Griswold packet *Toronto* carrying cabin and steerage passengers and a cargo of cheese, coal, clocks, oil, and lard to London. The crew were hard-bitten "hoosiers" who worked on the packets in summer and the cotton droghers to Mobile and New Orleans in the winters. To Charles their one virtue was their repertory as chanteymen, gathering on the forecastle to sing melodious insults to the packet rats on the rival Black Ball Line, which was British:

> "On a trim Black Ball liner I first served my time,
> And in that Blackballer I wasted my prime.
> To me way—aye, blow the man down!

> "It's when a Blackballer's preparing for sea
> You'd split your sides laughing the sights you would see,
> At the tinkers and tailors and sojers and all
> For you'll seldom find sailors aboard a Black Ball.
> To me way—aye, blow the man down!"

In London Charles had been unloading cheeses for a week, wondering just how he was to find Harriet in the vast city, when John Hillard came aboard, looking very elegant as usual. When Charles was arrayed to go ashore with him he was proud of his own clothes: sailor trousers and short blue jacket, a white shirt with a rolling collar, a blue navy cap and big black neckerchief.

His clothes became him, for Nature had cast him for his work. He was just under six feet, and developing a broad chest and good muscles. Like all the family, he was light on his feet and had a fine resonant voice, which was to develop power on the quarter-deck. He had the bright skin and ultramarine eyes of the born sailor; his straight brown hair bristled above his round forehead. For years to come he would bear a rather defiant expression, which evolved into one of quiet authority.

But Charles was still in the polliwog stage, and once in his sister's house near Marylebone Lane he reverted into the youngest son. Still on affectionate probation with his brothers, he was the sort of "mother's boy" who basked in the company of the women in the family, and was rather diffident with strange females. He had grown up as the darling of Grandmother Porter and his mother and older sisters, who loved him for his rollicking good nature and his endearing way of getting and giving unclouded affection. Finding Harriet and Sarah flanked by two small nieces was worth slushing all the masts on the seas.

Kate was now four, and Frances had just had her second birthday. Kate, whom her mother claimed was the wonder of the Tribe of Seth, could recite long poems from end to end, pretend to read the papers to her parents, exclaiming impatiently, "No news there!" and drive her little sister in a nanny-goat chaise in Hyde Park.

Harriet was never to have a son. Her firstborn had died at birth, and the twin sons born that April had lingered only a few months. But with her usual gallantry she managed to show Charles her usual self. London was an amusing pageant; having conquered the Company in Macao, she could look with detachment on royalty. Now and then, she told Charles, she saw Queen Victoria driving out in the park, looking cross and ugly. She had gone to

St. James's Palace with her friend Mrs. Putnam to meet the ladies of the Drawing Room, not very beautiful, either, but tall and elegant in figure.

"And, Charles, the gentlemen! Really, they were done up like great dolls in their silk stockings and knee breeches. I thought they were footmen, my dear. Then I noticed the ladies taking their arms. I said to Mrs. Putnam, 'How strange for the ladies to take hold of the footmen's arms!' She was scandalized, and told me they were great gentlemen in court dress. Well, I was so overcome with my blunder that I left my purse somewhere in the palace, so I couldn't have ice cream in Bond Street on the way home."

This reminded her of an earlier blunder when she and Aunt had stopped in London on their way home from Macao. She had taken umbrage at the statue a group of Englishwomen had set up in Hyde Park to honor the Duke of Wellington. "Quite naked, my dear. I was horrified—but now John tells me that it's really a statue symbolizing Achilles."

The next day Harriet took her sailor brother to the park.

"Charlie," she said when they were home, "I can't go to walk with you in that dress. Everyone was staring at us."

"What's wrong with my dress?" he demanded.

She was measuring him with a practiced eye.

"You're about John's size, dear. That settles the problem."

The next morning he found neatly folded on a chair in his room the horrible clothes Harriet considered proper. Sweating and swearing, he maneuvered himself into John's skin-tight breeches. He was sure they would rip if he took one step, and fervently hoped they would. But they kept him trussed like a frog through that day's walk.

"Harriet," he said, "I can't go walking in those togs again. Everyone was staring at us."

He saw the sights of London in the sailor clothes he had spent his life to earn.

10

Captain Nat

When Charles scrambled up the mainmast of the *Horatio* to send down the royal yard he had an inkling of his own future as a great sea captain. To his brothers the moment heralded something more: they now added a third dimension to the family enterprise. So far they had functioned in two regions half the globe apart; now the seas that linked them became the field of their endeavors.

Born at the right moment, with temperaments that made them responsive to the commercial drives of their day, the Lows were ready to go forward with the nation into its most exhilarating age—conquest of the seas by the greatest sailing ships that ever met the brine.

Without being great in themselves, the brothers were perfect tools for helping to shape an era of national greatness. You could not find another family that more perfectly expressed America's golden age on the seas. Their success came partly from their tight cohesion as a trading family, and even more from the fact that they were guided by three extraordinary men.

The now lost arts of fatherhood, the incessant, watchful guidance of each generation during its apprenticeship to the older one, had a great part in the rapid development of the New World. Every man brought up his own sons and also any young men who happened to be close to him. Seth Low gave his sons the heritage of the young republic, and in spite of his personal prejudice, that meant the Gloucester and Salem lore of two centuries during which the sea was the chief American reality.

Their second father was Houqua, who expressed the paternalism of China. He opened to them a vast alien land which they learned to respect and enjoy and to a certain degree understand, because they could understand Houqua himself. Intricate as he was, the steel-hard merchant, the austere aesthete, and the fabulous oriental prince, their relation to him was simple and clear: he was their Cantonese father.

Now the moment had arrived when the Lows needed a third father—or, one might put it, when a man with no sons of his own needed the Lows to carry out his bold dreams. When Nathaniel Brown Palmer discovered the Low brothers great forces were set in motion. They were now firmly rooted in New York and Canton, but the slow communication between their bases was holding them back. Only Palmer could show them what to do about this problem. He was the country's greatest salt-water man.

Captain Nat was the only man of his fraternity who combined all the experience and skills necessary to create the golden day now on the horizon. He knew three things: how to build ships of a new order, how to get maximum performance from them, and how to train the new breed of captains to command these great ships. Not only did he create the first clipper ships, but he stimulated younger designers, John Griffiths and Samuel Pook and Donald McKay. Evolving a science of his own for sailing at top speed without squandering men and masts, he was to go down in history as father of the clipper captains. From Beachy Head to Anjer, "Captain Nat" meant just one man, the big, lusty sire of proud ships and masters.

"My home is here in Stonington," said one of his brothers, "but Nat's home is the world."

Stonington, the beautiful little Connecticut port where Nat was born on August 8, 1799, was a good beginning for such citizenship. Like Salem, this harbor unloaded the excitement and smells and tales of the round globe for the instruction of its children. Nat's father was a lawyer and shipbuilder in a town which produced fine brigs, schooners, and ships. Nothing in the conception and gestation of watercraft was a mystery to Nat; he was born with a tiller in his hand.

The town produced sealers as Nantucket bred whalers. As Nat grew into boyhood the chief promoter of sealing expeditions was Edmund Fanning, one of eight brothers who made their careers at sea. The oldest, Nathaniel Fanning, had been a middy with John Paul Jones, and never ceased to recount the part he had played in the immortal battle between the *Bonhomme Richard* and the *Serapis*. Edmund Fanning had more to boast about. He had earned his name as "Pathfinder of the Pacific" by his amazing voyage around the globe on his tiny brig *Betsey*, when he discovered the group of islands which bear his name. He came home the year before Nat Palmer was born, and as a climax to his adventures, presented the owners of the brig a net profit of over fifty thousand. After that he shuttled between his Stonington shipyard and the offices of New York financiers, getting backing for no less than seventy sealing and exploring expeditions in the Southern Hemisphere.

The War of 1812 interrupted this work but gave young Nat the sort of experience which was soon to make him Fanning's best explorer. He joined the blockade runners by which Stonington men managed to keep a supply line open between New York City and New England. The British had strung a rope of ships between Montauk Point on the outermost tip of Long Island and Point Judith, opposite on the sound. These waters were Stonington's front yard, and the runners, knowing every shoal and current, could slip past the British patrol on foggy or moonless nights. Young Nat got pricelsss training in these years of navigating under conditions rather like those he would encounter below Cape Horn.

The British, infuriated at Stonington for breaking their blockade, bombarded the town, first warning the inhabitants to leave. The men sent off their families and stayed, putting out the fires started by the cannon balls and returning the fusillade with what weapons they possessed. After four days of this the British gave up, and the small boys of the town had a new chant:

> It cost the King ten thousand pound
> To have a go at Stonington.

The war was to be fought all over again south of Cape Horn, where British sealers challenged Stonington's priority in the seal trade, incidentally adding new islands to the Empire. Nobody will ever know how many of these islands had already been found by the Stonington men; secrecy about new rookeries was the essence of the game. Big profits were at stake. The sea otter of the Pacific Northwest had been all but exterminated to supply the China trade and new furs were needed for this market. Also, Americans had developed a passion for sealskin coats, hats, and trunks. There had been such a tremendous slaughter in the Juan Fernández and other islands near South America that the sealers had to push farther and farther into the antarctic ice.

When Edmund Fanning sent off his first postwar expedition in 1819 he gave its commander, James Sheffield, various hints that might lead him to fresh rookeries. During his voyages Fanning had sailed well south of Cape Horn, and surmised from berg drifts the location of large islands or perhaps a land mass above the Circle. This intuition of a southern continent was as old as human guesswork. The ancient Greeks had decided there must be land around the South Pole to keep the world in balance; in one of his unaccountable flashes Leonardo da Vinci had come close to guessing Antarctica's actual size; Captain James Cook had zigzagged back and forth across the Circle, vainly looking for the Unknown Land of the South.

After the failure of Cook's meticulous effort there was less belief in a polar continent, but rumors multiplied about a group of islands called the Lost Auroras. Fanning had a shrewd idea where these fabled islands lay. He had studied the notes of the Dutch explorer Gherritz and had himself, after a west-northwest gale, seen icebergs floating toward South Georgia. A little calculation suggested the location of the shores from which the bergs had calved. Since any new islands meant possible seal beaches, Fanning must have given his commander a careful briefing.

For his sealing fleet he chose men, as the local saying went, "who could smell their way through fog by night from Hellgate to Providence." Nat Palmer had proved himself of this breed, and was made second mate of the brig *Hersilia*.

At twenty Palmer had reached his mature height of well over six feet. Shaggy and powerful as a polar bear, he was cast in the mold that turned out Charles Low a generation later—ruddy, blue-eyed, with an open countenance expressing good humor, resolution, and utter serenity. Physically a deep-sea man was a definite type.

The sealers made a practice of stopping at the Falklands, where they kept half-wild herds of cows, sheep, and pigs, and picked up birds' eggs and certain grasses good against scurvy. Nat was left behind to collect provisions while the *Hersilia* went on the prowl for seal herds. A few days later a British sealer, the *Espirito Santo*, arrived, and Palmer obligingly gave the captain some of his freshly slaughtered meat. During this fraternizing he gathered that the English were bound for a newly discovered region swarming with seal. They did not confide the fact that the previous year the islands now called the South Shetlands had been sighted from an English ship. But Nat's mind was full of the Lost Auroras, and when the British ship left he climbed a hill to watch her course. When the *Hersilia* returned, and the commander heard Nat's account, the Yankees quickly sailed in the wake of the rival brig.

There is a pretty legend that Nat was able to guide Sheffield straight to the South Shetlands because he had seen the direction the brig took after she had started out on a false tack to mislead the Yankees. The legend has persisted because Nat Palmer did possess almost telescopic vision, and at sea would sight a ship or a landfall long before anybody else. The more probable explanation is that Fanning's clues, reinforced by Nat's eyes, led the Yankees to the new seal grounds.

There they found the dumfounded crew of the *Espirito Santo*, and several other English sealers, busily clubbing seal by the thousand. There were more than enough for everybody, and the *Hersilia* came home with a huge catch. It was impossible to keep the secret of the rich new rookeries, and the next year vessels from Nantucket, New Haven, and other ports followed the Stonington fleet. It was now increased to two schooners, two brigs, and the little sloop *Hero*, in command of Palmer. His sloop was the scouting vessel, a peanut shell of forty-four tons, with a shallow draft for nuzzling among floes and shoals.

The young captain's mate was Phineas Wilcox, his second Richard Fanning Loper, who was later to marry Nat Palmer's niece and become a brilliant inventor and shipbuilder. The crew were sixteen-year-old Stanton L. Burdick and the patriarch of the lot, the Negro Peter Harvey, who was thirty-one.

Nobody pretended that a sealer's life was comfortable. The inner walls of the ships forever dripped water because of the icy temperature around the hull. The only heat came from the galley while the salt meat and beans were cooking. At the rookeries the crews liked to build rough shelters ashore, and vary their diet with penguin eggs and tender seal pups, which they liked almost as well as the salt codfish that as true Yankees they carried down the length of the globe to this fishy empire. Even in the antarctic summer it was a hard life, brightened only by the fact that sealskins were still bringing five dollars apiece.

At the South Shetlands they found no less than thirty English and American vessels, rapidly exhausting the bonanza. The year before the *Hersilia* had loaded nearly nine thousand skins; now most of the seal herds had gone elsewhere for the whelping season.

On November 14, 1820, there was a consultation on the *Hero*, which ended in the dispatch of the little sloop to scout for seal beaches. Palmer at once sailed south, and the next day discovered the most curious island in the Antarctic—the partly submerged crater of a volcano forming a round bay five miles across, its waters kept warm and steaming by volcanic activity under the surface. The steam-heated haven of Deception Island soon became the favorite rendezvous of Yankee sealers.

At this midsummer season the evenings were still bright, and Captain Nat, climbing to the masthead, sighted snowy mountains fifty miles to the south. Here was land not laid down on any chart, a great expanse of land. Here, his thumping heart told him, was the Unknown Land of the South. And though he never bragged about it afterward, Nathaniel Brown Palmer's was the only name that could now stand beside that of Christopher Columbus as the discoverer of a continent.

At ten the next morning he stood over for the land.

"I pointed the bow of my little craft to the south'ard," he told the tale years later, "and with her wings spread she speeded her way like a thing of life and light."

Actually he was making four knots, respectable enough in these waters. He covered the forty miles to what we now call Trinity Island, which lies off the mainland of Antarctica, and since the sea was covered with immense icebergs he hove to under the jib and laid off and on until morning. At four in the morning of November 18 he made sail again and explored the strait lying between Trinity Island and the mainland.

Since Captain Nat was too busy all his life to record his adventures in any detail, and most of his papers burned with his brother's house in 1850, there remain only a few letters describing his voyage, and the *Hero's* log, written merely for sealing information. For nearly a century there was such ignorance about Antarctica that this log was so much Sanskrit. Now geographers have found it a precise description of Trinity Island and Orleans Channel; Palmer's observations, corrected for magnetic variation, are precise. Modern hydrographic surveys have merely filled out his laconic notes:

"At 4 A.M. made sail in shore and Discovered a strait. Trending SSW and NNE. it was Literally filled with ice and the shore inaccessible we thought it not Prudent to Venture in ice Bore

137

away to the Northard and saw two small islands and the Shore every where Perpendicular we stood across towards friesland Course NNW. the Latditude of the mouth of the strait was 63.45 S Ends with fine weather wind at SSW."

Without any doubt, Palmer was the first to lay eyes on the peninsula which bears his name, the best part of Antarctica, as all later explorers affirm. Palmer Peninsula is a long, mountainous tongue of the seventh continent which stretches well north of the Circle. Why the United States never pressed its clear title to the continent is too long and convoluted a tale to recount here.

Captain Nat had discovered the fabulous land, but failed to find seal. Sea leopards were the only mammals he encountered. He sailed back to his commander, on the way discovering Yankee Sound between Friesland and Greenwich islands, and a few small seal beaches.

Still, Palmer's steam-heated island was a valuable find, and the reality of a great land expanse to the south an invitation to further scouting. By the middle of January 1821 Palmer was again on a voyage of discovery. He made full notes of this passage on ten blank pages in the back of the log, which were later torn out and lost. But from nine independent sources it is clear that he explored his continent as far south as 68 degrees, which brought him to Marguerite Bay south of the Circle. He satisfied himself that the new land was not an island, he entered Marguerite Bay, Pendleton Strait, and several fiords without finding seal, and then turned northward again, drifting along under easy canvas, and laying to at night.

One night the sloop lay in a thick blanket of fog, and Captain Nat, on the midnight watch, struck one bell at twelve-thirty. Instantly there was an echo from starboard, and another from port. He thought this was a trick of the fog, and went on pacing the deck, building air castles. But at one o'clock the echoes came again from either side.

"I could not credit my ears," he said later. "I thought I was dreaming, because save for the screeching of the penguins and the albatrosses, the pigeons and Mother Carey's chickens, I was sure no living object was within miles of the sloop."

138

But when this uncanny echo was repeated every half hour, the watch below stirred in their chilly bunks and told each other the kraken or some other malevolent demon of the ice was after them. They were in a region where no human beings had ever penetrated, and clearly the spirits of this godforsaken realm resented the intrusion.

At three-thirty Phineas Wilcox rushed on deck.

"I hear voices, Nat. They sound like human voices."

"I hope it's seal pups," said Nat, knowing better. He went below at four, and slept for three hours. Then they all waited for the sun to burn off the fog. What they finally saw startled them as much as the ghost of a drowned ship. They were anchored exactly between two fine vessels, a frigate off the port bow, a sloop of war to starboard. Captain Nat hoisted the Stars and Stripes from the maintop, and the warships ran up the imperial flag of Russia. Soon a cutter was lowered and made for the *Hero*.

During the fog the tiny sloop had run between the ships of Czar Alexander I's exploring expedition commanded by Admiral Fabian von Bellingshausen. The frigate *Vostok* and war sloop *Mirni* had spent two mortal years trying to outdo Captain Cook in discovering land south of the Circle. They had crossed it several times at points where Cook had kept north, but so far had succeeded only in sighting an island from a great distance, which Bellingshausen had of course dubbed Alexander Land.

All this was explained in fair English to Captain Nat when he was rowed over to the flagship and stood in the cabin surrounded by versts of gold braid. The Russians had donned their full-dress uniforms; Nat was in his homemade coat, sealskin boots, and battered sou'wester. But the gold braid began to take him seriously when he informed them of the regions under the lifting fog.

Bellingshausen had glimpsed the South Shetlands before the fog closed down, and thought he had at last made a major discovery. Captain Nat explained that all the sealers on earth had already visited the islands, and then to cheer the admiral offered to conduct him to the steamy warmth of Deception. To make him feel even better, he described the new continent which he had just explored for the second time.

139

The admiral swallowed his chagrin and invited the young Columbus to breakfast while the cutter went over to the *Hero* for Nat's log and maps. The meal was princely, and so was Bellingshausen's tribute after he had examined the records.

He rose and made Nat Palmer a bow.

"What is this?" he exclaimed. "A mere boy, in a tiny ship the size of my launch, has pushed to the Pole and found a land that I, in my fine ships, and after two years' search, have looked for in vain. What shall I say to my master the Czar? But my grief is your joy. Wear your laurels proudly, young man. I now name the land you have discovered Palmer Land, in honor of a noble boy."

And as Palmer Land the new continent went down on the early maps, both in Russia and England. However, the English soon found that an Englishman had discovered Antarctica (though the man himself never made any such claims); and when Palmer, sailing in company with a British sealer the next year on a scouting mission, discovered the South Orkneys, this archipelago, too, became part of the Empire.

Altogether, between 1819 and 1831, Nat Palmer made seven exploring voyages to the Antarctic, the last one a three-ship expedition carrying scientists which Edmund Fanning, Captain Benjamin Pendleton, and Palmer financed themselves by sealing on the side. Though Washington belatedly spent money to send Lieutenant Charles Wilkes south in 1838, his work was ignored almost as profoundly as Palmer's.

As Captain Nat gradually pulled away from the fascinations of the ice, he found excitement in the political turmoil raging in South America, and for a time helped General Simon Bolívar by shuttling his troops and arms from Panama to Colombia.

In 1826 Nat Palmer married Eliza Babcock, and four years later took this Army major's daughter along on a sealing voyage in his brig *Annawan*. The Juan Fernández herds were now returning, so they made for the island where Alexander Selkirk had spent four glorious years teaching his castaway cats and kids to caper to Presbyterian hymns—a symbol of Man Alone which degenerated into poor old Robinson Crusoe with his umbrella and his miser's hoards when Daniel Defoe got hold of the story.

The island had also degenerated; Chile had made it a penal colony for its most dangerous felons. When the brig anchored offshore the convicts saw a chance for escape. They killed their guards and informed Captain Nat, landing in his longboat, that they were seizing his brig to take them to the mainland three hundred miles away. According to one story, they were about to murder Captain Nat when he made a secret Masonic sign recognized by one of the convicts. More probably they kept him alive because they needed a skipper.

At any rate his first anxiety was for his wife. He managed to get word to his mate to lock up Eliza in a spare cabin with a supply of food. For ten days she was an undetected prisoner while Captain Nat stood on deck just over her head, roaring his orders so she would know he was still alive. He landed the hundred-odd villains on a lonely part of the Chilean coast, where they preyed on the countryside and were soon recaptured.

After that voyage Nat Palmer looked things over and decided that the biggest adventure offering was in the packet trade. For the last decade there had been a busy traffic between New York and the cotton emporium of New Orleans. The earlier packets had V-shaped bottoms and were forever getting stuck in the silt and sand bars of the delta. Rather suddenly in 1831 five different New York shippers ordered a new type of cotton drogher with a nearly flat mid-section and lines longer and narrower than those of Navy frigates. The shipbuilder in Captain Nat approved, and he was not surprised when these new packets, built to slide over sand bars, also turned in surprisingly fast runs.

He took command of the new *Huntsville*, partly owned by his uncle Amos Palmer, and sailed under a new company organized by the young and highly intelligent Edward Knight Collins. Captain Nat promptly made a sensation by bringing the *Huntsville* up to New York in ten days, and then rolling up an average of fifteen, while the rest of the cotton fleet took nearly three weeks. This was partly seamanship, but Palmer was convinced that the small dead rise of the new droghers made for speed, an idea to which for some time he got only one convert, Collins himself. A

Cape Cod man and fine naval architect, Collins found much sense in Captain Nat's theories, and between them they built increasingly fast packets. By 1834 Collins came out with his big *Shakespeare*, and sent Captain Nat to Liverpool with her. When she docked the waterfront characters crowded the piers and the merchants came running from their countinghouses. Finally the police had to clear away the crowds, but for a week Captain Nat held open house on his packet.

This was no waste of time, for he had arrived on one of his scouting expeditions. Among his many gifts Palmer had an excellent head for business, and he was now to size up the situation and help Collins decide whether there was room for a new transatlantic line.

The famous Black Ball Line had begun running between New York and Liverpool in 1816, making a fortune carrying freight, mail, cabin passengers, and a constantly mounting tide of immigrants. The Blackballers departed from the old haphazard system of a vessel sailing when loaded, and ran on schedule, leaving New York the first and sixteenth of the month. This transformed business methods on both sides of the Atlantic, since merchants could now make their purchases in line with a definite market, and get a quicker turnover on their investment.

When the Erie Canal opened in 1825 and New York became the emporium of the East the volume of trade grew rapidly enough to justify new lines, the chief ones the Red Star of Liverpool and Grinnell, Minturn's Swallow Tail Line of New York. All these liners were the finest ships on the Atlantic, constantly increasing in size and the luxury of their cabin appointments, but they were not notably fast.

Captain Nat dreamed of prouder and swifter ships, and he came back to Collins with a hopeful report. Since the *Shakespeare* had made such a sensation, Collins decided to begin his new line with her and call his packets after famous dramatists. Thus the Dramatic Line was born, and Captain Nat, as the designer of the vessels, with the *droit de seigneur* for their maiden voyages, set mighty forces in motion.

The famous yard of Brown & Bell at the foot of Stanton Street had built all Collins' New Orleans packets, and it was now commissioned to lay down the *Garrick* and *Sheridan,* and later the *Siddons* and *Roscius.* No shipbuilders stood higher; the yard's founder, Noah Brown, was so revered that when he boarded a vessel the sailors manned the shrouds. His nephew and adopted son David was now building a variety of vessels in partnership with Jacob Bell.

When they looked at Captain Nat's designs for the new liners they shook their heads. A small dead rise midships had proved useful for the Mississippi sand bars, but the Atlantic was a deep ocean. All the Blackballers had V-shaped bottoms.

As Palmer argued in his lusty quarterdeck voice his revolutionary ideas of ship design reached the ears of two young men busy in the molding loft. One of them was John Willis Griffiths, trained as a shipwright by his father, and with a few years' experience in the Navy Yard at Portsmouth, Virginia, behind him. He was now working as a draftsman for Brown & Bell, in his spare time writing articles on naval architecture that revealed a truly scientific approach to the problem. Captain Nat's science was pragmatism; he tried out every new model himself and watched how it behaved, then he was ready for the next modulation. Palmer proceeded in everything with instructed intrepidity.

Much more cautious than Captain Nat, and without his creative fire, was the young Scot from Nova Scotia, Donald McKay, who had come down to New York to learn "the art, trade, and mystery of a ship carpenter," as his indenture papers put it. He was now a journeyman shipwright at Brown & Bell's. He was twenty-six, and Griffiths a year older; Captain Nat was a decade ahead of them in years, and his fame as captain gave his arguments weight. Griffiths was soon to proceed implacably along his own line of reasoning, and then swerve back to Captain Nat's. McKay was to watch all designers and finally weave their ideas into the magic of the *Flying Cloud* and the *Great Republic.*

Clearly McKay's ships were magic; but he never pretended to have originated one major principle in the design of his clippers. Palmer's *Roscius,* built in 1839, fathered the *Flying Cloud,* which fled down the ways a dozen years later. The liner was in fact such a glorious vessel that for years to come every big ship imitated it, but the *Flying Cloud* was clearly her father's daughter. The largest merchantman afloat, the *Roscius*, 1009 tons, carried a daring cloud of canvas which McKay's clipper, seven hundred tons heavier, reproduced with a shade of caution. The liner's mainmast sprang 160 feet above the deck, and McKay left well enough alone here, but increased the main yard from Palmer's 75 to his 82 to carry the increased tonnage.

Like all the Dramatic Line, the *Roscius* set and held amazing records for speed, on the downhill run to England and the uphill climb back against the prevailing westerlies. The Blackballers averaged forty days for the westbound voyage; the Dramatic liners cut this down to a median of twenty-eight, though once the *Siddons* flew to New York in fifteen days. On the eastward run Captain Nat made Cape Clear on the Irish coast in twelve days from New York. None of the other packets could beat the Palmer ships, which could even run out of sight of the Navy ships, much larger and heavily manned for quick shifting of sails. Navy officials admitted publicly that the Dramatic packets could beat anything under the flag.

Captain Nat got his ships built as he wanted them, and took them out on their first runs to analyze their performance. His younger brothers, Alexander and Theodore, were also packet captains, an arduous life with big financial rewards. Liner captains got a nominal salary of only thirty dollars a month, but their percentages on freight and passenger receipts brought them as much as twenty thousand dollars a year.

But sailing a packet as Captain Nat did, to create such speed records as to put the Dramatic Line ahead of its older rivals, to create them for the further reason that the relation between ship design and speed was a mystery he proposed to solve, meant hard driving for captain and crew. Palmer was never a driver in the sense that earned the competing packet captain, Robert Waterman, his sobriquet of "Bully," nor did he, like Waterman, tear the heart out of a vessel in two or three years. Captain Nat was thrifty, even "close," in using man power and ship substance; it was the elements with which he fought a vigilant, defiant battle.

th Low of Salem. Crayon portrait
unknown artist. Photograph by
bert Andrew Adams.

ptain Charles Porter Low. From
daguerreotype. *Courtesy of Miss*
elen Low. Photograph by Albert
ndrew Adams.

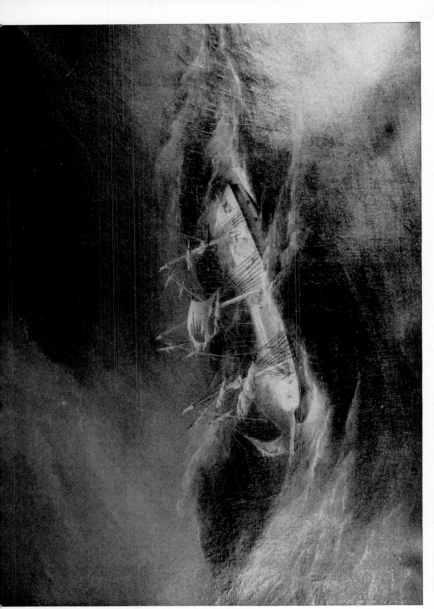

The *Houqua* Dismasted in a Typhoon, as imagined by a contemporary artist. *Courtesy of Miss Helen Low.* Photograph by Albert Andrew Adams.

He was a full-sail man in close-reef gales, but that meant he watched his sails with an eagle eye, daring to fly every kite up to the topgallants under the furies of a West Indies hurricane, and never losing a yard or a scrap of canvas. Phil Dumaresq, too, knew the dangerous secret of making a storm work for the ship, still keeping the ship whole; when Waterman "cracked on" he might lose a man along with a falling spar.

Captain Nat could hardly learn more as a shipmaster, but as a designer he was still studying and dreaming. Meanwhile he and Collins had started an era of reform in the home shipyards, and had even jolted the British out of their archaic ways. One expert confessed, "The mercantile navy of England is the least speedy and most unsafe that belongs to a civilized nation." Parliament appointed a committee to go into the sad state of shipping, and it reported that while the American merchant fleet grew apace the British was not even replacing its worn-out tonnage; moreover, English shippers were favoring American ships for the westward run. Brutal conditions on the Blackballers made "packet rat" a descriptive insult, and many of the crews deserted for American ships with their higher type of officers. Finally British consuls reported such disgraceful incompetence on the part of shipmasters that the Board of Trade set up a marine department and began building up a fine merchant marine.

After a few years of slamming packets back and forth, Captain Nat was physically tired. During stormy seasons he kept every watch, pacing the quarterdeck all night and most of the day, sitting down for his meals and strong coffee in the big armchair the steward lashed under the weather rail.

During the 1820s he had done more sealing and exploring than any man in his meridian; during the next decade he carried the packet ships to glory. As the golden forties got under way Captain Nat set his skysails and went into the China trade.

11

The

Houqua

The young house of A. A. Low & Bro. was coming up fast in that small group which controlled the China trade. The Griswolds, Grinnell, Minturn, and more particularly Howland & Aspinwall, were in a race with the Lows to capture business under the easier conditions that now obtained in China. Badly as it had come out for the Chinese, the Opium War had blasted away obstacles and anachronisms, and a greatly expanded commerce was now beginning. Here communications played a crucial role.

With only Abbot's capital to work on, the Lows operated on a margin which might be wide or narrow, all depending on their luck with ships. With luck, they could rush off a last-minute market report and final orders to William and Edward on a fast sailer, telling them what to buy and how much. With luck, the brothers in Canton could find another fast sailer in Whampoa to speed home with the goods and find a favorable market. But there wasn't enough luck; the China traders were often too slow.

There was always the monsoon, the slow metronome of the China trade. It laid down an expensive pattern of maintaining a ship and crew for three years for two round trips. The rhythm of the trade winds was made for oriental leisure, the ships blown comfortably up to China, then the long wait in Whampoa till the monsoon finally shifted to blow them home again.

The rival houses took an increasing interest in the speed of their ships. Grinnell, Minturn's *Horatio*, on which Charles had made his debut, was getting back and forth to Canton in 104 days. Howland & Aspinwall's *Ann McKim* laid down a new record in 1842 by romping home in 96 days. The Forbes brothers and Russell & Co. were doing brilliantly with their sharp-lined *Akbar*, built in 1839 by the fine Boston yard of Samuel Hall, who had watched the Dramatic liners to his profit. Next he built the *Paul Jones* for R. B. Forbes, and it was in command of this ship that Captain Nat broke into the China trade.

The day before Palmer left Boston, early in January 1843, his old Blackball rival, Robert Waterman, arrived in China on his first voyage to the Orient. For some years "Bully" Waterman had been in the South America trade for Howland & Aspinwall, loading the old drogher *Natchez* with hides and copper at Valparaiso, and getting notable speed out of her, as he did out of any ship he commanded.

Just thirty-five, Waterman already had a fabulous and dark reputation for driving ships and men to their last ounce of breath, but soon he was to drive them harder. He was a dashing figure, snapping with energy, and handsome in a saturnine fashion. The willfulness and excess of his character were plain in his straight mouth and ugly long chin. Still, he was considered a great beau, as fastidious about his clothes ashore as the trim of his ship at sea.

Captain Nat had usually managed to beat Waterman by two days on the packet run, but in this, their first China run, Waterman had the winds both ways. That may have been a small element in the fierce thinking Captain Nat was now doing, but his first voyage around Africa and up the China Sea had shown him what a complete assortment of climatic and wind conditions a China trader had to deal with.

Canton stimulated further thought. He met the William Lows, who were to sail back with him because Ann was expecting a child. William, like everybody at Russell's, was talking of what the opening of new ports would mean in the China trade—a sharpening of competition at both ends of the line demanded faster sailing. Russell and Black Ben Forbes could be proud of their *Akbar* and the new *Paul Jones*, and yet in Canton their lovely opium clippers, *Ariel* and *Angola* and *Zephyr*, and the newest and best one, the *Antelope*, just out, inspired the sort of pride that racing yachts evoke. Running between Bombay and Chinese ports, these beauties were piling up till-warming profits.

The *Paul Jones* started home late in the summer against the monsoon, and for weeks Captain Nat clawed down the China Sea. That did not improve his temper, which always went to pieces when sailing was slow, but it made him ponder the knottiest problem of the China merchantman, the monsoon. Every now and then he would call William Low to pace the quarterdeck with him while he cursed and snarled at the contrary wind, meanwhile watching every pitch of his ship, every slatting of sail.

"Mr. Low," he yelled, "a ship must be designed for this China work. There must be a ship that can beat this damned monsoon."

"If one could be built," said William, "it would be worth a fortune. Build 'em sharper, like the opium brigs and schooners."

"But not too sharp. Not a brig or a schooner or a packet ship. Even the *Roscius* isn't for this work." Captain Nat took off his white beaver hat and absently kicked it in front of him as they paced. "Not too sharp. In heavy weather sharp bows would take seas aboard, you'd get a labor and a drag. Low, on this run you've got seven bands of weather before the Cape of Good Hope. Westerlies, horse latitudes and squalls, then the cursed doldrums, and all the rest. Then the Indian Ocean and typhoons, then the China Sea, worry and fret, calms and baffling winds—and the monsoon."

He picked up his hat and crammed it on his head.

148

"Chips," he yelled, "bring me a block of white oak."

The carpenter dived out of his house. "How big, sir?"

"Big enough to model a ship for the China trade."

William watched day after day as Captain Nat whittled out his model. Long before it was done he had decided that the Lows must build this ship. He wasn't quite sure how Abbot would feel about going into the shipping business. But if the Lows were going to give Howland & Aspinwall and the others a race, they needed ships, like their rivals.

"Captain Nat," he said one day, "Ann and I have been talking this over. I'll take a three-quarter interest in this clipper ship, and I'm sure Abbot will manage the rest."

The *Paul Jones* made a respectable trip home, after all, for once out of the China Sea she sped, making New York in 79 days from Anjer, matching the *Ann McKim's* record of the year before. Captain Nat marched ashore with his precious model under his arm and set it down on Abbot Low's desk. As they talked, Botus kept glancing at the portrait of Houqua over the fireplace. A fire was in the grate, taking the edge from the October chill, and perhaps it was the firelight that made Houqua's somber dark eyes come alive, as they used to in Canton when the old merchant was pleased with some idea of Abbot's.

"We'll call her the *Houqua*," he said.

So it was settled. The first clipper ship would be built to honor the China trade which had evoked it. Abbot was not quite ready to become a shipping merchant, and decided that the vessel should be pierced for guns and offered for sale to the Chinese government, or perhaps to Houqua himself. At any rate Brown & Bell were to lay down her slender hull without delay.

In January 1844 Charles was back with the latest news of Harriet and Sarah and the bewitching nieces. The news waiting for him eclipsed even family affairs. Captain Nat was taking the *Houqua* out by spring, and Charles could go with him as third mate. He went to Brown & Bell's to see what a clipper ship looked like.

Slenderly built, but not too sharp, she was fine-boned, lissome,

149

her lines clean and long from her light rounding stern to her arching head. She was built to carry a light, precious cargo of teas and silks, and clearly, when her taunt masts were set, she would be a tall ship for her tonnage. Charles sighed to be on her; he filled the time by sailing down to Rio for a cargo of coffee.

William meanwhile had gone back to Canton, and missed the *Houqua's* launching and the birth of his son in April. William Gilman Low was named for his father and his father's best friend in Canton, Joseph Gilman, of Exeter, New Hampshire. He sent his namesake a Bible and a silver mug and spoons made by a Cantonese silversmith. The Bedell aunts arrived in the new plaids, with their hair *en classique*, looped down below their ears and pinned up behind in a cascade of curls, to coo over the baby.

When the *Houqua* was launched and towed down the river for her rigging the maritime community was aware that something momentous had occurred. James Gordon Bennett saluted her in his Locofoco *Herald:*

"One of the prettiest and most rakish looking packet ships ever built in the civilized world is now to be seen at the foot of Jone's Lane in the East River. . . .

"We never saw a vessel so perfect in all her parts as this new celestial packet. She is about 600 tons in size—as sharp as a cutter —as symmetrical as a yacht—as rakish in her rig as a pirate—and as neat in her deck and cabin arrangements as a lady's boudoir.

"Her figure head is a bust of Houqua, and her bows are as sharp as the toes of a pair of Chinese shoes."

Flush-decked, the clipper was 142 feet long, 32 wide, and 17 deep. She was unusually high 'tween decks, which would be a blessing for her crew. She was pierced for eight guns on a side, and though she was beautifully appointed, Captain Nat had kept her cost down to $45,000. In their first try the Low brothers and Captain Nat had arrived at the formula which expressed the personality of house and designer. Their ships were built more economically, stood up longer, and turned in, year after year, a steadier high performance than all the dazzling fleet in the clipper-ship era they now initiated.

Working by intuition and the wealth of his compounded experience, Captain Nat had finally arrived at a successful design for a China trader. But a China trader had to have the utmost versatility, bearing a cloud of canvas to offer the brave winds below the Cape, shaped with such cunning in hull and sail plan that she could beat against the monsoon or tempt the lightest airs of the doldrums; she must be free as a bird, yet sturdy and spunky when the typhoon came down. In other words, a China trader had to be the ship every designer from the Phoenicians on had dreamed about—perfection. What Captain Nat had really evoked was the genius of his age, when after thousands of years of striving and shipwreck and longing men could actually build perfect ships. This moment lasted only ten years, a decade transfixed forever in the sort of wonder which attends a complete harmony between the forces of nature and the human spirit. Such a moment was of course a miracle, and in the clipper ships its expression was beauty.

The moment was felt even on Mount Olympus. From the earliest days Hermes, and his Roman successor Mercury, had been the god of trade. His winged sandals expressed a need and a human hope—fleetness in exchanging goods between nations. When finally Americans gave the god his winged sandals he himself was transformed from the old symbol of trade into its new essence: flight.

John Willis Griffiths, working by mathematics as Captain Nat worked by love, began at this moment to lay down his China trader the *Rainbow*. This clipper, and much more the *Sea Witch* which followed, had the cutting brilliance of logic. Made to defy Nature, not to woo her, they fought to the limit of her patience, and then she destroyed them both.

There was something dark about these ships of Howland & Aspinwall, just as there was in their famous Captain Waterman, a link with black magic—which never belonged on the sea. The men of the maritime world who watched the *Rainbow* shaping in the stocks—very slowly, because Howland & Aspinwall were terrified at Griffiths' logic—felt this in their blood.

"She's much sharper than the *Houqua*," they said. "She's much too sharp. Her bows are turned inside out. She's contrary to the laws of nature."

So it was to prove. The Griswolds played safe with their third *Panama*, but the house of William S. Wetmore ventured toward the new sharp lines in their *Montauk*, a handsome ship launched less than a month after the Low clipper. Between the launchings Waterman came home from China in the old *Natchez* in 94 days.

The *Houqua* was loaded with pig lead deep in the hold to keep her steady on the homeward voyage with teas, and then towed down to Peck Slip to take on a cargo of lumber, cotton sheetings, naval stores, pitch, tar, and turpentine. The thrifty Lows loaded her so full that there was no room 'tween decks, and a house had to be fitted over the main hatch for Chips, sailmaker, and third mate Charles.

Escorted down the bay by all the Lows and their friends, the clipper sailed on May 31, 1844, a Friday. She had been launched on a Friday, towed downtown on a Friday, and was to arrive in Hong Kong on a Friday, but for four years she was a very lucky ship. She was a happy one, too, for Captain Nat fed his crew generously, and any man who sailed with him was apt to boast about it the rest of his life.

Captain Nat quietly watched his third for a few days, and then adopted Charles, not as one of the Lows, but as a born deep-sea man. He told his first mate, Thomas Hunt, jovial, stout, and cross-eyed, to keep an eye on the third—whichever eye was really looking at him. Hunt taught Charles seamanship, from turning in a deadeye to heaving a ship down. They progressed to navigation, dead reckoning, and shooting the sun. Dead reckoning was the mate's job, and only the captain used the chronometer, but Charles was to learn a master's work as quickly as possible. He learned, too, the rare happiness of finding in Nat Palmer his personal and lifelong ideal.

Frank Hillard, a younger brother of Harriet's husband, was on the ship, and he and some of the other passengers made evening visits to the deckhouse when Charles had his watch below, to smoke and tell yarns. After his hard voyages as boy and seaman, Charles could now enjoy the social side of life at sea, which he was through the years to develop into an art. But deeper even than his feeling for Captain Nat was his sense of the *Houqua*. His first love, this creature of grace and courage lived in his blood stream; he was identified with her.

Such identification was by no means unique, it was perhaps the final attribute of the good shipmaster, explaining why a captain with a beloved ship under him could make her do the impossible. It must even explain experiences which landlubbers dismiss as superstitious lies. (But of course sailors are "superstitious"; there is no vocabulary for explaining some things that happen at sea.) Because Edmund Fanning loved the *Betsey*, he was awakened in the South Pacific with a sense of her peril, and thus saved her from a reef beyond his sight and hearing, but perhaps not beyond hyperesthesia.

Going up the China Sea, Charles Low had a much stranger experience. He dreamed, in precise detail, what was going to happen in this spot when the *Houqua*, months later, sailed for home. The next day this dream so haunted him that he recounted it to steward, second, Chips, and sailmaker, and it was a lucky thing that they all remembered it.

He dreamed that the *Houqua* was bound home and racing with the *Montauk*, the Wetmore vessel launched about the same time. The second mate, William Gardner, was ill in his room, and Charles was standing his watch. He came on deck at four in the morning to relieve Mr. Hunt. There was very little wind, but Hunt warned him to expect a sudden squall. Soon after the mate went below the wind hauled ahead, and Charles had the yards braced forward. At once they had to be braced again, and then again for the third time. The wind was still light, but as Charles helped the men brace the main yards the squall pounced. He had the main brace in his hand, slacking away, and yelled, "Let go the skysail and royal halyards."

At that moment Captain Nat and Hunt rushed out of the cabin, and someone called, "The main t'gallant mast is carried away!"

"It's not the main t'gallant, it can't be," Charles protested. Then he let go the main brace, speechless and helpless, and the dream was over.

153

He soon dropped this strange nightmare deep in his mind, for the *Houqua* made Hong Kong in a triumphant run of 94 days, and then they were at Whampoa, where William and Edward got their first sight of the new ship. The three brothers and Captain Nat soon made a ceremonious visit to Houqua's palace on Honam to present him with a beautiful full-rigged model of his namesake. The fact that she was considered too small for the Chinese government, and was after all to remain a Low ship, only heightened the old merchant's happiness at this tribute from his American sons.

They spent a long golden afternoon walking through his gardens, now coming into the glories of the chrysanthemums, and feasting for hours on delicacies created for subtler palates than theirs. Always about Houqua there was an air of lightness and grace, substance bewitched into poetry, something they could understand in a ship. He was fragile now, his exquisite hands almost transparent, and as he bade them farewell, standing in his jeweled gardens, he seemed a figure painted on a screen that would stay so forever in their minds, wise, paternal, smiling at them, of all mysteries the most familiar.

He did indeed leave them that year, having ended, as he would have said, a cycle worthy of a rich gift to the Fung Shuy, the gods of wind and water who had brought him a beautiful ship to thank him for half a century of kindness to young Americans.

When they sailed home in early December William Low was on the ship he had first glimpsed as a fit of creative rage in Captain Nat. Ever since his sunstroke during the sack of Canton, periods of overwork had left him in a state of nervous exhaustion, when his moods swung wildly between depression and hilarity. On the voyage he was excessively gay, for several of his Canton friends were along, and every night until the ten o'clock lights-out the cabin rang with songs and toasts to the *Houqua*, fairly dancing home.

In the China Sea Charles's strange dream came true. They were racing the *Montauk*, with Charles in the dead of night standing the second's watch. The disaster unrolled exactly as he had dreamed it, but he remembered his dream only when he stood with the main brace in his hand and the men shouted that the t'gallant mast was gone. That moment of consternation had ended his dream, and now he was dumb-struck. Hunt brought him to his senses by ordering him aloft to send down the wrecked mast.

Later Chips and the three others to whom he had told his dream months before explained to Captain Nat that what had happened was fated, and Charles was not at fault. He agreed, and the incident was closed. The second mate was ill for six weeks, and Charles took his place, busy beating the *Montauk*, gloating over the log: 15 days to Java Head, 70 to the Line in the Atlantic, 90 days for the voyage of 14,272 log miles.

But before that final triumphant entry he and Captain Nat knew they had been too busy with the ship; they should have been watching William. He seemed his gay, charming self, but he had entered some private hell where he was alone and lost, and the gay drinking parties in the cabin only deepened his nightmare. One night when his ship was nearly home he walked forward to the bows. Below him the Atlantic creamed softly around her head where Houqua rode in his mandarin robe; ahead, Ann waited with the little son he had never seen, the son he was never to see.

The seas took William then, closing over whatever phantom woe it was that kept him from his landfall.

Captain Nat was dreaming of a new ship; the *Houqua* had taught him much of value. He approved her performance, but she was small. And Waterman had just come back from China in the incredible time of 78 days, which meant that he had driven his men without mercy—and yet the waterfront crowds were giving him an ovation.

"Lucky for Waterman that he's in the middle of a triumphal procession," he growled. "Otherwise, he'd be arrested for spreading too much belaying-pin gospel among his men."

No, he didn't envy Waterman his hard-bought records. Nor did he fear the rivalry of the *Rainbow*, launched with the scoffers yelling, "Aspinwall's Folly," and now well on her way to China.

But big days were coming, and his next ship would be twice the size of the *Houqua*. He was out of sorts with his old friend Collins for selling the Dramatic Line and going into steamships, like the British, just when the great days of sail were ahead.

"Let my brother Alex take out the *Houqua* while I whittle," he urged Abbot and Josiah. "And tell him that Charles is to be second. If he goes on as I expect, your young brother will be ready for the quarterdeck before I can build a ship big enough for him."

They nodded gratefully. It was good to think of a new ship and a sturdy young brother. Josiah had his own comfort in his bride, Martha Mills, and Abbot was taking out his grief in doing all he could for Ann. She had gone home to live with her parents and sisters, and was taking the shock of her strange widowhood with great courage. But they were glad Captain Nat was going to stay ashore for a while; he was a specific against the doldrums.

The *Houqua* sailed out in mid-May with cotton goods and lumber, and private adventures—everything from raisins to iron safes—from the three brothers in New York. Haskell was now helping Abbot and Josiah, but never became a partner. Late in September the *Rainbow* was in from her first China voyage, not at all proud of her long homeward run of 105 days. As Captain Nat had predicted of the oversharp vessel, she took water over her bows in heavy weather and tended to plunge into seas. Still, the Lows chose her to carry final instructions for the year to Edward in Canton.

The family was worried about Ned's health. "For God sake!" Haskell wrote. "Do not stay in such an unhealthy place too long! Better come home than lose your health."

Ned's attacks of illness frequently upset the family, but he lived to a ripe old age, and managed to keep up the China end of the business for years without breaking down. The family saw that he took frequent vacations at home. Haskell should have worried less about Ned's health and more about the possibility of war with Mexico.

"We have had a little war fever on for the last two or three months," he wrote, "but it is now dying out. . . . The great fear has been that Mexico would grant letters of marque and prey upon our commerce, and at one time war clauses were put in marine policies. But we shall have no war in my opinion, Mexico has delayed too long."

As for business, Haskell had sold his musk and cassia oil well, and hoped more was coming on the *Houqua*. Ginseng and Labrador otter were offering on the market, but opium was very high, because of a drought in Turkey and heavy purchases by English houses. "I know Abbot has bought about $20,000 worth within a day or two and has stored the same for two months."

Charles was back on March 10, 1846, in the fine time of 91 days, and back as first mate. Alex Palmer was a touchy and rather suspicious soul; in Canton he had rashly discharged the cross-eyed chief, Mr. Hunt, and since it was next to impossible to find a good first mate in China, he had decided that Charles would have a take a big step up in his rapid career.

"And what is more," said Charles, "he taught me how to take lunars."

A month later the *Rainbow* was in, very proud of her 79-day run. Her veteran captain, John Land, was no talker, but now he talked loud.

"The *Rainbow*," he said, "is the fastest ship that ever sailed the seas, and moreover, the ship can't be built to outsail her."

"We'll see about that," said Captain Nat, who was busy on his second clipper for the Lows.

"We'll see about that," said the mathematical John Griffiths, who was building the *Sea Witch* for Captain Waterman.

Howland & Aspinwall had to console themselves with their clipper's speed, for the Lows had the first of the new teas that year. By riding a gale home their ship beat the Griswolds' *Panama*, the *Ann McKim*, and the rest of the fleet. Though the Griswolds and Howland & Aspinwall dumped every chest they had in storage on the market, the Lows managed to sell their whole cargo before any other tea ships arrived.

"The result," Abbot wrote Edward, "though not brilliant, is satisfactory. I think *Houqua's* teas will yield a profit of 8 or 10% over and above commissions and charges."

157

He was crediting Ned with one sixth of this profit, and a fourth of the profit from rhubarb and white and damask shawls. The house was now dealing with Houqua's Number Two son, who succeeded with a younger brother to the old merchant's vast business, and who carried on the tradition of friendship with the Low brothers.

What with disposing of the *Houqua's* cargo and loading her as quickly as possible to get the best on the China side of the market, the Lows worked many an evening by candlelight. They managed to turn the ship around in four weeks flat, loaded with cottons, all the otter skins they could buy cheaply enough, and many coils of cordage. In this last item Edward and Charles held third shares, and Captain Nat, who was taking the *Houqua* back, had his own venture in cordage.

Abbot warned Ned that camphor, cassia oil, and gamboge were dull, but good sound rhubarb root was wanted. His last letter, on the eve of sailing, urged Ned to get rid of the goods promptly, as the *Ann McKim* would be in the *Houqua's* wake. Besides the thousands of dollars' worth of family ventures, Abbot was sending ten thousand dollars to Russell & Co., with discretion to invest. The modest young house was emerging into big business.

Ned was fretting about the delay in his winning a partnership in Russell & Co., and Abbot, always willing to move heaven and earth for his brothers, wrote him in June that he might get his wish unexpectedly. In other words, Botus was skillfully bringing pressure to bear. He had made up his mind to buy Captain Nat's new ship, which was slow in building, but he was much too diplomatic to give his brother more than an outline of the proper strategy.

"Ere long," he wrote, "I think it likely our business with Canton may be increased by the purchase or building of another ship, and an arrangement with some other house must be made if not with R & Co., but I feel now, as hitherto, that some present sacrifice had better be made than to lose sight of a connection with R & Co."

In other words, go softly, Brother. Leave it to Botus. For his good friend Edward King, a power in the company, had just come into the office, and Abbot managed to draw him out about partnerships.

"This is how it lies," King told him. "The next candidates are Pierce, young Sturgis, and your brother. I may say that Ned's prospects are very good."

By that fall Ned was admitted as a partner.

The turbulent year of 1846 was straightening out; the nation was on its new course. America became a continent and an empire. The Mexican War was on, but Texas had been formally annexed and the Oregon question settled without another war. Seth Low was pleased by the Whig victories, and his oldest son by the fact that the news of the Whig convention came over the new magnetic telegraph. There was now a wire connection between Washington and Boston. The farseeing Abbot was interested in clipper ships and Morse's invention for the same reason: they were speeding up communications.

In October Manhattan and Brooklyn were briefly linked by a telegraph laid down on the East River bed in an unjointed lead pipe. A week later a Liverpool liner dragged it up with her anchor and broke it. Some other system must be devised, but Abbot was not among those who considered the whole idea mad.

Old Mr. Philip Hone, once mayor of New York and still a strong voice in the bedlam, was angry at the human slaughter involved in the new mania for speed. The railroads, he said, did the retail business, the steamboats the wholesale; and indeed the times were full of disasters, along with the chronic fires.

"This world is going on too fast," he fumed in his journal. "Railroads, steamers, packets, race against time and beat it hollow. Flying is dangerous. By and by we shall have balloons and pass over to Europe between sun and sun. Oh, for the good old days of heavy post-coaches and speed at the rate of six miles an hour!"

The old days were over. In spite of the new Cunard Line, heavily subsidized by the British government, Americans were still competing in the packet business with larger and larger vessels. Collins was building steamships because the English had definitely been making something of these detested "teakettles." In August there was a great portent in the arrival of the leviathan of steam, the 3000-ton *Great Britain*. Her material was new: solid iron plates; and she had the new Archimedean screw instead of paddle wheels. This was too much for a country brought up on wood and canvas, and the American packet ships, though they might be steamers, loyally stuck to paddles and wooden hulls.

August was a good month for the Lows, bringing them a new brother to help compensate for William's loss. Edward Hutchinson Lyman, a young merchant from Northhampton, Massachusetts, married Sarah Low and settled down in Brooklyn. He was such an excellent businessman, and so sympathetic to the family, that soon Abbot took him as partner. The firm was now stabilized with Ned, the invaluable Josiah, and Edward Lyman as Abbot's permanent partners, and operated as A. A. Low & Bros.

Captain Nat and Charles were well out of the hurly-burly of 1846, bowling happily along in the *Houqua*, with Mrs. Palmer and a pretty niece for company. Charles may have had a romantic thought or two about Miss Fanning, who kept him company in his evening watch, but this was no time to think about a lovely girl. Every moment he sailed with Captain Nat meant that he was learning under the greatest master of them all.

A born teacher, Captain Nat showed Charles the mechanics of taking longitude, keeping the log, or putting the ship about. Then he would vanish into the cabin, leaving Charles master of the deck, to make his own decisions about making or taking in sail.

But when they were making for the Cape of Good Hope and lost the steady northeast trades to enter that region of rains, capricious airs, or complete nullity which were the doldrums, Captain Nat would suddenly appear on deck. He would take off his white beaver hat, hurl it to the deck, and jump up and down on it, yelling curses. This little ceremony braced up the men. He never swore at a man, only at something non-existent—a breeze.

Soon they had more wind than they needed, and one evening when Charles took his watch at seven the *Houqua* was rolling frantically under close-reefed topsails and foresail. Captain Nat stuck his head out of the cabin scuttle.

"How's the weather, Mr. Low?"

160

len Almira Low with Her Children, Harriet,
len, and "Gus." Portrait by Daniel Huntington.
urtesy of Mrs. William Raymond. Photograph
William Leftwich.

The *Jacob Bell* Entering the Harbor of Hong Kong. Painting by an unknown artist. *Courtesy of Miss Helen Low.* Photograph by Albert Andrew Adams.

"More moderate, sir. But I think it will blow again in an hour."

"Mr. Low, shake the reefs out of the main topsail, set the main t'gallant sail and main royal, and let her roll over shipshape and Bristol fashion, with all her canvas on her!"

He vanished until eight, when, as Charles had predicted, the blow began.

"Mr. Low, take in the main royal, the main t'gallant sail and close-reef the main topsail, and let her roll over and be damned to her!"

That was Captain Nat. He struck a close bargain with the elements, but he never gambled, and he never lost.

12

Typhoon

"Very soon now," said Josiah in the spring of 1847, "the Lows must have a house flag."

Abbot nodded. It had been no problem to decide the name for Captain Nat's big clipper, soon to be launched. She would be called the *Samuel Russell* in honor of the merchant who, next to Houqua, had been most responsible for their rising fortunes. But a house flag for the Low fleet . . .

"Let's ask Ann," he said. "This is a matter for an artist to decide. Besides, the *Houqua* is mostly hers. And she needs something to occupy her mind."

Before the question was settled, Seth and Mary Low, Grandmother Porter, and their own wives had been drawn into the game of designing the flag. When everybody was in a welter of luffs, flies, and diamonds, Abbot suddenly simplified the whole matter.

"We'll make them sit up," he said. "We'll have the one house flag that isn't blue and white."

For Howland & Aspinwall, the Griswolds, Grinnell, Minturn, and even Russell & Co. had flags using blue and white in various designs, though the swallowtail of Grinnell added red.

Ann was daring. "Yellow, Abbot? That's Chinese."

So the flag bore red and yellow horizontal bars with a white L in the center. Even the Lows didn't dream how famous this ensign was to become around the world.

Captain Nat had come home early in March, his head seething with ideas for finishing up the *Samuel Russell*, and left the *Houqua* in Charles's hands. She had made three round voyages and now needed new rigging and sails. Captain Nat had a great way of sailing a new ship and spending little or nothing on her, then turning her over to another captain, who would have to make good. The captain for the next voyage was to be his brother Theodore.

"Make out a list of rigging to be replaced," Theo Palmer told Charles. "I know Nat like my own hand. He's let her ropes get frayed and the sails battered to hell. If I'm to take command, I'll have everything shipshape."

Charles made out a careful but not niggardly list. He went along with Captain Nat in a certain sort of thrift by which a careful captain could save the owners money. One trick he had picked up from Palmer was the fine art of docking a ship without a tug, simply sailing her to her berth without scraping an inch of paint. He was to take pride in such delicate feats, and the economy and seamanship involved in dispensing, when he could, with river and harbor pilots. But worn-out rigging was dangerous.

One day Captain Nat came aboard to find the riggers bending sails and reeving new ropes on the main- and topsails. He was furious.

"Take out those ropes and put back the old ones," he bawled.

"The old ropes won't make another voyage, sir," Charles said bluntly. "If you remember, we almost lost our sails coming in through that last gale."

Captain Nat gave in, but he fought Theo over every penny as

long as they were in port. There was plenty of sulphur in these wrangles, for Theo's ugly temper was seasoned by years on the Liverpool packets. Charles did not enjoy the voyage with him, but the youngest Palmer and the youngest Low made a quick passage.

Captain Nat's fits of rage were mostly creative. Griffiths' masterpiece, the *Sea Witch*, came home from her maiden voyage late in July, rushing against the monsoon in just under 81 days, the first of her many records. She was Waterman's creature, for he had supervised her building, and only he could have sailed her so fast. His black magic held for three years, during which the *Sea Witch* was the fastest creature afloat. Captain Nat still thought Griffiths had gone off on the wrong tack, though in this new ship he had tacked back in the direction of the Palmer doctrines.

However, the *Samuel Russell*, launched the middle of August, was his answer to Howland & Aspinwall and their rainbows and witches. Designed as the most powerful ship in the China trade, she was 957 tons, fifty tons heavier than the *Sea Witch*. In her Palmer made a shrewd balance between his greatest packet, the *Roscius*, and the climates of the China passage, which called for a sharper bottom and heavy spars, with plenty of light canvas for moderate winds. She was not so much a brilliant compromise as a new evolution.

Dispensing with a forecastle and all deckhouses except one for the galley, longboat, and fowl coop, her deck was almost flush. Her cabin was a half poop lighted by a skylight and seven square stern windows.

"The external appearance of the vessel," said one of the papers, "is strikingly beautiful; her great length, towering and well proportioned spars, her sharp bows and clean, graceful run, give her a dashy, man-of-war air. Her bow is formed according to the new style, no lumbering heavy cutwater, the planking running chuck up to the stem, and is ornamented with a finely carved billet head, and gilded carved work along the trail board. . . .

"The hull is black with a narrow red and white ribbon streak

164

around her waist. The yards, black, the jib and flying jib-booms varnished and tipped with black."

The day the *Russell* was launched the *Sea Witch* got out to sea in double-quick time, for reasons explained in a South Street legend. On that river-front street Howland & Aspinwall and many of the great merchants had their countinghouses, and the ships tied alongside poked their long jib booms almost into the windows.

Waterman was ready to leave for China, and was in the upstairs office of his owners, getting their final instructions, when a clerk bounded up to announce that a sea lawyer was below with a policeman to serve papers on Captain Waterman. This was routine, for Waterman ended every voyage with at least a few of his men ready to cut his heart out. The difficulty was that the police were blocking the one exit.

"We'll simply have to wait them out," said Gardner Howland.

"No." Waterman had been thinking fast. "Have you got a bosun's chair and tackle block in the warehouse below?"

"Ah," said William Aspinwall. "We have. Dear me, what a bold idea!" He went to the window and looked out at the *Sea Witch* just across the narrow street.

Waterman's mate was with him, and he absorbed instructions and made for the ship. Soon the captain sailed over South Street from roof to foremast in a bosun's chair, and the fat little tugboat, trembling for her life, got the *Witch* the nineteen miles to Sandy Hook in an hour and three minutes by Pilot Hyer's watch.

Captain Nat got something better than summonses from his men. In the crew that sailed out to China with him that September was a common seaman, Robert Steigh. Exactly four years later he sat down to write a long letter "to the Skipper of the New York *Herald*." He was indignant that in that great year of '51, when the *Flying Cloud* and other new ships were the sensation, the *Samuel Russell*, "one of the sweetest crafts that ever danced through old Neptune's dominions," was overlooked. Bob Stay, as his messmates called him, declared that the *Russell* could compete with any of the new clippers, he'd stake a year's wages on that.

"When I made a voyage to China in that 'ere ship, under command of old Captain Nat. Palmer (a captain, let me tell you, as *is* a captain) we had an experience of so wonderful a character that it has often been a wonderment to me, that the ship's owners, or some of her relations, did not blow on it through the newspapers. Scores of vessels, on the same tack with ourselves, were overhauled and ran away from with just the same ease as the America beat the Royal yachts of England. Occasionally, to be sure, some brother Yankee would put the good ship to her mettle before we could shake her off; but as to anything foreign—whether English, or French, or Dutch, or what not, and we had chances with all sorts of them—why, Lord bless you, sir, it was the merest baby play in the world.

"But, lest you should consider this only a sailor's yarn . . . allow me to state one fact that may be proved by her log-book. One day, we took a pretty smart breeze upon our starboard quarter, and it continued to blow tolerably steady for the space of ten days. At the end of that time we had skimmed upwards of forty-five degrees, making, as you will preceive, hard on to 3,200 miles in ten days. The handsomest run, in any one day, was 328 miles. Now, sir, I humbly submit, is that not a feat to boast of? Is that not an achievement to entitle a ship to be classed among the clippers? But the most astonishing fact of all remains to be told . . . from the time we left Sandy Hook until our return (being the first to report our own arrival in China), I never saw scarce a gallon of water on her deck.

"I could tell you many interesting facts connected with the history of this favorite ship—how, on a subsequent voyage, all hands wrote home from Hongkong, by a ship that sailed nearly a month before us, and how beautifully we overhauled and passed her, having thereby to deliver the contents of our letters by word of mouth. How—but I must haul up the slack. . . .

"In my humble opinion, if the *Russell* were somewhat more heavily sparred, there is not a ship afloat in the world that could outsail her . . . while she is sixty tons larger than the *Sea Witch* and is, in all respects, fully her equal, yet she carries one-fifth less canvas than that justly celebrated clipper."

Perhaps Bob Stay had a point there. But Palmer's ships had better staying powers, and lived longer, than the extreme models.

The *Houqua*, Captain Low. The sweetest ship afloat, the youngest clipper captain, just twenty-three. What a home-coming that had been, Abbot running down the wharf with his light elastic step to tell him, "Captain Nat says you can command now." And his mother standing in the doorway when he got to Brooklyn, crying, "Charlie! Captain Charlie!" She was happy; even his father was proud and excited. The brothers and sisters teased and feasted him, and sister Ann told him he must be sure to copy Captain Howland. For some reason she thought the stiff master of the *Horatio* perfection, perhaps because she and William had sailed with him early in their marriage when everything was perfect. How long ago it seemed, that voyage when Charles was slushing masts. But it was only five years. Through the hawsehole and up to the quarterdeck in only five years—that was quick work indeed.

The *Houqua* was making quick work of her China passage. They had rounded Africa in 45 days, and now she was running up the Indian Ocean with all sail set. It was January 15, 1848, the moon was shining in a cloudless sky, Low and his mate, Stevens, enjoyed their pipes and for the hundredth time remarked that at this rate the *Houqua* would beat her own previous records to China.

At ten Charles took his watch below. Before he turned in he looked at the barometer, which was steady at 29.80, as it had been for several days. He woke up at two, sweating from a nightmare. He had clearly seen the *Houqua* going down headfirst with a great sea rolling over her bows. He rushed up on deck, looking at the barometer on the way. It hadn't moved.

"How's the weather?" he asked Stevens.

"No change, sir."

Low shivered, feeling an actual chill in the air. He went below again and looked at the barometer. In that short interval it had fallen two tenths. Somehow that was a relief; evil was working surely, and now the barometer, too, knew it. He hurried into thick trousers and monkey jacket and heavy sea boots. When he got on deck the sails were chattering; now they, too, knew a storm was coming.

"Mr. Stevens, I'll have the port studding sails taken in. Furl the jibs and spanker."

The barometer fell another two tenths.

"Call all hands to shorten sail!"

The men tumbled out. The wind increased as fast as they could clew up, haul down, and furl. The nightmare had not roused Low a minute too soon; by four they were scudding under a close-reefed main topsail and reefed fore-topmast staysail, and the wind was blowing a furious gale. The sky was covered clear to the horizon with thunderclouds, and all over the ship was a lurid electrical show, all up and down the masts to the lower yards, and out along the yardarms the camposants rolled and balanced like fiery balloons.

"Hell's fireballs," the men muttered as they rigged in the stun-sail booms. "And a typhoon to follow."

Five in the morning, the *Houqua* scudding and rolling like mad. One heavy heave, and she rolled the starboard topmast stunsail booms under, on both the fore and main yards, snapping them off short like sticks of candy. She shuddered, rolled to port, and snapped the port booms off. With a quivering sigh she rolled again, and the starboard quarterboat was snatched from its davits.

Six o'clock. Without warning the wind shifted from southwest to south, blowing a hurricane now, and broaching the ship to. She was hove down with her port leading trucks in the water.

"Haul up the foresail and brace the main yard with the port braces!" Low yelled through the trumpet.

Now the typhoon began stripping the ship in obscene haste. The close-furled foresail and main topsail were rags in an instant, then one by one every sail was peeled from gaskets and reefs, bursting from the gaskets as if exploding, blowing to leeward in ribbons.

"There goes the jib boom," the men bellowed.

Fore, main topgallant masts followed the jib into the churning sea, carrying with them the topmast head. The mizzen topgallant mast bent like a reed, nearly double, and then broke off just above the cap.

The port quarterboat was now pounded to kindling and snatched overboard, with the stem and stern left foolishly hanging to the davits. All eight ports to larboard were sliced off, and the monkey rail was stove in fore and aft with only the stanchions left.

Low, shouting to Stevens beside him, could hardly be heard through the trumpet. They lay flat and held on. There wasn't much left to be blown overboard now.

Nine o'clock. The wind pulled in its talons and crouched, gathering breath before it leaped again. The ship, without a rag to cover her agony, shuddered, lifted her head, and righted, falling off before the wind. The barometer was now 27.50. Without thought of food, the men were using the respite to clear away the wrecked spars and let them go overboard.

At noon the typhoon pounced, a murderous gale blowing from the southeast in gusts that lasted a quarter hour, then paused, only to blow harder than before. The ship now had her larboard side to the wind, and when the men passed the open ports they bawled and cursed with the pain, for the wind gushed at them like jets of live steam.

The *Houqua* was keeping her brave head up, but she couldn't scud much longer. Low hove her to under her bare poles, on the port tack, with her head to the south. On the starboard side the rails and ports were still whole; the lower masts and topmasts were standing, with the wreck of the main and topgallant masts hanging to windward. The wind was hauling against the sun, from southwest to south, and from southeast to east.

At four in the afternoon the mates and sailors were lashed under the main rigging, and Low was standing just abaft, holding to the pinrail, when he saw the spoondrift, a solid mass thirty feet high, coming down before the hurricane. Shrieking, infernal gusts of wind fled before it, hurling themselves on the ship. Then the spoondrift engulfed the *Houqua*, driving through the ports like cannon shots, forming an arch of water over her so that they could see the deck fore and aft but above the tops nothing but that ghastly bridge of heavy brine. Trapped between sea and spoondrift, the men choked and gasped, drawing into their lungs an air that was almost water.

For ten mortal minutes the *Houqua* fought for her life. Then she was hove down on her beam-ends. She was over so far that the deck inclined *in*, and the water rushed down the forecastle scuttle. Low, clutching the weather rail with one hand, saw the men scramble for the main rigging, climbing out of the flood. One of the crew, sick abed in the fo'c'sle, was about to drown when the water rushed down, but he saved himself by swimming out of the scuttle and catching the rigging.

The *Houqua*, Captain Low. The sweetest ship afloat, the youngest clipper captain. The *Houqua*, hove down on her beam-ends. The anguish Charles Low felt was the ship's, not his own, the brave ship violated, stripped, and all but drowned, laboring and fighting still to preserve her first and last function—to keep afloat.

She was going over so fast that suddenly he lost his footing and was swept to leeward. He was drowning on his own ship. When he fought to the surface he could see the mizzen rigging almost within reach. Then a big sea rolled over him. Now it was very dark, now it was the end when you say a last prayer with agony in your lungs. . . . He was up again, and there was a line before him. The captain was still on his ship, but they were drowning together. He caught the line and painfully hauled himself up, fouled with his heavy boots and coat, and finally his head struck the pinrail around the mizzenmast. Then his feet were on the deck. He got on the weather side of the mast and looked at his ship. The *Houqua* was so deep in the water that the tops were submerged. The deck was perpendicular.

He was incapable of thought, but he knew what must be done, and instantly. Get the masts down, relieve the ship of their weight. While Stevens and the men slashed the lanyards of the mainmast, Low cut away the mizzen. Down went the main, breaking off about four feet above deck. Then the mizzen went over.

The *Houqua*, after a moment of dreadful suspense, lifted herself from the sea.

"Thank God she rights," sighed every man in his heart. In two minutes more she would surely have foundered. She might still sink, with the weight of water she had taken aboard.

"Mr. Stevens, have a look at the fore hold."

He came back shaking his head. "She's a-sinking, sir. The water's up to the break of the deck."

"Cheer up," said the captain. "We'll soon pump her out."

What really worried him was that the masts had been swept under the bottom and were battering against it, threatening to stave a hole in her hull. Low and his men fought their way through the wreckage, cutting away every rope they could see that was holding the masts to the ship. The men were crying out that there was a hole in her bottom. At last the masts were cut clear, and Low could breathe again.

The *Houqua* had four feet of water in her hold and was lying like a dead log in the water. Dismasted, stripped, the deck swept clean of carpenter's house, galley and cookstove, and gear, the casks of drinking water flooded with brine, the clipper was still alive, and not a man had been lost. The storm had done its worst; now it was a question of staying alive till morning.

Low set the men to work at both pumps and they labored till dawn, captain and mate taking their turns with the rest. He had a small sail rigged to the boat davits (there was nothing else left) and the wind was still so strong that this small defiant rag brought the ship to the wind and she lay comfortably under the ebbing storm.

When he went below, for the first time since noon, he found his cabin a pool covered with flotsam from the pantry and storeroom just forward of it. His chronometers were full of water, but one was still working. His watch and sextant were ruined, his bed and clothes a soggy pulp, everything was soaked but six volumes of Channing's sermons, dry as ever.

His Filipino cabin boy had tried to climb up through the skylight when the ship was flooded, and had cut himself badly. Other casualties turned up, so Low played doctor while he wondered how he was going to feed his men. His steward, Essex, managed to break out some dry bread, and every three hours the men had a glass of cider. As soon as the pump crews were relieved they lay down on the deck and slept with the seas washing over them. But the captain kept on his feet.

About midnight a group of seamen sloshed down the deck to him. "Where's the second? Why don't he take his share at the pumps?"

Where *was* the second? Low found him in his room, praying.

"Hustle out of that quick, and go to the pumps! What's the good of praying?"

"Is the ship going to the bottom, sir?"

"We'll know better when we get the water out of her."

By seven the next morning they had her dry. She had stood the battering of the masts without being stove in. Low sent all hands below to sleep.

Charles Low found some dry paper and wrote long letters to his parents, to Abbot and Josiah, trying to make them understand how, on his first command, such a disaster could have overtaken him. The *Houqua* was now limping under a jury rig contrived with no ropes or blocks, and only a hatchet and gouge left of the carpenter's tools. He had taken a daring decision, and tried to explain his reasons to the sympathetic Josiah:

"Fear I had none, but we were 450 miles from the nearest land, 1200 miles dead to leeward of the nearest place for fitting the ship out, 3000 miles and more from Hongkong, and to go there the ship had to be worked through straits, among islands and shoals, which for a full rigged ship is none of the easiest work. But to Hongkong I was determined to go; there I could find advisers and friends, it was the most likely place to get fitted out, and so, if God spared me and the ship I meant I would try it."

Was he being foolhardy, trying to make Hong Kong with one damaged chronometer, a pitiful jury rig, no drinking water? He was at least giving the men hot food, for the stores in the fore hold were intact, and Chips had improvised a cookstove. But his brothers could never collect enough from the underwriters to make the *Houqua* shipshape or absorb the loss on cargo; this typhoon was going to cost them heavily. Soon after the storm he had all the hatches opened, in the nick of time, for the cotton goods were on the point of spontaneous combustion.

To bring his wounded ship and damaged cargo three thousand miles to port was the enormity of daring. But he was pretty sure Captain Nat would have had the same reaction: bring her to her port of destination, and be damned to her! Only other captains like Palmer and Uncle James Low and Howland could understand what he was trying to do now, and what he had done during the typhoon. He copied out his log to send back by the first homebound ship he should meet, and urged Josiah to let an informal panel of captains explain to the underwriters what the log meant.

"Let them examine how I shortened sail on that night, and what condition my ship was in when she was knocked down, laying to under bare poles, with only lower masts and topmasts aloft, without a sail on the yards, the ship with as good a cargo as ever steadied a vessel—show this to them and I have no fear of the judgment that they will pass."

At least, not much fear.

The *Houqua* reached Hong Kong very much as the typhoon had left her, for Low, with a small boy's pride, refused to accept more than a minimum of help from the ships they met. From one they got a few tools and cooking utensils, from the next a spar and some ropes and blocks. They stopped at Boero Island for water and bought standing timber for a mainmast. When they were through Dampier Strait north of New Guinea Low began to worry about pirates, who would be apt to attack a limping ship. He bought bows and arrows from the natives, and with these weapons, about as useful to them as slingshots, the men watched the war canoes making for them one day when they were becalmed. Some of the pirates had fifty stark-naked, yelling savages aboard. At the right moment a squall came up, and the *Houqua* got clean away.

Brother Ned was home on furlough, so Charles put himself in the hands of the Low agents in Hong Kong. He decided to abandon his cargo to the underwriters and act as their agent. The cotton goods were badly damaged and scorched on the outside. And yet, when he put them up at auction, they sold for more than they would have brought if he had delivered them in Shanghai. His luck was taking strange twists.

Making the *Houqua* seaworthy was more of a problem, and in the end his own crew did most of the work cheerfully and well, on the system of grog three times a day and liberty every evening. By June the ship was made over, and Low took her up to Shanghai with a cargo of cotton goods. They took on teas, carried them down to Canton for repacking, since the Shanghai coolies had not yet mastered this art. Then they went back to Shanghai, where Charles found a pile of letters from home.

The *Houqua*, Captain Low, was the talk of the seaboard. Everybody from Lieutenant Matthew Maury to the family pastor praised him as a hero. The newspapers and marine journals had published his log. Even the underwriters loved Charles Porter Low like a son. "Mr. Hale of the Atlantic," Seth Low wrote, "said your resolution to carry the ship to Hongkong was deserving of great praise, and had saved a great deal of money for the office. Capt. Hudson of the Navy read the account which I send you from the *Journal of Commerce* with great interest. He said he had read it twice and his wife wept like a child while he read it . . . you will never want a ship to command as long as your character stands as well as it does now."

The family had suffered a month of dreadful suspense between the first news of the disaster and the announcement of Charles's safe arrival in Hong Kong. But they had managed to keep his mother in ignorance of "the lawless depredators of the sea" and all the other perils of his long passage under jury rig. Seth Low made religious capital of his son's miraculous escape, enclosing their pastor's letter, which credited it to Providence and the goodness of his parents. Charles was too well aware of the truth in this to disagree, but as the youngest son who had fought for a place of his own, he was warmed by his father's praise: "you were inspired with a presence of mind, courage, resolution, fortitude, prudence as well as with health and strength to endure."

Abbot, approving fully of everything Charles had done, wrote two long letters about business details, and then paid him the ultimate compliment: "I leave everything to you. You hardly need instructions from me."

His little sister Ellen, so like him that they might have been twins, wrote him a spate of family news. Everybody but Charles was home for the Fourth of July, even the Hillards and their five small daughters, Katherine, Frances, Mary, Sarah, and baby Harriet. John's business affairs had been going badly in London, and the family was now going to settle in Brooklyn.

"It is right good to get Harriet back," Ellen wrote, "and not have to be screwing up our courage all the time to bid her good-bye again.

"We all miss your joyous spirit and long to hear your merry voice. By the time you come, Neddy will have left us. We have enjoyed very much since his return, and particularly myself, for I have been the favored one."

In June Ellen and Ned had spent two weeks with the Lymans in Northampton, then made the pilgrimage to Niagara Falls and up to Canada, circling back to Lake Champlain and Lake George and visiting the new fashionable resort of Saratoga, "Edward and I in a chaise by ourselves, and the rest of the travelers in stage coaches. We passed two days amid the fashionable throngs of Saratoga Springs but were rather glad to leave. Dining with three hundred people will do very well occasionally."

Now she was keeping house for Abbot and his wife, who had gone up to Wakefield, taking dear William's widow with them. "I have Abbot's two youngest children and Harriet's Kate and Fanny under my care and I can assure you I feel some responsibility."

Charles folded up the letters and stowed them carefully in his pocket.

> Old Low, old Low's son,
> Never saw so many Lows
> Since the world begun.

Never had he loved them all so much. His heart was bursting with happiness and relief. But there was still Captain Nat. Until he looked over every foot of the *Houqua*, Charles could not be sure that he had kept faith with the most exacting standards of his calling.

Captain Nat beamed like a steady beacon through the home-coming party for Charles. Engulfed in the adoration of the Tribe of Seth, it was a relief to hear Captain Nat's protesting roars.

"Why doesn't somebody praise me? Why are you all choking Charles to death? Who thought of the *Houqua* in the first place? Who trained up Third Mate Charlie to be Captain Low? I'll be blessed if there's any justice here. Not one of you beautiful ladies has offered me a kiss."

Ann came laughing and tripping over to him. "May I bestow the first one, Captain Palmer?"

Abbot watched with a twinkle in his eye as the big handsome giant stood the siege of billowing skirts and bobbing curls that followed. Then he laid a hand on Charles's shoulder and drew him to one side.

"Jose and I have been over the figures," he said. "If you had made the voyage as we laid it out in New York, we'd have lost about fifty thousand dollars. But the delay, and your two trips to Shanghai, and your coming home now with the first of the new teas means that the voyage will clear more than sixty thousand dollars."

It was hard to understand such luck, but there it was. Charles shook his head in bewilderment and went over to talk to Grand-mother Porter. Her memory had gone lately, but she was still her cheerful spunky self, and Charlie was still her idol.

The next day he went over to the ship, and with fear and trembling saw Captain Nat coming down the wharf. He knew the rigging was too large, and the new quarterboats below standard. For the next hour Charles keep pointing out all that was wrong.

"Don't you worry," said Captain Nat. "You saved the ship, you saved the insurance companies a lot of money. They'll have to make everything good, and I'll see that they do."

A few weeks later the *Houqua* was her beautiful self again, and Charles and Captain Nat went to Negus & Co. to buy an eight-day chronometer.

"This is the finest we have," said the clerk. "The price is eight hundred dollars."

Charles blinked, but Captain Nat had his orders.

When the chronometer was delivered it bore a silver plate:

> Presented by the Atlantic, Sun, Mercantile, and Union Mutual Insurance Companies of New York and the Insurance Company of North America of Philadelphia, to Captain Charles P. Low, late master of the ship *Houqua*, as a testimonial of their approbation of his good conduct in saving said ship and cargo, after having been thrown on her beam ends. . . .

Whenever he looked at the chronometer that moment of agony came back, when he and the *Houqua* were drowning together. It was a wonderful timepiece, and for the next two or three years kept mean time, no gain, no loss. Just as faithfully, the *Houqua* sped back and forth to China, fresh and beauteous as a little Manchu princess. Apparently she did not remember.

13

Gold Rush

Catching up with anything but the family news was always a bewildering task to Charles when he returned from a voyage. But he had a politically-minded father and brothers who watched everything, so while the *Houqua* was being rejuvenated he was given his bearings.

Seth Low was pleased with the Whig victory and the election of Zachary Taylor, with the Mexican peace and the purchase of New Mexico and California at the bargain price of fifteen million dollars. John Quincy Adams had died, a firebrand Abolitionist of whom Seth Low could not approve, but he repeated to his son Adams' final words, "This is the last of earth; I am content" as worth remembering. In March, a few weeks later, John Jacob Astor had died without giving a phrase to posterity, but testate to the tune of twenty millions, the first great China trade fortune.

Abbot was elated because the telegraph now extended as far west as Milwaukee, and market news leaving when the Exchange closed at three reached this distant city by nine the next morning. He was happy with the flourishing state of the country and especially of shipping, though part of the activity on the seas was caused by the Irish famine, which crowded the westbound packets with immigrants, and the eastbound with tons of wheat and Indian corn.

"Our friends Grinnell, Minturn are heartbroken about the famine," he observed with less than his usual gentleness. "They have a house dinner to celebrate the fortune it is bringing them, and dine on terrapin, salmon, peas, asparagus, strawberries—all out of season, of course—then Mr. Grinnell gives the famine fund $360, which he had lost on a bet with Mr. Wetmore. That, my dear brother, does not remind me of the way Houqua used to do things."

One more piece of news had arrived as a rumor during the heat of the election campaign. It was said that gold had been discovered in California, and that the whalers had left their base in Honolulu to desert to the gold fields. It happened that Howland & Aspinwall's new steamship *California* was just ready to initiate their latest venture, the Pacific Mail Steamship Co. At once they sent her around the Horn to San Francisco, followed by three ships chartered by the government to carry food and troops. By early spring the forty-niners were on their way.

From every port large and small along the seaboard the fortune seekers embarked in droghers, brigs, sloops, schooners, anything that appeared capable of sailing, out for seventeen thousand miles of the hardest going on earth. Some of the vessels got safely around the Horn, many of them limped into Rio, others dumped their passengers along the Isthmus of Panama, to find their way across to the Pacific afoot or on muleback. William Aspinwall, very much the pioneer in this boom, sent surveyors to Chagres to lay out a railroad line across the Isthmus. That year ninety thousand vessels from all over the world were to go through the Golden Gate in an almost continual procession.

The Low brothers shared the general excitement and told

Charles, who sailed for Canton early in April, to make a quick voyage and avoid typhoons. They followed with letters urging him to hurry back and join the gold rush fleet. By the time he arrived in China his father had been honored by the Harvard authorities with the degree he had missed getting many years before; and Ellen was married to Ethelbert Smith Mills, whose sister Martha was Josiah's wife.

By that time Charles had probably forgotten the sight of the black dragon on the *Sea Witch's* prow, swimming up the East River just before he sailed. Waterman had brought his ship back from Canton in 74 days and 14 hours, an incredible record which was never to be broken under steam or sail. This time the men who were always claiming that Waterman had found a new route home from China were justified; somehow he had cut more than a thousand miles from the route ships usually took during the northeast monsoon.

This feat gave a fillip to clipper building. Not that the gold seekers could afford to take clipper ships to California; it was fourfold freight rates that started the shipyards humming.

But the Lows were first and foremost China merchants, and their thoughts were on a grandiose project: the moment would soon come when foreign ships could compete with the British in their own ports. The old Navigation Acts, which had kept England dragging at her anchor for two centuries, were at last repealed. In general the acts forbade the carrying of goods to England or her possessions in anything but British bottoms. Archaic measures dictated by stubbornness and fear of Holland's sea power, the acts had been concocted by Oliver Cromwell and reaffirmed by Charles II. They were an underlying cause of the American Revolution, but after this war had lost Britain her richest colonies she simply tightened the laws and forbade British subjects even to own a foreign-built vessel. Thus was bred the era of the secure East Indiamen and apathy in the British shipyards.

By 1850, for the first time in history, an American ship could carry teas to England. The Lows and Captain Nat decided to mark this moment with a superb gesture, the clipper ship *Oriental*. She was built early enough for a trial run to China and back before she broached the sacred waters of the Thames.

Their builder, David Brown, had now retired to live in the country, and his partner, Jacob Bell, laid down the *Oriental*. She was the largest China clipper so far, a proud creature of 1050 tons, with the slender black hull of a racer. Her rails and deckhouse were pure white, her decks of clear pine holystoned to ivory, her hatch coamings, skylights, pinrails and companions of Spanish mahogany, her brightwork a dazzle. Her cost ready for sea was $70,000.

Launched August 4 from the Bell yard at the foot of Stanton Street, this two-decker created excitement even in the midst of the gold rush hysteria. Said the *Commercial Advertizer:*

"Her launch was exceedingly beautiful. She was taken to the dry dock to be coppered. Her model gives promise that she will be both a safe and fast ship; and Capt. Palmer is a gentleman likely to do the Oriental justice in both respects, being well known as a cautious and enterprising officer."

"Well," said Captain Nat, "we'll see how she sails."

He took her out September 10 on her maiden voyage, and his last as master. He had turned fifty that summer. A pretty thing happened on the voyage out; he met his brother Theo, homeward bound in the *Samuel Russell*. This ship had been doing the Lows proud; on the previous voyage she had come home in 83 days, making her the fastest ship afloat with the eternal exception of the *Sea Witch*. On this voyage she was against the monsoon, but ran to New York in 90 days, while her time from Java Head was 64 days, a record rarely matched. As for the *Oriental*, she went out in 109 days and came back in 81, putting Theo Palmer in his place.

From November, when the *Russell* got home, until early January 1850, when Captain Low pleased everybody by his speedy return, the Lows loaded the clipper with goods for San Francisco. There was no point in keeping out of the gold rush, with freights at sixty dollars a ton. By the time the *Russell* was loaded her freight list was seventy-five thousand dollars, more than her first cost ready for sea. For the next few years all shipowners made money, but the Lows, as established China merchants, could make a great deal more. Instead of the easy voyage around Africa they began sending their ships around the world, piling the steady China profits upon the spectacular rewards for delivering goods to San Francisco.

Time was literally money, and Charles was given two or three days to wind up the *Houqua's* voyage and get ready to command the *Russell*. Fortunately they were tied up at the same pier, congested with boxes of teas for New York, and boxes of tools for gold miners, as the ships discharged and took on their cargoes. Charles had to wind up all his accounts of the voyage just finished, from his master's wages of a hundred dollars a month to the various port charges for towing and pilotage, dockage and stevedoring, from new copper for the *Houqua's* bottom to new china for her cabin.

Meanwhile everybody in the family wanted to see him before he took the dangerous voyage around Old Cape Stiff, so he ran all over Brooklyn Heights, eating two or three dinners in succession. His first visit was to Harriet and her five little girls. Then at the Bedell house on Cranberry Street he discovered that his orphaned nephew Will, who was nearly five now, was a young man of his own kidney. Not only did he command an infant hook-and-ladder company for fighting fires on the Heights, but he had a Newfoundland dog named Hector.

"So have I," exclaimed Charles, "and he's coming with me on the *Russell*. Chips is building him a house. But of course," he went on with a wink at Sister Ann, "a huge dog like that may sink us. The clipper's loaded deeper than a sand barge now, with her scuppers only a foot out of the water."

The story went over so well that Charles repeated it to Abbot's children on Washington Street. Harriet, Abbot Augustus (understandably called Gus), and little Ellen were duly impressed with Uncle Charles's defiance in taking along his pet, even if it did sink the ship. Dogs they understood; disaster had never come near these children of serene and happy parents. The pleasant house was particularly happy now, because Ellen was expecting a fourth child.

Ten days after Charles sailed Ellen died in giving birth to her frail little son Seth, whose own life was almost despaired of. In the sudden benumbing darkness that fell on him, Abbot found one comfort: Sister Ann, too, had faced the inexplicable. Day after day it was she who helped him and the children through the darkness, who stood vigil over the ailing baby as if he were her own. She brought them all through; and Abbot's second son lived to become the most famous of all the family.

Much as he loved his first dainty clipper, Captain Low could see that the big *Russell* had powers far beyond hers. He had, too, a fine first mate, Joseph Limeburner, soon to be one of the greatest of the Low captains. Leaving New York in mid-January, they made the Line in 20 days, and scampered down to the Horn in 44, amazing speed for that or any later day. The ship proved equally handy in light or heavy weather, but she had been designed for the passage around Africa, and taking an overloaded ship around the Horn for the first time was a test.

In the conventions of sailing, rounding the Horn meant getting from 50 degrees south latitude in the Atlantic to the same latitude in the Pacific. Even in the antarctic summer it meant a fight against brute elements that drained the last reserves from officers and men. Burdened as she was, the *Russell* was in no condition to fight back if the Horn was in a petulant mood.

Old Cape Stiff threw a gale at them. Low and Limeburner stood together on the quarterdeck, bawling orders to men wading waist-deep through the cataracts of water boarding the ship, men climbing rigging stiff with frozen spume, dodging flailing spars, pulling at ropes turned to steel.

A tremendous sea boarded the *Russell* abaft, and swept master and mate like puppets sixty feet down the deck. They fetched up in the main rigging, and held on while the monster wave rolled down the deck. It had swept the man at the wheel into the mizzen, and carried off the binnacle and two large compasses as spoils for Davy Jones. For moments the ship was at the mercy of the next trick of the gale, but in those moments Limeburner fought his way aft foot by foot and took the wheel. They rode out the storm, and Chips used the doghouse to make a new binnacle. Hector had already developed a fondness for the snug cabin, and did not mind.

Captain Low now understood why so much of the gold rush shipping went across the Isthmus. Aspinwall's *California* was busy on the Pacific side, in three years carrying gold worth $122,000,-000, besides mail and passengers, between San Francisco and the Isthmus. The Panama railway was soon to be completed, and then letters from California could reach New York in five or six weeks.

Early in May the *Russell* stood outside the Golden Gate, with a ship that had left New York nearly a month before her just sighted astern. The pilot at the Farallones asked such a staggering price for bringing the ship into port that Low decided to dispense with him. Knowing nothing of San Francisco Bay, he sailed in between the beautiful headlands and brought his ship neatly to anchor opposite the Low agent's office. Captain Nat could not have done better.

At once the agent, F. W. Macondray, Harriet's old friend of the storeship *Lintin*, came aboard. The *Russell* brought news of her own run—109 days flat. San Francisco went wild. Placards all over the sodden streets announced "Shortest Passage ever made from New York—109 days." Not only, as the *Daily Pacific News* exulted the next day, was the *Russell* "one of the most beautiful specimens of naval architecture afloat," but she had shown the world what a clipper ship could do. She had cut two weeks from the record made by the *Memnon* the year before. But the feat was more significant: up to now the average voyage of the gold fleet had been 200 days. Thus Low and Limeburner, despite their overloaded ship and the gales they had fought, were the pioneers of what was to be the greatest sailing of all time.

That year the *Houqua* followed them in 130 days; the *Memnon*, 123; the *Mandarin*, 126; the *Natchez*, 150 days. It was not until July 24, long after Low had cleared for China, that the *Sea Witch*, now under Captain George Frazer, came romping through the Golden Gate with the record for that year of 97 net sailing days.

The next year a Low ship was to do even better.

That spring of 1850 the *Oriental* came back on her splendid 81-day run to find her sailing orders waiting. She was to return to China at once and pick up a cargo of teas for England, thus winning a place in history as the first United States merchantman to trade in a British port. Captain Nat, as usual, was building the Lows a new ship. He decided to give Theo Palmer command for the voyage, but went along as passenger.

They sailed out May 19, reached the Line in 25 days, passed the Cape of Good Hope 45 days out and Java Head 71, and reached Hong Kong in 81 days. That remained the record for a New York-to-China run, and also surpassed any run from England to China, though it was reckoned as a shorter passage because of favoring winds from England to the Equator.

At Hong Kong Russell & Co., by arrangement with the Lows, chartered the *Oriental* to load teas for London. They found plenty of shippers ready to pay six pounds sterling per ton of forty cubic feet, when the British ships then loading got little more than half that rate. This was due partly to the prestige the *Oriental* had won, partly to the fact that long voyages deadened the delicate flavor of teas. The clipper was loaded with sixteen hundred tons of new teas, with a freight list of forty-eight thousand dollars.

Just twenty days loading, she sailed out August 28, beat down the China Sea against a strong southwest monsoon, and on December 3 tied up at the East India docks in London. Her 91-day passage to the Lizard had never been matched, especially against the monsoon, and has seldom since been surpassed. In ten months and eight days this clipper had made two 81-day voyages between New York and China, and the third one from Hong Kong to London.

England was profoundly stirred. Brother Jonathan had timed the historic gesture perfectly, and made it with stunning success. The English had never seen a clipper ship, and day after day the throngs came to worship the *Oriental* as she lay at her mooring, her tall raking masts and skysail yards belittling all the shipping in the river. The Palmers kept her groomed like the thoroughbred she was; the men were forever holystoning her decks, polishing the brightwork, tucking in the last inch of snowy canvas under bunt, quarter, and yardarm gaskets. England feted ship and the Palmers.

Could the *Illustrated London News* print her picture?

"Certainly," said Captains Nat and Theo.

The Admiralty begged the privilege of taking off her lines as she lay in dry dock; the Admiralty was obliged.

The august London *Times* printed an editorial:

"The rapid increase of population in the United States, augmented by an annual immigration of nearly 300,000 from these isles, is a fact that forces itself on the notice and interest of the most unobservant and incurious. All these promise to develop the resources of the United States to such an extent as to compel us to a competition as difficult as it is unavoidable. We must run a race with our gigantic and unshackled rival. We must set our long-practised skill, our steady industry, and our dogged determination, against his youth, ingenuity and ardor. It is a father who runs a race with his son. A fell necessity constrains us and we must not be beat. Let our ship-builders and employers take warning in time. Short voyages and the coal trade will take care of themselves, but we want fast vessels for long voyages, which otherwise will fall into American hands."

"One has already," Captain Nat chuckled. "The British haven't been so mad since the Boston Tea Party. The *Times* says we can all start together now with a fair field and no favor. It says the Britishers aren't complaining, only they want to beat us at this game. Let them try, Theo—even with the *Oriental's* lines at the Admiralty."

They tried, but for the next seven years the best British ships were built in American yards. The *Oriental* started a procession of Yankee tea ships to London, and five years later there were two dozen ships in the trade, getting not only the greatest tonnage but the choicest teas. The Lows, having pioneered the tea run to England, kept the lead with the *Oriental* and with the new clipper *Surprise*, launched the fall of 1850. That year the New York shipyards were so overwhelmed with work that the Lows commissioned the ship to Samuel Hall, the East Boston builder who had turned out the Russell opium fleet. It was the first clipper ship built outside of New York.

Though Captain Nat watched over her building between his voyages, the *Surprise* was designed by an unknown young man of twenty-three, Samuel Harte Pook. Like Griffiths, Pook had received his first training from a father who built ships for the Navy. There any resemblance between them ceased. Griffiths arrived at a marvel, but also a dead end, in the *Sea Witch*, and soon turned to drafting steamships. Pook, who followed the Palmer principles of design, was to create some of the very greatest clipper ships.

The *Surprise* was the queen of the 1850 fleet, which included the *Celestial, Mandarin, Witchcraft, White Squall,* and *Stag Hound,* all destined for fame. Her launching was one of the events of Boston that year; for one thing, she was fully rigged in the stocks, against all tradition, and launched with her three skysail yards across and colors flying. A great many of the multitude who watched expected her to capsize, but she flew down the ways like a gull.

Mr. Hall was making such an event of her debut on October 5 that several of the Low family went up to Boston, as their mourned Ellen would certainly have wished them to do. He erected a pavilion near the stocks for the ladies, and after the launching took his guests to a banquet at his house, while in the mold loft every man who had helped build the *Surprise* feasted and toasted the clipper.

A giant of 1261 tons, she was 190 feet long, her mainmast 84 feet from heel to cap, her main yard 78 feet across. Like most Low clippers, she was painted black from the water line up. Her figurehead was a finely carved and gilded eagle, and her stern bore the arms of New York City—just to remind the Bostoners.

Then she was towed down to New York by the festive steamer designed by Pook and named for Bob Forbes. The *R. B. Forbes* had her utilitarian moments as the best wrecking steamer in the Atlantic, but she was at her best acting as godmother to a clipper ship. Her hull was a brilliant red up to her bulwarks, which were black on the outside and bright green inside, as were the deckhouses and fittings. At Fourth of July celebrations, regattas, and launchings such as this, the *Forbes* broke out a rainbow of bunting from her mastheads, and shipped aboard hampers of festive food, cases of champagne, and a band of musicians.

The *Forbes* and her newest debutante had a gala reception in New York. The *Herald* declared the clipper was the handsomest ship ever seen in the port, running out of superlatives before the *Flying Cloud* came on the scene.

The Lows decided to give the clipper to Philip Dumaresq for her maiden voyage; few captains stood higher. His big crew of fifty included four mates and two cooks. He took her out for California December 13, and she made San Francisco in 96 days. At last the Lows had beaten the *Sea Witch*, on the run which all the world watched. Every California voyage of the new clipper ships was now a race on which tremendous bets were placed.

A San Francisco merchant, perhaps Mr. Macondray, had bet heavily on the Low ship's breaking the *Sea Witch's* record of 97 days. On March 19, 1851, it was 96 days since the *Surprise* had sailed, and she must come in or he would lose a small fortune. He rode over to North Beach, hoping to see her coming into the bay, but the fog was too thick for him to see anything at all. He rode back to his countinghouse to find it in an uproar. The *Surprise* had already come in through the Golden Gate, and by noon Dumaresq was on shore. He had sailed 16,308 sea miles in just over 96 days, and reefed his topsails only twice. His cargo manifest was twenty-five feet long, and his freight receipts were seventy-eight thousand dollars.

Brooklyn Heights was a happy place for a six-year-old boy. Will Low understood vaguely that his father had died at sea, and his first memory was of his mother Ann singing "Lightly May the Boat Row" at bedtime, and of feeling tears on her cheeks when she leaned over to kiss him good night. But these memories were now as faint as the fragrance of musk that clung to the knick-knacks from China Ann kept in their sunny front bedroom.

Will was embedded in family affections. The Bedell house on Cranberry Street was always animated, with one young uncle and eight aunts, most of them married now, running in and out with their children, and Grandmother Bedell, who looked so remarkably like George Washington, marshaling her brood like an indulgent general. Will had more Low and Bedell cousins than he could count.

He was full of responsibilities. His black-and-white Newfoundland was one; his volunteer fire company another, pulling their little truck piled with toy ladders madly down the streets, yelling like Mohawks, and ending the race with a feast in his grandfather's barn. But he never forgot that the Heights was a lookout for ships, perhaps one of Grandfather Bedell's coasters up from the Carolinas, or on great days a Low clipper ship, sure to bring him a present from China. Uncle Charles never failed him, and sometimes the three Palmer captains remembered too.

But on the whole Will's best times were at Uncle Abbot's house. He and his mother were often there, because the children had lost their mother, and baby Seth was still delicate. Of all his cousins his closest friend was Gus, who was about his age. They worked busily in the garden back of the house, where all the children had their own plots. Gus had title to the tulip bed, and was experimenting with peanuts. Will was so industrious that his uncle turned over the raspberry and gooseberry bushes as his special charge. His mother used to sit in the garden with baby Seth on her lap, directing operations. On their way home they would often stop at Grandfather Low's house around the corner on Concord Street, and Will was an important person there too.

That fall he started school, and two weeks before Christmas the *Surprise* started off on her first voyage around the world. One midwinter day Will came home from school to find a bevy of aunts using his best white drawing paper to wrap slices of cake. He was put out.

"But it's wedding cake," said Aunt Susan Bedell.

His mother knelt and put her arms around him. "We're going to live at Uncle Abbot's, dear. Isn't that wonderful?"

"Yes. Can I have a piece of cake now?"

The Lows and Bedells took the coming marriage with almost the same calm acceptance. It was inevitable, it was perfect, almost

189

as if fate had been in this from the first. When Ann had been widowed, her closest friends were Abbot and Ellen, watching over her with angelic kindness. Abbot had taken charge of her business affairs, he had played the part of father to Will. In any case he would have shouldered his brother's responsibilities, but from the first there was a deep affinity between him and Ann. She was sensitive, gifted, gently bred, with a beauty and grace rather like Ellen's.

These mid-century women were deceptive; under their artless femininity were formidable powers. Abbot, having learned the paradox of his sister Harriet—fortitude under inconsequence—recognized the strength in Ann. She had weathered her tragedy, and helped him through his own. For months she had mothered his children, just as for years he had been the only father Will had ever known. In Abbot's life there was always an equipoise, and now it was Ann who perfectly filled the balance.

Charles was home just a month before the wedding on February 25, home in 88 days, the most brilliant run of the China fleet that year. Limeburner's part in the victory was rewarded by his getting command of the *Samuel Russell* for the next voyage. Abbot had other plans for Charles.

The young captain and Edward, who had come home with him, had mapped out plans for a trip over inland waterways—from New Orleans up the Mississippi to the Great Lakes, down the St. Lawrence, across Lakes Champlain and George, and then through the White Mountains into Maine. The trip was all described in a book Ned gave his young brother to read.

"That's the most fascinating book anybody ever wrote," said Charles. "It's time I had a vacation, Ned. We'll take that trip."

But when they got in, Abbot proposed a visit to Westervelt's yard. Jacob Westervelt, a pioneer shipwright and public figure who was soon to be mayor of New York, had built the *Russell*, and now had the newest Low clipper nearly ready to launch.

When Charles Low saw her a shock ran all through him. This was the most tremendous ship he had ever seen; already, without her top gear, she was flight, she was perfection. He ran up and down her great length, scanning her lines—and the continuous curves from bows to stern were lines you could scan, like poetry. Oh, how honorably they were building her—white oak, live oak, locust, and cedar! Look at her treenailings, not driven blunt into the timbers, but coaxed through timbers and ceiling and then wedged inside and out. And her knees—no hackmatack here, but the finest oak in clean lengths . . .

"Well," said Abbot when they were back in the office, "how do you like the *N. B. Palmer?*"

"She's the most beautiful vessel I've ever seen, Abbot."

"I'm glad you like her. She's your command, Charles. I want you to go to Westervelt's tomorrow morning and take charge of her, and then see to her fitting out."

Charles felt his heart and lungs surrender their functions while his brain slowly absorbed this dazzling moment. For every captain there is the perfect ship. He had found his soul on the *Houqua*, but the *Palmer* opened his heart. He was in love.

"I gather," said Ned, "that our inland trip is off."

"Our inland trip? Oh yes. You can't blame me, can you?"

Ned laughed. "Not after seeing the *Palmer*, my boy."

Charles made his pilgrimages to the yard every day, though there was little he could do but worship this masterpiece. They sent a full-rigged model to be exhibited at the Crystal Palace in London that year, and before she met the water she was famous. In years to come "the Yacht" meant one clipper, the *N. B. Palmer*. It was like "the Factory" meaning the power and glory of the British East India Company.

The year 1851 saw some of the loveliest of all ships into the world: Donald McKay's *Flying Cloud*, the *Witch of the Wave* and the *Nightingale*, the *Challenge*, which Waterman was to command, the *Sword Fish* and the *Northern Light*. Forty royal clippers came out that year, almost every one of which justified the hopes of their admirers. There was amazing range in their design, for builders and draftsmen were now competing with each other to find new elements making for speed and sturdiness. America was still maritime, in spite of the Conestoga wagons going west, and a large public, whose hearts were bursting with pride at the clipper ships, were also able to understand the fine points of construction.

Thus, when the *Herald* came out February 9 describing the *Palmer* literally down to her bolts, hundreds of readers could nod their expert approval.

Her proportions, said the account, "will be admired by those versed in the art of marine construction, more especially by those experienced old salts, who well understand the necessity, in heavy weather, of a ship having not only buoyancy to her mid-ship body, but are also aware of the fatal fallacy of having little or no buoyancy in the after body. We have examined several vessels in this port lately, which although extolled as pattern ships, may, like those of the British Navy . . . disappoint their most sanguine admirers."

Then followed a discussion of Baltimore sterns and English overhanging bows, of the *Palmer's* meticulous construction, of her sturdy made masts, well proportioned with good doublings or long mastheads for security. "In fact, she must be acknowledged, up to the present, one of the most perfect specimens of naval architecture seen in this port."

Captain Nat had poured his heart, and the Lows' money, into the *Palmer*. Of 1490 tons register, she was 214 feet long, 39 broad, and 22 deep. Her hull, yards, and bowsprits were painted black, the lower masts white to the tops, with the tops and the doublings above scraped bright and varnished. The quarterdeck ran a third of the ship's length, and at the break of it steps went down to the main deck on either side of a covered companionway leading to the cabin.

Charles was to have a comfortable, even luxurious home. The cabin was divided by a partition of rich paneling and stained glass into dining room and saloon, both richly carpeted, with plump cushioned seats. There were four staterooms on a side, and even the Liverpool liners could not offer their passengers beds wider or furnished with springier mattresses, or prettier paneling of bird's-eye maple and mahogany. The captain had a suite of rooms.

By March all spars were aloft, the royal and skysail yards were crossed, and the *Palmer* was ready for her launching. Captain

Nat insisted on being launched with his newest treasure, sending Charles to the steam tug with the guests. He swallowed his disappointment in the joy of watching the beautiful ship slide down the ways. She came down with such an eager rush that a sea washed over her stern and set the carpenter's chips afloat.

There was nothing whatever for Charles to do while the *Palmer* was loading.

"Why don't you find a pretty girl and get married?" Haskell suggested.

The family was in a romantic mood, happy about Abbot and Ann. Charles was now twenty-seven, and quite able to support a wife. Spring was coming, and he hadn't seen the lovely girls of Salem for years.

Early in April handsome young Captain Low registered at the Essex House in Salem, and for miles around there was a flutter of ribbons and laces and hopeful young hearts.

14

Philopena

In South Danvers, next door to
Salem, the Cutlers had a party every night for Charles. Haskell
and his wife Rebecca Ann Cutler had arranged this by letters
explaining that Charles must soon take out his new ship and
needed expert guidance in choosing a wife. To expedite matters
they had told Charles that Miss X was probably the girl for him.

He couldn't quite agree. She was charming, but so were the
dozen misses in each evening's fresh bouquet. He was beset by
lovely girls, any one of whom would have jumped at the chance
to marry this famous young captain. They all began to look alike
to him, Mary Jane and Paulina, Eliza and Harriet. One Thursday
evening they all acted alike; invited to sing, they all had excuses,
perhaps knowing by then that Captain Low had a sensitive ear
for singing.

Then without a word a small prim girl went to the piano. She played, she sang like a lark. She went on without prompting. She looked almost Indian with her dark eyes and black hair parted in the middle and slicked down over her ears; music brought out the fire under her stiff shyness.

Charles, for the second time that spring, fell in love. When he saw the *Palmer* he had known instantly that she was his ship. This was his girl, honest, warm, no fuss about her. He went over to the piano and leaned against it, keeping her singing because he enjoyed it, and because he dreaded the moment when they would have to talk. He felt completely tongue-tied, and sensed that she wasn't going to help him out.

About all he learned when they were introduced was that she was Sarah Maria Tucker, eighteen, the only child of a widow, and was related to half the people in the room.

The next evening nearly the same company was at the Shillabers', and Charles monopolized Sarah Tucker. He even made her eat a philopena with him.

"But it won't do you any good," she protested. "I shan't ever see you again."

He was up early the next morning, and at the livery stable hired a horse and a green chaise, the most elegant one they had, and drove to her house.

She opened the door and cried, "Philopena!" which delighted him.

"Here's my forfeit," he said, pointing to the carriage. "Will you go riding with me, Miss Tucker?"

"I must ask Mother."

Mrs. Hannah Tucker was like the new steamships—boiling and bubbling with inner warmth, bursting with energy, as excitable and inconsequential as her daughter was self-possessed—or pretended to be. On the long ride to Phillip's Beach Sally Tucker, trying to look severely dignified, heard what a clipper captain's life was like, sailing clean around the world.

She heard about the Bella Union in San Francisco, where a thousand miners gambled their piles of gold dust as the band played, where Charles, prudently coming ashore with three dollars, won and lost and won again, breaking even for the evening, besides sampling the free-lunch counters in the four corners of the huge hall.

"But the next day was really exciting," he went on. "I'd just got a crew aboard at the wicked price of a hundred and fifty dollars apiece for Honolulu, when San Francisco caught fire. I rushed ashore, because our agent, Macondray's on Market Street, had seventy-five thousand dollars in freight money I'd just brought in. I spent all that day and night keeping the fire off. You know, in Brooklyn I used to be torch boy——"

Sally Tucker wanted to know about Honolulu.

"Oh, I had the King aboard for dinner, of course."

"You mean, the cannibal king, Captain Low?"

"No, King Kamehameha and a lot of his ministers. They wanted to see the *Russell*. They'd never seen a real clipper ship, and the King went into raptures. Then they invited me ashore for a real bang-up native feast——"

It was easy to talk to Sally Tucker. The next day was Sunday, and Charles described the captain's suite on the *Palmer*. Monday morning Sally went over to Salem and had her miniature taken for him. He left for New York the next day, but was back that week end with a length of China silk for Sally and a delaine for her mother, and before they knew it, Charles and Sally were engaged. He had to leave much too soon, for the *Palmer* was almost loaded, so they said farewell for a year.

When Charles got home on Tuesday night he found his mother sitting up for him.

"Charles, where have you been?"

"Getting engaged."

The family was delighted that Charles had managed this important matter with such expedition. It seemed a good omen that at the same moment the news came via the Isthmus that the *Surprise* had beaten the *Sea Witch* and all the ships that had ever sailed to California. At the Astor House merchants, sea captains, and builders paid off the bets they had made on their favorites, and began laying new ones on the *N. B. Palmer*.

By Saturday she was still not ready to sail, and Captain Nat and

Abbot came aboard to find the young captain in a stew. Abbot took his arm.

"Charles, you'd like to go to South Danvers, wouldn't you?"

And Captain Nat said, "Yes, why shouldn't he go?"

"You can catch the boat at five, if you hurry," said Abbot. He gave Charles a roll of bills. "Be off with you, now."

Charles flew to Brooklyn, packed a valise, and got to Pier 1 on the North River in time for the Fall River boat.

On Sunday Sally stayed home from church to write her first love letter, which she must get to Charles before he sailed. At noon in came Mr. Cutler.

"Sarah, you must come over to our house at once." He rushed her over without explanations—and there was her clipper captain. The next day they went driving, to escape hordes of mere people, and said a final farewell.

The *N. B. Palmer* sailed May 6, and the captain tested her first in the heavy weather that plagued him all the way to the Line. She behaved beautifully, and in 60 days out they rounded the Horn and she was flying, faster than he had ever sailed, pressing her sharp breast forward like a mallemuck under the arctic white of her great wings. He got her to San Francisco in 106 days and laid her alongside the wharf without taking a pilot.

"This is the prettiest piece of seamanship ever seen in San Francisco," Mr. Macondray told him.

It was also the fastest voyage so far that year, and it was now August 21. Captain Waterman had made 109 days in the *Challenge*, and the *Sea Witch*, Captain Frazer, had lagged with 111 sailing days. At the very end of 1851 the *Flying Fish* and the *Sword Fish* came in with 101- and 94-day voyages, the only ships beside the *Flying Cloud* to beat the *Palmer*.

Ten days after Captain Low arrived his old friend Josiah Cressy, of Salem, brought in the *Flying Cloud* on her maiden run, in the wholly incredible time of 89 days. This was the absolute climax of all clipper races; the record was never surpassed, and was equaled only twice, once by the *Cloud* herself three years later, once by the *Andrew Jackson* in 1860.

In creating this perfect ship (but not the only perfect ship of her day) Donald McKay arrived at his full stature as designer. He had studied and pondered and no doubt prayed over her lines, he had based himself firmly on the principles of Palmer's *Roscius* and his clipper ships, and then had added those final inspirations that turned bulk into breathless beauty in flight. Her record and her lovely name made her the symbol forever of the clipper ship, the damosel among damsels as hauntingly beautiful, and sometimes as fleet.

This year was the high point in sheer excitement on both coasts, with the New York *Commercial* calling the *Cloud's* log "the most wonderful record that pen ever indicted." It was also the low point in Robert Waterman's career.

All captains during the gold rush had to sail out with crews they would infallibly lose to the mines in California, men who shipped only to get free passage and high wages, the offscourings of ginhouses and dives. Waterman left New York just after Captain Low with such an unsavory crew that he almost turned back to dump them at the nearest wharf. Instead he scuttled their bowie knives, knuckle-dusters, pistols, and caches of rum.

The crew was riddled with syphilis, and during the voyage five men died in the crowded sick bay. Off Rio de Janeiro there was a mutiny and Waterman killed two men with an iron belaying pin. Off the Horn three of the crew fell from aloft and were killed. The survivors roused the mobs in San Francisco, and Waterman barely escaped lynching. He never commanded another ship, and settled down in California, a tired old man of forty-two.

His *Rainbow* was already a ghost; she had left New York in 1848 and simply vanished. The *Sea Witch*, after her three years of amazing records, was a tired old ship waiting for a storm off Cuba to put an end to her misery.

It was a mad year. Captain Low got a crew together in San Francisco and sailed out under ballast, his only cargo the bodies of seventy-five Chinese being taken home for burial. He was amused at the quick advantage at least one captain had taken of this custom. Captains were paid one eighth of cabin fares, so he

198

listed his dead Chinese as passengers and collected seventy-five dollars apiece on them.

On the voyage to Shanghai Low caught sight of a dismasted ship eight miles to windward and hauled on a wind and beat up to her. She was the *Austerlitz* of Boston, caught in a typhoon four days before, and not worth saving. He took off her captain, who had his wife and child along, and the crew, and then burned the ship to keep her from endangering passing vessels. In spite of this delay he beat the *Flying Cloud* to China by ten days. As a Grinnell, Minturn ship she was on the tea run like the *Palmer*. Again, getting back to New York in the spanking time of 82 days from Whampoa, Captain Low beat his friend Cressy by ten days. He was home April 2, 1852, covered with glory, but with one more feat of navigation to accomplish: getting through the tides and reefs of the wedding at South Danvers.

The Lows were rushing the California trade for all it was worth, and it was worth a fortune. Their new ships paid their first cost ready for sea in the single voyage to San Francisco, then went on to China to pick up teas at a bargain. It was now safe to delay purchases of the new crop for three weeks, letting their competitors pay the top prices, and then buy a cargo at reduced rates, with the confidence that it would arrive in time to command the New York market.

Their competitors were of course trying to do the same thing with their glorious new clipper ships, and now and then a brilliant run by one of them would put the Lows at a disadvantage. But they excelled by having a large fleet under the red and yellow flag, every one of them in the very first rank. Captain Nat's formula had worked; in designing the perfect ship for the China trade he had shown all builders how to evolve clippers ready to sail around the world, encountering every sort of wind and weather. The sharp principles Griffiths had borrowed from the frigates were now abandoned in favor of Palmer's packet lines, infinitely varied by cross-fertilization between yard and yard.

There was a tremendous amount of building in 1852, which saw sixty-six clipper ships launched, doubling the fleet. The Lows added to their *Houqua, Samuel Russell, N. B. Palmer, Surprise,* and *Oriental* only one new ship that year, the *Contest,* built by Westervelt, a beauty with a dazzling future.

After her maiden run under Dumaresq the command of the *Surprise* went into family hands—the Charles Ranletts, father and son, who ran up eleven consecutive voyages from China home in 89 days or less. During his hard-pressed years in Salem Seth Low had opened his home to his widowed sister Abigail Ranlett and her four sons, and his own sons were now rewarded by the steady high performance of the *Surprise.* Her sustained record was the more remarkable because most clippers got waterlogged and tired, and slowed markedly after two or three voyages. But the *Surprise* equaled the *Oriental's* record of 81 days from Shanghai to New York in 1857 when she was an old lady, as clippers went.

The Lows did not get involved in the Australian gold rush, which had begun the year before and within two years had attracted so many gold seekers that two hundred full-rigged ships from all over the world lay together in Melbourne Bay. This gold frenzy was to beget more fast ships than the world needed, for the English were rushing vessels in their own yards and ordering many from American builders. McKay built four clippers for Australia, meanwhile producing the new giant of the American fleet, the *Sovereign of the Seas,* 2421 tons and 258 feet long. He loved big ships.

How the clipper captains managed their circumnavigations of the globe and their swift sailing to completely unfamiliar parts of it is explained mainly by their high caliber. The only systematic work on winds and currents was now in process under Lieutenant Matthew Fontaine Maury, and it was the clipper captains who furnished most of his material. Lame from a stagecoach accident, given only niggardly backing by the Navy, Maury was just coming into his own. Since 1847 he had been issuing wind and current charts and sailing directions that cut down passage time to California, and in every mail he got more and more logs and notes from grateful captains.

By 1853 he had organized an international congress in Brussels which set all the navy and merchant captains in the world at work recording data by a uniform system. The same year the Lows and other New York merchants and underwriters presented him with a silver service and a much-needed purse of five thousand dollars. Not long after that the Lows named a clipper barque in his honor.

Abbot Low felt a special kinship with Maury because they were together in backing the project for a transatlantic cable, both of them working closely with Cyrus Field. Maury made a chart showing the profile of the ocean floor between Europe and the United States, pointing out the "telegraphic plateau" that simplified the tremendous undertaking.

England was doing her best to emulate Brother Jonathan in the tea run to London. The Americans had eighteen ships in this work in 1851 and 1852, and twenty the next year, which turned out to be the peak. They were still getting double the freight rates given British carriers, and were taking the tea trade of the London markets almost out of English hands. Good British vessels would lie for weeks in a China port waiting for a tea charter, while the Yankee clippers loaded up and sped to London to capture the market.

Under the impact of the *Oriental*'s first visit, Jardine, Matheson & Co. of London built the first British clipper, the *Stornoway*, followed by the *Chrysolite*, which was faster and closer to the American formula. On her first voyage she made Liverpool to Anjer in 80 days. At once this was hailed as a record, though the *Oriental* had made the much longer run from New York to Anjer in 71 days—longer in miles, and always longer in sailing, since English ships met favoring winds going down to the Line, and American ships had to make a point near the Cape Verde Islands and wait, sometimes *ad nauseam*, for the northeast trades. Aside from the *Oriental*, which the *Chrysolite* was built to beat, a dozen American ships had run from New York to Anjer in less than 76 days, and for many years to come no foreign-built vessel could do better.

But the English papers made much of it. There was even a fable that England's pride had beaten the *Flying Cloud* and the

Bald Eagle to London in 1851—though the *Cloud* was then in San Francisco after her famous run, and the *Bald Eagle* was still in the stocks. However, the British clipper was lucky enough that year to get the winds the Low captains whistled for in vain, and arrived in Liverpool from Whampoa in 105 days. Dumaresq in the *Surprise* sailed earlier, against the monsoon, and rolled up 106½ days, while Theo Palmer made a longer voyage from Woosung in the *Oriental* in 128 days of labor and cursing.

From London Dumaresq wrote the Lows: "The English flatter themselves that they can build clippers that can compete with ours, but I fancy that idea will be a short one. Their ships in the race had a fine fair wind, while Palmer and I had easterly gales and calms to contend with."

Early in 1852, soon after the Low ships reached London, the *Illustrated London News,* much read in the United States, came out with such praise of the new British ships that certain of the old China hands decided it was time to take the Britishers down. Some of the Lows' best friends—Thomas H. Perkins, John Cushing, John Forbes, Warren Delano, and Edward King—founded the American Navigation Club for this specific purpose. It promptly issued a challenge to the British which was printed in the leading shipping papers of England and in *Bell's Life,* then the great sporting paper overseas.

The terms of the challenge were an American-British race from an English port to a port in China and back. Each nation was to put up a ship of from 800 to 1200 tons American register, to be designed, commanded, and officered by citizens of each nation respectively, and to rank A1 at Lloyd's or an American insurance company. The stakes were to be ten thousand sterling a side, the judges mutually chosen. If the challenge was not accepted within thirty days the British would be allowed a head start of fourteen days and the stakes doubled.

Bell's Life and the London *Daily News* urged taking up the challenge for the sake of British prestige, but there was silence on the part of English shipowners. The most that came of it was an informal race that year between four American and three British clippers from Canton to Deal, and though the Yankees happened to buck the northeast monsoon, they won handily.

Late that year the *Oriental* came foaming up to Sandy Hook, which she had last seen two years and seven months before. In that time she had sailed ninety-seven thousand miles, earned tremendous sums for the Lows, and won a festoon of new sailing records. She looked as fresh as the day she was launched, too. Captain Theo Palmer at that point established a new record; he allowed himself the extravagance of taking a tug.

Another Stonington stalwart, Captain William Brewster, was now on his way around the Horn in the Lows' new *Contest*, beginning her brilliant career in a great deep-sea derby of no less than fifteen princesses of the blood that happened to sail within a few weeks of each other. It was the happiest moment of gold rush days, when freights were still high and sail the nation's poetry. The fifteen splendid clippers that filled away from New York and Boston represented the utmost that designers, shipwrights, and riggers could produce, and Captain Brewster was sailing against a royal line of masters, every one of them conscious of the skill and hardihood of the others.

It was all a matter of getting the winds when you needed them, and of the ships that sailed in November under much the same conditions, the *Contest* was first with a run of 100 days, and a noteworthy spurt of 42 days from Cape Horn to San Francisco. She was third among the fifteen ships; the *John Gilpin* and *Flying Fish* made the passage in 93 and 92 days, sailing almost in company a month earlier. That still put her two weeks ahead of the famous Pook ship *Game Cock*, and eighteen days ahead of the Boston ship *Northern Light*, with which she was soon to race home. To star in a company which included these great ships and the *Telegraph, Queen of the Seas, Wild Pigeon, Dauntless, Trade Wind*, and *Westward Ho* was no mean feat for the youngest ship to fly the red-and-yellow house flag. The Lows decided she had earned her name on her maiden voyage, but when the *Contest* sailed back through the Golden Gate she was on her way to fresh triumphs.

15

Log of

a Honeymoon

A Yankee sloop came down the river,
Hah, hah, rolling John.
Oh, what do you think that sloop had in her?
Hah, hah, rolling John——

Mrs. Charles Porter Low preferred not to hear the end of that particular chantey the men were singing as they scrubbed the deck over her head. Not that the thought of "monkey's hide and bullock's liver" was going to spoil her appetite for breakfast. She sorted out the delicious promises coming from the galley—coffee, ham and eggs, and yes, without a doubt, pancakes! And her mother had been sure she would have nothing but codfish and salt beef on the *Palmer*.

The captain's lady took a quick turn on deck, listening to her husband bawl, "Clap a watch tackle on the lee forebrace," or some equally cryptic order before he came down to breakfast. Then she took her book on deck to watch Charles finish his watch. In the cabin then he read *Handy Andy* aloud while she sewed on her warm hood for Cape Horn. A snack at eleven preserved them for dinner at one, a sustaining meal of oyster soup, salmon, roast chickens, half a dozen fresh vegetables, and two or three desserts.

They had sixteen passengers, half of them children, and since the *Palmer* was becalmed, the captain took the ladies for a row around the ship so they could gaze up at her and feel her might even with idle sails. The crew went fishing and caught a shark, and Sally sampled a bit of it at tea. There was a moon that evening and they had a country dance and a quadrille on deck, winding up in the saloon, singing around the piano as Sally played.

She couldn't imagine why people thought a clipper voyage anything but a continual round of pleasure. Nor could she quite understand the change in her husband when the gale came up. No *Handy Andy* now; he was always on deck. When the ship careened and the seas rushed past the cabin portholes, the three lady passengers began to twitter, but she assured them the captain was taking care of things.

At noon he came down to look at his chronometers, and whooped.

"Dear darling," he told her, "while the ladies were twittering the *Palmer* ran up a record."

"Of course," she said staunchly.

"I mean," he said, "that she made 390 miles this day—over sixteen knots. That's the record, Sally. Last year the *Flying Cloud* rolled up 374 in a day, steering north and west under t'gallants."

"Wait till you see Mr. Cressy," she glowed. "How will he feel about that?"

"Well, the *Cloud* left New York ten days before we did. How do you expect an old barge like the *Palmer* to catch up with her?"

"Fiddlesticks, Charlie. We'll overtake her."

On June 7 Sally came up on deck to find Charles and Mr. Haines, his mate, looking through the glass at a clipper ship far ahead. They kept her in sight, off and on, all day. At one in the morning Charles came down and woke up his wife.

"Do you want to watch the *Palmer* pass that ship?"

She scrambled into her clothes and ran up on deck. It was the *Gazelle*, which had left New York six days before them. After they had run past her Sally began talking about the *Flying Cloud*, but Charles said that was bad luck.

A week later they crossed the Line with the usual ritual of ducking the green hands. Then there was an interval of dead calms and gales in which they lost one sail but no men.

On July 1, off the coast of Montevideo, the captain shot the sun and sighted a ship dead to windward. He took the spyglass to the mizzentop and looked again. It was the *Flying Cloud*. Twice the year before he had beaten her by ten days, and now for the third time he was ten days ahead of her, only forty days out of New York. Both ships were running before the wind, and he felt sure that he could outsail the *Cloud* as long as the wind was precisely aft. He hauled up close to the breeze with his studding sails shaking, and waited two hours for her to come up.

Cressy drew close alongside at two in the afternoon.

"*Palmer* ahoy," he yelled. "When did you leave New York?"

"Ten days after you, Cressy."

Their Salem friend did a solemn dance of rage. Then he exchanged genial remarks with the bride and groom, and told them he'd see them in San Francisco.

"We'll be waiting there for you," the Lows called.

The race that began then was against the *Palmer* at the start, since she was at a standstill and waiting for a breeze. Soon there were cat's-paws from the south, and a breeze made an indigo line across the horizon. Both ships got ready for the wind, rigging in their booms, taking in their studding sails, and started off on the starboard tack sharp by the wind. Soon the *Cloud* shook her snowy petticoats and scampered away, for the wind hauled ahead and Low had to brace sharper than the *Palmer* liked.

"As long as the *Cloud's* on a wind," he told Haines, "she can beat us a mile an hour."

By four in the morning the wind freshened and the *Cloud* took in all her studding sails, gaining on the *Palmer*, but not as fast as Low had expected. By daylight the *Cloud* was still in sight, then a thick mist closed in and they lost her. For the next week there were westerly gales, and the racing ships could only guess how the contest was going.

A stove was put up in the cabin and everybody wore his warmest clothes. Sally's twentieth birthday was July 3, and the Fourth was her mother's, but there was too much excitement to think about birthdays.

At midnight on July 8 Captain Low was just turning out for his watch when there were sudden heavy noises on deck. As he hastily pulled on his boots he heard Haines call the steward.

"Bring me my musket," he said.

Mutiny? Low rushed out.

"Don't go on deck, sir," Haines warned. "There's trouble."

Then Low saw a red stream running down Haines's left leg.

"Dublin Jack shot me," the mate said.

When the steward came up with the musket Low took it and told him to call the carpenter and sailmaker and come on deck with a lantern.

The watch was hoisting the mizzen topsail. When it was set Low ordered the men to pass in front of him and Haines. When the seaman Dublin Jack passed, Haines said, "That's the man that shot me."

Low ordered the second and third mates to put him in irons. To his amazement, a seaman called Lemons then came up and announced coolly that he, not Dublin Jack, had shot the chief. That looked more like mutiny.

"Where's your pistol?" Low demanded.

"I threw it overboard."

The captain was still suspicious. "Or was it a revolver?"

"No. If it had been, neither you nor your mate would be alive now."

"You're mighty cool about it," the captain said. He had no choice but to release Dublin Jack and put Lemons in irons in the booby hatch.

Fortunately there were two English surgeons among the passengers, and they reported that Haines had only a flesh wound in his thigh, but would have to keep his berth for some time. Haines said his assailant had aimed at his heart, and only a timely lurch of the ship had saved him.

That was by no means the end of it. Low came back on deck to see his second mate with his arm in a sling.

"What in tarnation's wrong with you, man?"

"Dublin Jack knocked me down with a handspike, sir. While the third and I were putting Lemons in irons."

"Then both Dublin Jack and Lemons are in it. Well, the watch has gone below, and there's nothing we can do till morning. You'd better go below and see the surgeons."

The captain was now minus his first and second, and the third was not going to be much help rounding Old Cape Stiff in a midwinter gale. He felt quite capable of standing incessant watches until the Cape was rounded. The worst ordeal came the next morning when the watch changed at eight.

He called all hands on deck, thirty able seamen, six ordinary, and four boys, and lined them up on the other side of a rope stretched across the deck. He took out his pistol.

"Now," he said, "anybody who steps across this rope will be shot."

Dublin Jack cackled and put one foot over the rope.

Low made a bound and caught him by the throat. In a minute he had him ironed and trussed up to the mizzen rigging. Then Lemons was brought out of the booby hatch and triced up beside him.

"Give them two dozen lashes apiece," Low ordered the third mate.

"Sir," he protested, "I've never lashed a man in my life."

"Neither have I," Low roared, "but here's where I begin."

He took a piece of ratline and gave the men their strokes. After they had been locked up he eyed the rest of the crew.

"If you're not satisfied with this morning's work," he told them, "step out one at a time and I'll thrash you too."

Nobody seemed interested.

"Go below the watch."

208

The Low Clipper Ship *Contest*. Painting by a contemporary artist. *Courtesy of Harry Shaw Newman, The Old Print Shop, New York.*

The Tea Fleet at Whampoa Anchorage. Painting by George Chinnery.
Courtesy of the Frick Collection

But after breakfast Low made all hands come on deck again, and he worked the mischief out of them. After that he decided it was safe to have watch and watch again.

Sally looked dark and grave when he finally snatched a moment with her. "They'll go for you next, darling," she whispered.

"Never." He stroked her smooth hair. "We've got all their weapons. And they liked that lashing ceremony about as much as I did. Trouble's all over."

For the next eighteen days Sally saw her husband only when he came down to the stateroom to wind the chronometers and note down the time. He didn't sleep below, he scarcely slept two hours out of the twenty-four, and then he lay down in a corner of the house on deck in his wet clothes. Storm after storm brought high seas, snow, rain, hail, and even after they passed the Horn the gales continued, shredding the main royal to rags.

Sally Low learned what it was to be a clipper captain's wife. It meant music in the cabin and races with the *Flying Cloud*, it meant the icy infernos of the Cape through which the ship labored and groaned and hurled itself at the giant seas, it meant mutiny, treachery, danger, and the cruel strain of the captain always on deck. And it meant herself, snug and quiet in the cabin, keeping as calm as she could because, as her mother would put it, she'd lost no time. Young Charles was already on the way.

One day it was quiet enough so that she bundled up warm and came on deck to stand beside her husband.

"They tell me," he praised her, "that you're braver than any man in the cabin."

"That's because I know enough to trust the captain," she said.

Finally Haines was back on duty, and the captain began making up his lost sleep a few hours at a time; he still could not risk taking his full watch below.

They stopped at Valparaiso to send home Lemons and Dublin Jack to be tried for attempted murder on the high seas. The rest of the crew deserted, and Captain Low feared it would be next to impossible to man his ship at Valpo, which specialized in scoundrels and beachcombers. By great luck he picked up a fine crew who had worked up a business of shipping by the run at high wages, and was out again with a delay of nine days.

On the way to San Francisco the captain found time to write a long letter to Hannah Tucker, whom he considered one of the blessings of his marriage. She was like him in jovial good humor and invincible energy and a protective attitude toward Sally.

"My dear Mother," he wrote, "I am at a loss how to address one who has given up her only child, her only hope and comfort to bless me, but may it be your comfort dear Mother that in giving one child you now have two to love and take care of you, although my love will be but little, for my dear Sarah engrosses it all. . . .

"After leaving New York and entering upon the broad expanse of waters I was agreeably disappointed and made very happy to find that I had no baby for a wife but one who in storm and calm has proved herself a heroine."

She had been a little seasick sometimes, and missed her mother and her cousin David Galloupe, who took the place of a brother.

"If you want to think of us sometimes you must imagine yourself standing in our front cabin peeping in through the small door into the Bed Room. There you will see Sally with your Miniature in one hand and David's daguerreotype in the other, first kissing Mamma and then Grandma, and then David. You will then see Charles stealing in softly and saying, 'Well, Sally, what is the matter?' Sally replies, 'Oh I would give $10,000, yes $40,000 to see my mother.' I then set down and begin to talk about home. Dear Mother and dear Grandma, Dear Aunty David, Uncle Galloup, Uncle William, Mr. Daniels, Mr. and Mrs. Cutler, Mr. and Mrs. Parsons, Mary Jane Gordon and all Danvers included. By this time Sarah begins to cry a little, then I begin to think of my happy home and all the dear friends, and I sometimes drop a little salt water . . . after that, kisses, and Sarah's tears are dried up and we are as happy as any married couple in the United States."

They arrived in San Francisco the last day of September, and, everything considered, their voyage of 130 days had not been too bad. Before they arrived they had even overtaken the *Gazelle* again, and Captain Low had boarded her with a gift of potatoes and squashes from Valpo. The *Flying Cloud* made a passage of 113 days, twenty-four days longer than the year before, proving that she was as susceptible to the ups and downs of sailing as her sisters.

Despite its wicked reputation, San Francisco offered the Lows a different church to go to every Sunday, and the prices in the shops were at last within reason. They had a long dusty drive to the gold diggings at Sacramento, and exchanged dinners with various other clipper captains. Best of all, there were letters from home that had come across the Isthmus, those from Hannah Tucker with sly remarks about "little Charlie Low."

For weeks Sarah's letters to her mother had been full of hints any practical matron could read: her growing plumpness, her reveling in food, and her longing to have her mother with her. But she was determined not to have Hannah Tucker worrying about a grandchild arriving off the Cape of Good Hope, so the maddening hints continued. As for "little Charles" she admitted, "I think of it sometimes and wish it were so that we could have a dear little pet of our own. When we get home, perhaps the thing will be possible. You would be surprised to see how much I have altered. You need have no fears for my health. At present I am in excellent condition. Here comes my old husband to bother me and I think I will put by my writing for the present. He is the greatest bore imaginable, always plaguing me."

She had done a little plaguing of her own, and had made her husband promise to stay home for a year after the voyage was done. "And by that time," she confided, "I hope to persuade Charles to remain on shore the rest of his days. . . . He leads a very hard life, and I see the need for economy on our parts."

And yet she loved the *Palmer*. "Talk about the Flying Cloud and Gazelle, you had better talk of the Palmer, the handsomest, safest, and as fast as any. I would not go to sea in any other, but would trust this old ship anywhere. She rides through the gales so gracefully, and is perfectly bewitching in all her movements. I love her. She has been a happy home to me."

She was glad when they sailed out again with no children, and no other women aboard. "I find it much pleasanter having no lady passengers, always poking around. I am mistress of my own house now." She even helped the steward make mince pies for Thanksgiving.

They were in Canton for Christmas, after a stop in Manila for a cargo of hemp. For a while they lived ashore at Suy Hong, but Sarah was feeling too miserable to enjoy the freedom now granted Fanqui women, and was happy to go back to the ship at Whampoa. With his usual luck Charles found an ideal nurse to sail home with them. Miss Hemenway had tended some of the first families of Boston; she was a cheerful, talkative old soul, lyric about children, and a notable pastry cook. Two missionary couples took passage on the *Palmer*, one an elderly pair, the other a young man whose present wife had been sent out as replacement from a mission school in the United States when his first wife died.

Captain Low made one of the shortest Canton stops of his life. They sailed out in mid-January, and for once he wasn't thinking of speed for the honor of A. A. Low & Bros.

Ten days later they were through the Strait of Gaspar and in the Java Sea, flying under a fine breeze. It was all so beautiful in the moonlight that Captain Low called everybody on deck to share his enjoyment.

"Wait till you see Anjer, Sally," he said. "It's always one of the best things in the voyage. But it makes me wish the Dutch would open up their islands and let us trade with them. They're as hoity-toity as Japan about that."

He took the watch at four the next morning, and was still in the cabin pricking out the ship's position on the chart when there was a sound as if the whole ship were exploding, then a terrible quiver of her frame as she wrenched to a standstill.

"We're on Broussa's Shoal," he yelled to the mate as he rushed on deck. "Lay all sails aback, mister."

They moved everything they could aft, the water barrels and casks of salted meat, and ran out a kedge anchor astern. The wind freshened and helped them off the reef. They found the ship was leaking seven inches an hour, it looked as if the forefoot was gone, and Captain Low was so certain she had torn a hole in her bows that he could not understand how she kept afloat. Later they found a huge piece of coral, two feet across, stuck in her wood ends like a cork—a fluke that saved them from sinking within the hour.

As it was, the *Palmer* was close to foundering, and the nearest shipyard was at Batavia, ninety miles away.

"So we'll see Java, in spite of the Dutch," he told Sarah.

She nodded, pale and tight-lipped, and he went back to see whether the pumps were gaining, and how much canvas he could get up to push the laboring ship through the water.

At six that evening Miss Hemenway flashed up the companion.

"Can you come down to your little wife, Captain Low? The poor child's being so brave, but she needs you."

The sweat broke out all over him. A foundering ship, and Sally's time upon her, all untimely . . .

"Now you mustn't worry, Captain Low, everything will be all right, you'll just see——"

But she had to help him down to the cabin.

16

Cloak and

Dagger

A few hours before the *N. B. Palmer* went aground the turnkey of Weltevreden Prison in Batavia whispered some very bad news to one of the inmates, Mr. Walter Murray Gibson, of South Carolina. A secret tribunal had voted to execute Mr. Gibson for plotting to overthrow Dutch rule in the East Indies.

Having spent the last sixteen months arguing with the authorities that his yachting trip along Sumatra was purely for pleasure, young Gibson's command of Dutch and Malay had improved rapidly, but his fortunes had darkened. It was quite possible that they might go through with the sentence before official Washington learned of his plight.

Mr. Gibson bade the turnkey a cheerful good night, patted his dog Bassett, and blew out the candle. The moonlight revealed a special guard standing under the ketapan tree before his cell. Yes, quite possibly the secret tribunal meant business. He settled down to sleep, wishing that an American ship were coming for him over the Java Sea.

Since his life was arranged by kelpies, gnomes, and the local widadiris, the nymphs of the bulah batang trees, the *Palmer* obediently bruised her sharp breast on Broussa's Shoal and came down the coast to Batavia.

At thirty Walter Gibson had rolled up a saga that Nathaniel Hawthorne later declared had not been equaled since *Gulliver's Travels*. The same story, spread over 314 pages of a special Congressional Report, was to make the most lurid reading in all the national archives. There was a brilliant implausibility about the man, the more so because his legerdemain was conducted in broad daylight under the eyes of distinguished witnesses.

The bare outline of his life up to that January of 1853 does little to suggest his inner drives, which were always a good deal of a mystery. Born at sea as his English parents emigrated to America, he was orphaned early and went to live with the Indians. Then he drifted down to South Carolina and taught a backwoods school, while he gave himself the sort of education that made people think him a university graduate. At twenty-one he was a widower with four small children; he left them with their mother's relatives and went up to New York City, immediately making a small fortune as a commission merchant.

He sped on to a short career in public service, nominally United States consul general in Central America, actually carrying on the Gibson adventure of mesmerizing everyone he met, and he always met the people at the top. With the Russian envoy and an escort of soldiers he toured every state in Mexico; General Robles entertained him at Santa Cruz, General Santa Anna feted him at his country estate. In Guatemala he was instantly deep in the political ferment; he consented to build up a Guatemalan navy with himself as admiral of the fleet.

To this end he returned to New York and put most of his private fortune into the purchase of a fine United States revenue schooner, which he intended to sell to his Central American friends. However, the neutrality laws prevented an armed vessel from sailing on any such errand.

Gibson made a lightning switch of plans. The schooner was now a pleasure yacht, the *Flirt*, and Gibson was off to see the world. After several volumes of picaresque adventures he arrived off the coast of Sumatra to make the acquaintance of the beast-men who lived in trees, of the widadiri who lived in the bamboo glades, and of the local nabobs in filigree palaces on the canals of Palembang. They took him to their hearts, they told him all their troubles with Dutch rule and their plans for restoring their ancient kingdoms. He was especially close to the Sultan of Jambi, who had so far kept his little realm from Dutch sovereignty.

The Netherlands officials were puzzled by this purported wealthy yachtsman, and the more they surrounded him with spies, the more mystified they became. Anybody actually watching Walter Gibson's gyrations must have felt dizzy. However, they coveted the lovely *Flirt*, so one fine day they stripped and impounded her, and arrested skipper and crew. After many trials they released the crew but kept Gibson jailed, and for the most part incommunicado. One exception was Mr. Cramerus.

Captain Low came to see Mr. Cramerus as soon as he had his wife and young Charles Palmer Low comfortably installed in the suburbs of Batavia. Taking care of the clipper ship was far more complicated. It turned out that Batavia had no dry dock, and he must take the *Palmer* to the Navy Yard on Onrust Island five miles away, and heave her down. That involved a petition to the governor, and the payment of duty on all his cargo, which was unladed during the repairs.

Mr. E. W. Cramerus was the man to help him with all the arrangements. This Dutch merchant was the nearest thing to a United States consul in the islands since he represented the American house of Peele, Hubbell and carried on their business through his firm. He was extremely kind and effective in straightening out the *Palmer's* affairs, and his wife went almost every day to see Sarah Low and the baby.

"Now," he said one day, "I have a favor to ask from you, Captain Low. I wish you'd come to the prison with me and see this young Gibson. The officials here accuse him of trying to stir up an armed revolt against the Netherlands with help from the United States. He claims he was just making friends here for your country, and trying to open up the islands to your trade."

Cramerus had smuggled out letters for Gibson to the State Department in Washington, and to Humphrey Marshall, the new United States commissioner to China. Marshall had been so alarmed that he had considered coming down to Batavia himself, but had been forced to give up the idea. He had, however, made strong representations to Secretary of State Edward Everett, hinting that the American naval force off Hong Kong might send a warship to take off Gibson.

"But all this comes too late, Captain Low. This young gentleman is apt to lose his head if we can't get ours together in time."

They went to Weltevreden Prison, a compound enclosed by high walls, with the cells arranged around a hollow square. Walter Gibson received them with exquisite courtesy. He looked like an oriental monk in his native costume and long beard, and his cell was strewn with books and the "ingenious machines" he had amused himself inventing. Captain Low was instantly taken with Gibson, who had a genius for giving and inspiring sympathy, and who wore his hangman's noose like a man.

"It was my mistake, Captain, for going to a Chinese wedding that day and drinking too much arrack toddy," he explained. "You see, I wanted to write my friend the Sultan of Jambi to thank him for entertaining me as royally as if I were a sultan myself. At that time I could not write a decent letter in Malay, and called in a native scribe and dictated a polite note to him. Then I went off to the wedding, and when I came back, rather befuddled, I signed the letter and sent my mate up the river with it.

"It turned out that the scribe and my two cabin servants were agents of the Dutch police in concocting my ruin. The next day my beautiful *Flirt* was plundered and confiscated, we were all arrested, and I was brought down here to plead my own case in three trials. Instead of the harmless note on blue paper which I remembered signing, there was produced in court a forged letter on white paper which urged the Sultan of Jambi to join other native princes in an alliance with the United States to overthrow Dutch rule in the islands. Serious enough, you see, Captain."

"You're in a fix," the captain growled. "My ship's hove down on Onrust, but there's a room for you when she's ready for sea, that is, if you——"

"If I'm still alive," said Gibson calmly. "And if I can get out of prison. That may be a problem. Since my death sentence they've honored me with a private guard under that ketapan tree, and my native friends are no longer allowed visits. I haven't even seen my good steward, Pirez, for weeks, and suspect he's in jail himself. However, I'm allowing myself the pleasure of anticipating a voyage on a splendid clipper ship, Captain."

So they left things for the moment. Captain Low had his own interpretation of Gibson's errand in the islands: no doubt he had hoped to emulate Sir James Brooke, and carve out a delectable kingdom with himself as another white rajah. That did not prevent him from trying to rescue Gibson, if he could.

The Bosun agreed with the white rajah theory. This huge Englishman had been discharged from a warship and engaged passage on the *Palmer*. He was enthralled with Gibson's plight, which he considered hopeless. All over Batavia, he reported, they were saying that the Dutch would never give Gibson up alive, he'd made himself too agreeable to the yellowskins.

"Old Dutchy," he said, "thought he might wake up some morning and see the skipper of the *Flirt* riding through the streets of Batavia on top of an elephant, with a hundred thousand or so Malay run-amucks in his wake."

Gibson, a man of peace and diplomatic filigree, enjoyed having the bull-chested Bosun as champion. In one of the Batavia dives a local merchant with a reputation as an amateur prize fighter had aroused the Bosun by going up to him and pulling first one lapel and then the other off his coat. The Bosun threw him twice, and when three bystanders intervened he knocked them down on top of his fallen enemy, then piled a heavy table upside down on all four, and danced on it. At least that was the story.

All her life Sarah Low loved Java best of all the East. It was in Batavia that she discovered that the sum and substance of her existence was to be a mother. She was radiantly, fiercely maternal, and her fat, blue-eyed son was worth all the agony of his inopportune arrival as the ship anchored in Batavia Roads. "You will find me an entirely different person," she wrote her mother. "I am no longer a little girl, for now I feel that I am in reality a woman. . . . Charles is as happy a father as ever lived. . . . Miss Hemenway says Charlie is the dearest baby ever was, but you cannot have him when we get home."

The captain found a particular satisfaction in naming his son, born on the *Palmer*, for Captain Nat, thus fusing his greatest prides into one. In spite of Sarah's insistence that neither Charles Low must ever go to sea again, the captain had his own ideas. And amazingly enough Seth Low agreed with him. Forwarding some Batavia letters to Mrs. Tucker, he remarked, "The little boy is a regular screamer and one of these days will make a first-rate sailor."

While the *Palmer* was mending on Onrust Island the captain had to live in Batavia miles away from his family, taking the land breeze at dawn to the island. When the baby was a month old Sarah went forty miles out of town to stay on the sugar plantation of Captain Darling, and then Charles saw even less of them. But he was busy getting the *Palmer* ready for sea and finding a crew to replace his men, who were stricken with Java fever. And there were the final arrangements for rescuing Walter Gibson.

On April 22 family and passengers were all aboard out in the Roads, and Captain Low planned to sail with the dawn tide the next Monday. He arranged with two Englishmen who kept a ship chandler's store to have Gibson at the end of the jetty at nine some evening before sailing, where a ship's boat would be waiting.

But nobody knew how Gibson was going to get out of prison.

In his knightly adventures with women, Walter Gibson combined the more winning qualities of Lancelot and Galahad, along with a streak of evangelism. Thus he had developed a complicated and tender relation with the Sumatran damsel Sahyeepah in the

219

days before his arrest, a mere child, a "wild mischievous rock deer" who paused obediently enough to listen to his stories from the Bible. One must remember that he had taught a backwoods school and knew how to catch the attention of children.

On that crowded day when the *Palmer* went aground she had come to the prison with her father and brother to congratulate Gibson on his expected release. His last trial had actually ended in an acquittal, and it was only that evening that he learned the secret tribunal had cynically reversed the verdict. Sahyeepah threw off the coarse outer dress she usually wore, and revealed herself as a little girl suddenly transformed into a siren. She wore a bright sarong, an embroidered bodice caught with a gold and filigree girdle, brilliants in her ears, and gems on her slippers. He was overwhelmed at the change in her.

With his death sentence, the hope of ever again seeing Sahyeepah faded. The weeks went by, Captain Low and the Bosun made their last visit, and told him that the *Palmer's* longboat would be waiting at the jetty for the next three nights, but Sunday would be the last, and then the ship would sail. By Saturday night Gibson still had no idea how he was going to get out of Weltevreden. But he drilled through two bars in his rear window, with the nearly hopeless notion of climbing the high outer wall and getting across the moat in spite of the sentries on patrol.

He heard a vague sound, and then his old steward, Pirez, crept into his cell, rather proud of himself for breaking out of his own prison and into Gibson's. Pirez had been jailed in the police station, and the news of his master's plight had been brought by none other than the lovely Sahyeepah, pretending to sell filigree work in the jailyard. That night he had broken out, visited various allies to get a disguise for Gibson, and had scaled the high wall of Weltevreden.

Proudly Pirez laid out the things he had brought: money, a dirk, skin dye, a dark wig and mustaches, a suit and uniform cap, and a loose hunting coat such as the Dutch gentlemen wore on their excursions. As a final touch, he brought cigars, because Gibson was known never to smoke. Whereupon Pirez climbed back over the wall, landing like a giant bat on the sentinel and knocking him senseless.

The next day was a cloudless Sunday, and visitors were allowed until sunset. Gibson was to make his exit as a visitor. He practiced a new gait. He put on the suit under his loose garment, softened up his beard so he could shave it off quickly. As the sun sloped he stained the skin under his eyes, which gave him a new expression.

When the guard Tutup made his rounds, opening his door to look in, Gibson was in bed pretending to be ill and surly. Tutup went on. Conan arrived and set Gibson's supper inside the door. Now the guard was assembling in the gateway to inspect the visitors as they left. Gibson shaved like lightning, put on his dark wig and mustache, and tied up his poor little dog Bassett under the bed with his own supper to keep him quiet.

He flashed out of his door and joined the visitors moving toward the gate. He felt sick, the air was full of dancing shapes, and there was a buzzing in his ears. But he did not forget his anxiously practiced gait.

The guard was drawn up in a file headed by the sergeant, ready to start on their rounds. The sergeant had seen Gibson a hundred times; now he looked straight at him as he made a perfunctory salute. Gibson returned it and passed by. An instant later he heard the sergeant wheel; something had made him suspicious. Gibson was now in the archway. He took out a big cigar and stopped beside a soldier idling at the gate and smoking a pipe. He lighted his cigar from the pipe, thanked the soldier in Dutch, and walked through the gate. The cigar had saved him.

In a park some distance away a friend was waiting with a horse, and Gibson cantered through the by-lanes to the harbor. The *Palmer's* boat had not yet arrived at the jetty, but Sahyeepah and other friends were waiting. It was an ordeal saying farewell to his little rock deer, who wanted him to go to Singapore where she could join him. But he had business in Washington.

"We'll meet surely, in the bright city of the Great Brother," he told her as he kissed her cheek in the native *tchoom*.

When the longboat sped out to the Roads Gibson had another

agonizing farewell, for they passed close to his *Flirt*, now looking like a slut. He had loved her greatly.

The *Palmer* lay near the guard ship, a Dutch frigate, and Gibson was hardly aboard when she sent a boat to the clipper. He was hustled below to the mate's room, while the captain ran his handkerchief under the wilting edge of his collar. But it turned out to be a few officers coming for a farewell schnapps. By morning the *Palmer* was threading through the lovely islands of the straits.

The *Palmer* was home July 25 in fine fettle after racing the *Samuel Russell* and the *Wild Pigeon* neck and neck for twelve thousand miles. Night after night Mr. Gibson had held the ladies spellbound with his adventures in the spice islands, and he was to have the same effect upon Congress.

The House Foreign Affairs Committee had a field day with the Gibson case. Its special report read like a Dumas novel, mingling the perfumed airs of Banda with a suggestion of countinghouse odors. The committee found that Jambi was an independent state, and Gibson had a perfect right to deal with its Sultan as he pleased. It declared that the Gibson case had been whipped up by the Dutch as an excuse for taking over Jambi, and requested the President to treat with Holland for the payment of a hundred-thousand-dollar indemnity to Walter Gibson for his loss of the *Flirt*, and his sufferings.

The matter was put into the hands of August Belmont, United States minister at the Hague, and Gibson was sent over to assist him. For the next year the pourparlers went on, mounting to a crisis when Belmont made a peremptory demand for settlement with the plain implication that the United States was ready to go to war over the Gibson case. The Netherlands government curtly refused, and instead of war the United States got what it really wanted: the opening of the Dutch islands to American trade and consuls.

Walter Gibson never collected a cent of damages, but his career became more and more extraordinary, and the world had not heard the last of him.

The Dutch were angry with Captain Low for his rescue of Gibson, and refused to refund the duty he had deposited on the *Palmer's* cargo. He finally got it back, but he was forbidden ever to revisit Java, which was a great pity because he agreed with his wife that it was the loveliest spot in all the Orient.

17

The Great *Fleet*

Few men can end their lives
feeling that they have accomplished more than they set out to do.
Seth Low, who died June 19, 1853, must have felt that his family
had outstripped his fondest ambitions for them; even carefree
Ned and rebellious Charles were firmly established. He had been
father, too, of the little city of Brooklyn, of which he was an
incorporator and alderman, and had set his mark on it as president
of the Packer Institute and a founder of the Institute of Arts and
Sciences, of the Church of the Saviour, and of the Association
for Improving the Condition of the Poor.

He was fortunate enough to die at the moment when America
reached its crowning moments on the seas, when the mightiest of
all clipper ships was building, the *Great Republic*. There was deep
significance in this name which spanned the seventy years be-

Captain Low's Ship the *N. B. Palmer*. Painting by Charles Patterson. *Courtesy of the Columbian Rope Company.* Photograph by the Marine Museum of the Marine Historical Association, Mystic, Connecticut.

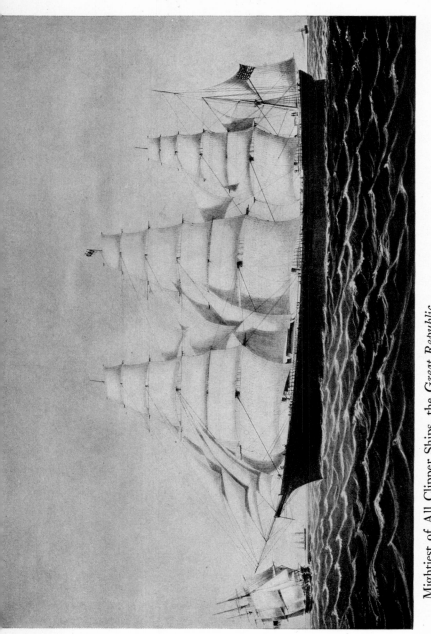

Mightiest of All Clipper Ships, the *Great Republic.*
Courtesy of Harry Shaw Newman, The Old Print Shop, New York.

tween the *Empress of China*, the first American ship to enter the Pacific, and the age when the United States had the greatest merchant marine on earth. That was the span of Seth Low's own life; he had watched a young country grow up to conquer the seas, and his sons were at the heart of this conquest.

A very different age was beginning, the age Jefferson had wanted, when Americans mastered their own continent and turned their backs on the sea and on the great world. That age was to involve many things which would have disturbed Seth Low: the dissolution of the old family pattern, and then the War Between Brothers. A country which had grown strong because each family was a tight unit was now tossed into chaos. Eight Fanning brothers might live on the seas and only bind the clan tighter, but when the young people of the fifties started west they cut the hawsers clean through.

Since the Lows were bound together in sea trade, they remained a happy anachronism. Seth Low's grandchildren, in New York or California or China, still belonged to the hive. They would always remember the dignified old man in his Sunday dress and his best cane, visiting them after church to hear them sing "While Thee I Seek, Protecting Power" and other favorite hymns. And his namesake, Abbot's small Seth, remembered his grandfather's final admonition, "Be kind to the poor," and was kind not only to the poor but to more difficult people like Negroes and labor leaders and the students of Columbia University, of which he was long the president.

Little Charles Palmer Low, having received due adulation in Brooklyn, was taken to further triumphs in South Danvers. Mrs. Tucker refused to be separated from him, he was too young to be snatched from his mother, and his mother, said the captain, was coming straight back to the *Palmer*. The only way out of the impasse was to take the whole family along.

The young Lows went down to Brooklyn while the ship was loading, and Sarah wrote her mother final instructions:

"I advise you mother to get all the old clothes you can—night-gowns, chemises, drawers, etc. You will find them much better than new clothing. Have a double gown, made like the one Abba made for me—of mousseline de laine. It will be warm for you at sea. Lined with a calico—mine is. Miss Hemenway thinks you will have to step round a little. Now mother you must not back out. Get plenty of your clouded and white wool and knitting needles, that we may knit Charlie some stockings.

"Charles thinks you had better take your money from the bank, as you will need to spend it, and he says he can make much more on it than it will gain there."

Then, knowing her mother's incessant interest in her neighbors —she was quite capable of dashing out to stop a runaway horse— she added, "If there should be an accident, do not go to see what is the matter, but remain quiet. Mother Low says she will preserve me some barberries if you will send them here as soon as you can."

They sailed for San Francisco on September 27, with a full cargo and all the passengers they could accommodate.

This was the year of the greatest California records, with ships under the red-and-yellow house flag capturing three out of the four top runs to San Francisco. Best of the three Low ships was the *Contest*, which had started her career in the fifteen-ship derby of 1852 only to go on to fresh triumphs.

In her maiden run she had beaten the Boston clipper ship *Northern Light*, Captain Freeman Hatch, to San Francisco by eighteen days. She did not go on to China, but turned around quickly for New York, clearing the Golden Gate at three on Saturday afternoon, March 12, 1853, with a good following breeze. Exactly twenty-four hours later the Boston ship was out after her. It was to be a race between New York and Boston, though the ships did not sight each other for five weeks. Both made the incredible time of 14 days to the Line. Then the *Northern Light* gained a day, and off the Horn, very snowy and glum in the growing antarctic winter, Captain Brewster first sighted the Boston ship, and set down in his log:

> Apr. 20—Lat 56.30 S. Lon 66.22 W—Comes in with moderate breezes, cloudy and light snow squalls (Latter-part) moderate breezes from SW with light snow squalls. Saw ship Northern Light.

Apr. 21—Lat 54.09 S. Lon 60.40 W—Latter, fresh gales and good weather. in company with her.
Apr. 22—Lat. 50.57 S. Lon 54.20 W—Fresh gales and pleasant. Middle, very squally. Latter more pleasant but not suitable to carry light sails—24 miles current NNE. Northern Light two points abaft the beam.
Apr. 23—Lat. 48.32 S. Lon 50.16 W—Comes in moderate —Latter squally with snow and rain. Northern Light 15 miles astern.

After that happy entry the ships lost sight of each other, but they made equal runs to the Line. Captain Brewster had every reason to think the *Contest* had won the race, for he arrived in New York in 80 days, a very fine passage, and the standing record for the shortest round trip of 180 days.

But the *Northern Light* had taken a more easterly route from the Equator, and must have found favoring winds, for her passage of 76 days and 5 hours from San Francisco to Boston Light was to remain forever the record. Freeman Hatch's gravestone was to say, more truly than most epitaphs, that this passage was "an achievement won by no mortal before or since."

A few weeks later the *Contest* was out again for California, and made one of her all-time records of 36 days to the Horn, and a splendid one of 97 days to San Francisco, the only clipper ship ever sailing in the unfavorable month of July to make such speed. Thus in less than a year she had made three brilliant voyages— out to San Francisco in 100 days, back in 80, and out again in 97.

The only ship that beat her through the Golden Gate was McKay's *Romance of the Seas*, commanded by Phil Dumaresq, who shaved a day from the *Contest's* time and thus headed the 1853 fleet. The third ship of the top four was the new Low clipper *David Brown*, arriving in 99 days, and the fourth was the *Oriental*, which lost her mainmast off the Horn but speeded to her port in a round 100. Well behind these favorites were the *Flying Cloud* in 106 days, the *Northern Light* in 122, the *Palmer* and the *Samuel Russell* neck and neck in 121, and the *Surprise* bettering her sisters with a voyage of 116 days.

It looked as if no ships could beat Captain Nat's, unless built by the men who had most profited by his principles, Samuel Pook and Donald McKay. A demonstration of the great closeness in the sailing mettle of the Palmer and McKay ships was made that year, when two of them raced around the world, the *David Brown* and the *Romance of the Seas*. Both launched late in 1853, they were about even in weight—1700-odd tons—but the McKay ship was longer and slenderer. The Low ship was built by Roosevelt & Joyce, who had taken over the Brown & Bell yard, and she was commanded by George Brewster, of Stonington, brother of the *Contest's* captain. Again it was Boston against New York.

The Low ship left New York December 13, 1853, and Phil Dumaresq sailed from Boston three days later. At the Horn the *David Brown* was four days ahead, but the *Romance of the Seas* caught up with her in the North Pacific and led her into port by a few hours. Then they sailed in company for Hong Kong and arrived after a passage of 45 days with the *Romance* one hour in the lead.

The *Romance* went to Whampoa, and the *Brown* to Shanghai, both loading for London. Dumaresq left June 9 and arrived in London 104 days later. Brewster sailed from Shanghai two days after Dumaresq, and in the Strait of Sunda went on a reef, the bow three feet out of water and the forefoot badly twisted. Two days later he got away again, running into a turbulent sea, causing the ship, his log noted, "to labor very heavy—*but she is a beauty in a gale.*"

He then proceeded to roll up a record of 69 days from Anjer to London, closing his log with the pious remark: "Altho it is not quite what I was in hopes of doing yet it is not bad when we consider the monsoons against us and the ships forefoot athwartships and copper off and rough.

"To God be all the praise, for his protecting care."

God was not so kind to the Lows' extreme clipper *Golden State*, which Westervelt had ready for them early that year. Ten days out of New York a sudden whirlwind carried away all three topmasts with everything attached, a cruel blow to Captain L. F. Doty, since he had been passing every clipper ship he sighted. However, she proved an excellent ship, and three years later made a record run of 90 days from Shanghai to New York.

Clipper ships continued to pour from the yards, but it was apparent that freights to San Francisco could not hold up much longer, and charters were getting more difficult to obtain. Many fine clipper ships entered the race to the Australian gold fields, and some of the proudest went into the guano trade, taking on odorous cargoes at Callao or the Chinchas, where a hundred ships waited their turn at the chutes—beauties like the *Flying Eagle, Radiant, Witchcraft,* and *Empress of the Seas.* Others had gone into the even more malodorous traffic of carrying slaves from Africa, or coolies from Canton to San Francisco.

Though the gold fever was abating, crews were still deserting for the mines at San Francisco. Captain Low managed to get hands for Honolulu, where he sped in 10 days, but there he was stuck, wholly unable to ship a crew for China. He was forced to accept the offer of a New Bedford man to assemble a crew for the *Palmer* from the whaling ships in port, on condition that the clipper carried a cargo of whale oil to New York.

The voyage planned to impress Mother Tucker with the delights of sailing around the world was thus drastically revised. The ladies were happy enough to turn around for home, as Sarah was expecting another child. And Mrs. Tucker had her fill of island royalty. Captain Low began the amenities with a dinner on the *Palmer* for King Kamehameha and his sons, and was pleased that the King was even more rhapsodic about the *Palmer* than he had been about the *Samuel Russell* a few years before. The next day the ship was turned over to the ladies, and the Queen and her suite dined aboard. Hannah and Sarah Tucker were far more interested in good Father Damon, the seamen's missionary, and went to stay with him while the captain went scouting for his crew.

"The Yacht" and her master always endeared themselves to passengers, and at the end of the voyage the ladies and gentlemen of the cabin presented the captain with a testimonial letter of thanks for the "remarkably pleasant passage we have had in the noble ship."

It was remarkably pleasant to the captain too. He kept his

whalers on their toes for two reasons, both indicating the need for cracking on canvas. One was the natural desire on Sarah's part to have her second child ashore. The second was the fact that he was making the same passage as McKay's *Sovereign of the Seas* the year before, which had obliterated all previous speed records and inspired a special report from Lieutenant Maury to the Secretary of the Navy.

Donald McKay's brother Lauchlan was commanding the *Sovereign*, which, like the *Empress*, *Romance*, and *Champion of the Seas*, was putting the great builder into first place as a designer. In these ships he had finally given up the sharp bottom in favor of Captain Nat's flatter lines. The *Sovereign* raced from Honolulu to New York in 82 days, the miraculous part of the record being her run in one day of 421 nautical miles, and an average of 378 miles for four consecutive days, an absolutely dazzling burst of speed.

Therefore Charles Low was jubilant when he rounded the Horn and reached the Line in the Atlantic in 57 days, cutting down the *Sovereign's* time by ten days, incredible as it seemed. Then from the Line to Sandy Hook he had nothing but calms, and often wanted to act like Captain Nat and throw his hat down on deck and dance on it, yelling curses. Still, he passed Sandy Hook on July 14, 1854, in 82 days, the same passage time as McKay's, and chalked up one of his standing records.

Sarah Low must have been sensitive to tensions. When the *Palmer* went aground on Broussa's Shoal, she had taken to her bed. Now at Sandy Hook, with a great record won, she was brought to bed again. The captain was not at all sorry that his second son, Josiah Orne Low, was born on his beloved ship.

Donald McKay loved big ships. Beginning with the little *Houqua* of less than 600 tons, the clipper ships had steadily increased in size, but McKay went beyond all builders in daring. The *Great Republic*, 4555 tons, was the supreme gesture in sail.

She was intended to carry immigrants from England to Australia, if McKay needed an excuse for her size. What he was really doing was to arrive at the ultimate in wood and canvas, a right he had earned. He was paying her huge first cost of $300,000 out of his own pocket, and when his brother Lauchlan returned from his remarkable Honolulu passage he took charge of the outfitting, since he was to command her.

When the world's largest sailing vessel was launched in Boston on October 4, 1853, the city declared a public holiday. The schools were closed, the shipping in the Navy Yard was dressed in gala bunting, and thirty thousand people watched her leap into the sea, the ways smoking and blazing under her. Because of the temperance movement she was christened with a bottle of Cochituate water, but she herself was a national intoxicant.

The *Great Republic* was a goddess of heroic proportions and quite unearthly beauty. Her sheer ran in one masterful line from the carved eagle's head at her bow through the finely molded midship section to her graceful stern, a line 335 feet long. She carried four masts bearing 15,635 yards of canvas; her rigging followed the new system devised by Black Ben Forbes. The old salts shook their heads at it, feeling it was too complicated.

She was a magnificent ship, not a practical one. Even with the innovation of a 15-horsepower engine on deck to hoist the yards and work the pumps, it took a crew of 130 men and boys to work her. Unable to find a purchaser, McKay decided to send her to England and put her in the Australian trade on his own account. More than half of the route lay through the steady westerly winds of the lower forties, the winds that blow around the world; he had built his ship to fly before them.

The *Great Republic* was towed to New York, where thousands came to see her at her anchorage at the foot of Dover Street in the East River. The Low brothers paid their homages, as did Captain Nat.

"She's beautiful enough to burst your heart," Captain Nat growled. "But there aren't winds enough on this planet for her. What was that farmer's lad from Nova Scotia thinking of—sailing her to the moon?"

She was nearly loaded and ready to sail for London when, the night after Christmas, a fire broke out on Front Street a block away. A little past midnight the watchman called the second mate. The wind was blowing sparks all over the ship. All hands were called and stationed over the ship with buckets of water, which were pulled up to the tops to moisten the sails. Soon the foresail burst into flames which licked up and up the 130-foot foremast. Then, one after the other, the tops and topgallants took fire. The men tried to cut the sails from the yards, but were driven back by the furious blaze. Now the fire engines arrived, but pump as they might, they could not reach the lofty spars. The firemen refused to work on board or near the ship for fear of falling blocks and gear. It was an intensely cold night, and firemen and crew suffered at once from ice and flame.

Captain Lauchlan McKay consulted the underwriters. They decided to save the hull by cutting away the masts. The fore and foretopmast stays and rigging were cut, and the mast went overside into the dock. But in falling the blazing topmast broke off short and came down on the ship, cutting down through three decks. Next the main- and mizzenmasts were cut away, and in their fall crushed the boats, deckhouses, and rails and disabled the steam engine. The decks were now a mass of burning yards, masts, sails, and rigging, but by dawn the firemen were aboard and put out the blaze.

Two ships tied up near by, bound out and almost ready to sail, the *Joseph Walker* and the *White Squall*, each worth about ninety thousand dollars, were caught in the conflagration and destroyed. The sight of three blazing ships on that snowy night had an apocalyptic beauty.

Once the deck fire on the *Great Republic* was out, a tremendous blaze was discovered in the hold; the cargo was on fire. Quickly the ship was scuttled in three places, and she sank ten feet to the bottom of the river. For two days, until the fire reached the water's edge, the clipper kept burning.

Then a cofferdam was built and the wreck was floated by steam pumps. The cargo of grain had swollen so much that the knees and beams of the lower hold were sprung, and the hull was badly strained and buckled. The *Great Republic* was condemned and abandoned to her underwriters; the insurance covered only half her cost.

Captain Nat had watched the great clipper ship's travail, and his temper was so short that the Lows knew he was laboring with mighty thoughts. Clearly the wreck could be bought at a bargain, and there were still more than two million feet of hard pine and white oak in her hull.

"I could change her aloft," he told Abbot Low. "None of that Forbes rig. Howes's double topsail yards are good enough for me. Cut down her tonnage, cut down her crew——"

"Yes, if you could make her a handy ship that we could afford to run, we might be interested," Abbot Low agreed. "Besides——"

There was no getting into words what they felt, what every man who loved brave ships felt about the *Great Republic*. Captain Nat, the bluff old giant with compassion in his heart and the arts of healing in his head, bought the blackened hull and sent it to Greenpoint, Long Island, to be rebuilt by Sneeden & Whitlock.

A year later the transformed *Great Republic* was ready for sea as the flagship of the Low fleet. She was still a four-master, the original beauty of the hull with its sheer line was preserved. But her tonnage was cut down to 3357 tons, which still made her the largest merchantman of her day. The sail plan was drastically revised; the fore and mainmasts were cut down seventeen feet and their yards twenty, and all the other spars in proportion. A crew of fifty able seamen and fifteen ordinary seamen and boys could now handle her.

The Lows sent her to England on her maiden voyage in February 1855 under Joseph Limeburner, and she made Land's End in 12 days, the first of her great records. In London there was no dock large enough to take her, and she lay at anchor in the Thames. The Crimean War was on, and France chartered her as a troopship to carry soldiers from Marseille to Constantinople.

While the *Great Republic* was rebuilding the Lows lost their famous *Oriental*. Theo Palmer had turned over the command to Captain Fletcher, who had loaded her with teas at Foochow early in 1854, and started down the river Min with a pilot. She was caught in the treacherous chowchow of the river and lost, a great blow to the Lows and Palmers and all who loved this pioneer of the London tea run. They kept the brilliant *Surprise* on the service to England, and added the *Golden State* and *David Brown* and later their clipper barque *Maury*.

That year there was a portent of what was to happen to all the clipper fleet. When the *Surprise* started out from Shanghai the new steam tug *Confucius* took her as its first tow. The English were pressing forward with steam; their famous P & O steamers were already on regular runs between the Orient and England, and their Australian fleet of "teakettles" was making good time. Some English clipper ships were fitted with auxiliary engines.

The American builders, however, were not done with wood and canvas. In the decade from the *Houqua* to McKay's *Champion of the Seas* 270 full-rigged clipper ships had been launched in the United States, besides barques and smaller craft. World commerce could not afford that many ships built for speed rather than burden, but the creative fury which possessed the designers had not yet spent itself, and a new type of clipper, more burdensome but still beautiful, was now evolving. Ships from new yards, like the *Andrew Jackson* of Mystic, the *Carrier Dove* of Baltimore, and the *Flying Mist* of Medford, were still to join their sisters as the loveliest apparitions ever to mount the blue horizon.

18

Hauling

the Bowline

Sarah Low managed to keep her husband in dry dock for a year and a month. They bought a roomy house in South Danvers, and the captain amused himself setting out trees and shrubs and whittling a model of the *Palmer* for his infant sons. This sympathetic magic got him back on the quarterdeck before he exploded with boredom.

When he and Sarah paid a spring visit to Brooklyn they found that Abbot Low was taking advantage of the lull in his affairs, and planning a summer trip abroad. It was a lull only in the sense that A. A. Low & Bros. had reached their competitive peak and were now stabilizing their business and their fleet. After 1853 they commissioned no new clippers, and while they were to buy vessels and build smaller ones, they wisely avoided having more ships than they could use. The wild rush to the California mines had subsided, and in another two years the sixty-dollar freight rates plunged to ten dollars.

Abbot and Ann were taking Will to Europe with them, and the other children were going up to stay with the Dows in Wakefield, after a delirious succession of treats. That year brought Franconi's hippodrome from Paris with its chariot races and tournaments. They had seen Tom Thumb in his miniscule swaggerings as Napoleon, plays at Niblo's Garden and Barnum's Museum, Christy's Minstrels and Signor Blitz's trained canaries. The coachman had taken them for nutting parties in the pleasant wilderness that was to become Prospect Park, and on Saturday mornings they went to their father's warehouse at Burling Slip to sniff the delightful odors of teas, cinnamon, and firecrackers.

Recounting these revels to Uncle Charles, Gus and Harriet then exchanged glances and plunged into the sad recital of what had happened to the chocolate-and-canary-colored squirrel their uncle had brought them from Java.

"He escaped from his cage," said Gus, "just like that Mr. Gibson you brought home. But we found him next door at Bartow's. He'd built himself a nest of sticks in a tree, and maybe we should have left him there. But we put him back in his cage, and then he caught an awful cold and died."

"Too bad," said Uncle Charles. "I'll have to see if I can find you a more durable pet this voyage."

He sailed in mid-August alone in the cabin, his only comfort at the China end the sight of his brother Ned, who had finally married his cousin Lucy Haskell. They had a pleasant life shuttling between Canton and Brooklyn, where they took frequent furloughs. The next August Sarah was back on the *Palmer*, and the little boys were left with their grandmother and the maids, Milly and Eliza, to look after them. Within six weeks Hannah Tucker missed her "dear darling children" so much that she wrote, "If you ever go to sea again I will go with you, if you have a dozen babies to carry."

They took the easy passage around Africa and arrived in Hong Kong to find that the British and Chinese were at it again. For years the Taiping rebels had been tearing China apart, and the

236

leadership of the empire was decidedly sick. Emperor Hsien-feng, who had succeeded to the throne in 1850, was a degenerate and weakling completely under the thumb of the baleful Yehonala. This beautiful Manchu woman had started her court career as a concubine of the third class, but she moved into first class when she bore the Emperor his only son, and after Hsien-feng's death was to become Empress Dowager Tse-hsi.

Yehonala hated the foreigners and she encouraged Governor Yeh Ming-chin to stir up a war with the British, on flimsy grounds this time. The French, aggrieved at the murder of a missionary, joined forces with the British, and for the next four years the war flickered up and down the coast.

It was not safe for the Lows to go to Canton and they stayed on the ship at Hong Kong, where Sarah's chief fears were the rats and cockroaches. She wrote her mother, "But I think Hong Kong will certainly be destroyed and all foreigners driven from the place. The Chinese however are not bitter against Americans. It is the English they hate. And they really *hate* them."

There was an aggregation of clipper ship wives in the harbor who did much to bolster Sarah Low's morale—Mrs. Caldwell of the *Fairy*, Mrs. Osgood of the *Sword Fish*, and especially Charlotte Babcock of the *Young America*. Her husband, David Babcock, was Captain Nat's brother-in-law, but only two years older than Charles Low. The two captains had a good deal in common, since they had both been trained by Captain Nat and had the same high rating in the clipper fleet. They were always glad to find each other in port.

Whenever the captains' ladies were inclined to bewail the inconveniences of their lot they thought of Mary Patten. She was only nineteen the year before when she started on her second voyage around the Horn on *Neptune's Car*. Before they reached the Cape Captain Patten was taken with brain fever and lay in the cabin blind, deaf, and for many days in a state of coma. The chief mate had already been put in irons for incompetence and neglect of his duties; the second was a good seaman but knew no navigation. Mrs. Patten had learned enough on the previous voyage so that she now took charge of the big heavily masted clipper ship and sailed it for fifty-two days to San Francisco, nursing her husband all the way. He died a few months later, but this girl had saved ship and crew, and had even beaten the *Intrepid*, racing with *Neptune's Car* from the start of the voyage, by ten days.

By February 1857 the Lows were on their way to Siam. It was impossible to do business in China, and Captain Low had decided to pick up a cargo of rice in Bangkok, where it was very cheap. He did well enough with this voyage to make a second one that spring, and by that time they were on friendly terms with the most fantastic royal family on the globe.

It was five years before Mrs. Anna Leonowens arrived to instruct the royal children and engage in her strange affair, half feud, half romance, with the irascible King Mongkut. At the moment Mongkut was emerging from his monk's retirement to take an owlish glance at the world, but he opened up enough to receive Sarah Low and her missionary friends at a birthday party for one of his queens, and to explain to them the dancing performance in her honor. Mrs. Low was fascinated with his diaper-like panome fastened with three elegant diamond brooches, but thought the palace "not much like Victoria's, not much appearance of royalty about," a remarkable enough reaction. She liked the Second King's palace and garden much better: "nothing could be improved." The Lows were invited by both kings to visit their pretty vessel, *The Royal Seat of the Siamese Forces*.

By this time it was understood that Captain Low was not going to give the Second King the *Palmer's* guns, much as he desired them. Phra Pin Klao had a positive passion for ships and artillery. As Mongkut wrote after his brother's death nine years later:

"As he pleased mostly with firing of cannon and acts of Marine power and seamen, which he has imitated to his steamers which were made in manner of the man-of-war, after he has seen various things curious and useful, and learned Marine customs on board the foreign vessels of war, his steamers conveyed him to sea, where he enjoyed playing of firing in cannon very often."

But not with the *Palmer's* cannon. As soon as the clipper ship anchored in the river Pin Klao came aboard. The captain was ashore, but the King informed the mate that the nine-pounders pleased him greatly. He was surprised, since this was Siam, not to receive them the next day, and took the matter up with Charles Low.

"I'm sorry, Your Majesty, but I can't give you the guns for the simple reason that they don't belong to me."

"To whom then do they belong?"

"Well, to my brothers in New York."

It took a good deal of explaining of the American *meum* and *teum* before the Second King gave up his campaign. An intelligent soul who loved astronomy and navigation, he had to content himself with picking up ideas "curious and useful" from the clipper captain.

They had eaten quantities of fruit in Bangkok, and on the way back to Hong Kong the captain was stricken with dysentery. In one week he lost sixty pounds, but fought his way to the anchorage, where he collapsed and nearly died.

At this point Mary Ann's son George Archer arrived by mail steamer to go into business with Caleb Smith, the Low agent in Hong Kong. He was twenty-four, the pioneer of the third generation of Lows in the China trade. The family letters he brought made Sarah and Charles Low cry like children; their little sons had been ill with scarlet fever. They were perfectly well again, and after weeks of convalescence in Macao Captain Low was up and about, but his wife was completely unstrung. Loving husband and children as she did, she could not bear separation from either, and began to hate sea life far more intensely than had Seth Low. Over and over during the next years she prayed that her sons would never go into the China trade, much less into their father's calling.

But her nursing had saved Charles's life, and he rewarded her by being angelically patient at her hysterics over the cockroaches in the cabin. They were glad to start home, and after the captain had soundly beaten the *Golden City* and the *Witchcraft* to Sandy Hook he felt himself again. But he took another full year off to recover, and to enjoy the twins, Francis and Frances. They were born two months after the *Palmer* docked, and even Miss Hemenway, who loved the ship, was glad that Frank and Fanny had arrived on terra firma.

Together Ann and Abbot Low planned every detail of their new mansion at 3 Pierrepont Street, a monument to the China trade and to dense Victorian domesticity. Because of the sweeping view of the harbor, it was also a shipping merchant's house, and often Abbot Low could stand at his library windows and see the ghostly loveliness of the *Surprise* or the *Great Republic* far out toward the Narrows. Sometimes the home-coming ships came in at sunset and docked below the house and the captain—big blond Charles Ranlett, or Joseph Limeburner, or Charles Low—came striding up through the gardens to report to the taipan.

Like a clipper ship, the house was built of costly materials, its big octagonal vestibule paved with foreign marbles, its broad staircase and wainscotings of hardwood, the double doors to the drawing room of rosewood, walls and ceilings frescoed, the massive cornices gilded. In short, it was a Victorian mansion. The drawing room boasted an Axminster medallion carpet woven to order, rosewood furniture with silk covers, great gilt mirrors, a carved and inlaid grand piano, silk curtains, lace curtains, portraits, landscapes, marble statuary, bronzes, and precious knick-knacks from Paris or Canton.

The family preferred the big library at the back with its matchless view of river and bay, its open fire and fresh flowers from the greenhouse on the lower terrace, and Huntington's portrait of Ellen smiling gently down on her children.

Unlike his father, Abbot Low took little interest in public life as such, but he was beginning to be a public figure because of his broad activities as a merchant. He was a director of the Brooklyn Savings Bank, and the year they moved into the new house, in 1857, he saved it during a run by bringing a drayload of gold from New York. He was such an effective spokesman for business that he ended by being president of the Chamber of Commerce. And he stood behind Cyrus Field until the first Atlantic cable was laid, broken, and finally put down to stay. On land, the telegraph had pushed to the Mississippi, and the new Pony Express was carrying on from there, rushing mail in twenty-four days from St. Louis to San Francisco.

By 1858 the country had struggled up from the financial depression and turmoil of the previous year, which had seen the Dred Scot decision and John Brown's marching. Despite the collapse in freight rates to San Francisco, ninety clipper ships went around the Horn. Their owners had to keep them busy at something. For two years the *Flying Cloud* was idle; famous clippers like the *Challenge* were stripped in China and sold for pitiful sums. Decidedly there was a plethora of first-class shipping.

It was plain by now that 1855 had been the peak of the country's maritime achievements. That year she had five million tons of shipping, only a small fraction of it in steam. The United States merchant fleet was much better than the British, and captured the most desirable commerce. Just when it seemed that America ruled the waves, the impulse which had carried her so rapidly forward died out, shipyards closed, masters and men went on the beach, and a decline in tonnage set in that lasted a generation.

What was it? The Civil War was casting a long shadow before, the gold rush and the sheer intoxication of the clipper ships had stimulated too much building. But the real reason was a rechanneling of the nation's energies. America's best red blood was pouring westward; the nation's sons no longer went into shipping and trade, but built cities and railroads over the face of the continent.

There was another reason which Abbot Low considered crucial: the fact that the government had never been interested in the merchant marine. He had smiled as broadly as anybody at the pampered Indiamen in the Pearl River, but he believed that merchant ships were part of a nation's power and should be subsidized to a healthy degree. Some years later he delivered an address before the Chamber of Commerce in which he described how England, with her subsidized Cunard Line, had driven the Collins packets from the ocean, and had done so deliberately and "just as effectually as they ever did drive an enemy from the ocean by their guns.

"I only know that the English have always, in peace and war,

241

manifested a determination to hold their supremacy on the ocean, and the supremacy which they have acquired by arms in war they have in peace acquired by subsidies. They have deliberately and intentionally driven the Americans from the ocean by paying subsidies which they knew our Congress would not pay."

Not that the house of Low was wailing for government grants. It had built its clipper ships for the China trade, not for the momentary delirium of the gold rush. It kept them busy in the China trade, which had been growing along with the port of New York until fifty good ships a year passed Sandy Hook with cargoes from Cathay. Boston still kept the India commerce and ran neck and neck with New York in the Philippines and Dutch East Indies business, but the China trade belonged to New York, and the Lows had as much of it as they could handle. During their generation the foreign trade of Manhattan had grown so fast that it was now six times that of all New England.

Being pioneers, they broached Japan before it was officially opened to trade, and the Low *Benefactor* brought the first teas and raw silks from the islands to the United States. They had a fleet of pretty clipper barques for the Japan trade, all built by Roosevelt & Joyce—*Maury, Penguin, Osaca, Sunda,* and *Benefactor*—and now and then some of the clipper ships on the China run went up to Yokohama.

The bets were not so heavy nowadays on clipper ship races, and no new beauties were coming down the ways to try their wings. But as long as the thoroughbreds lived every voyage was a race. Charles Ranlett was doing brilliantly in the *Surprise,* ringing up a standing record from Shanghai to New York in 1857. A month out she ran into a hurricane that stripped off her foresail, reefed mainsail, and other top gear, but she reached Sandy Hook in 82 days, under the conditions a miracle.

While Charles Low was recuperating, a very young Brooklyn captain, James Higham, took the *Palmer* over the same course as the *Surprise* in the same record time. He had fought every mile of the way, pouring the last of his strength into the ship, for he was dying of tuberculosis and it was nip and tuck for him and the ship. Five days after he brought the *Palmer* home every flag in the harbor flew at half-mast for one of the most gallant of all clipper captains.

The *David Brown* was proving herself very high in steady performance, sailing, as the skippers said, "in any weather, blow high, low, or flat calm." It may have been for sentimental reasons that the Lows bought the *Jacob Bell*, named for the partner of their first shipbuilder, but she had shown her mettle in four years of fast sailing before they added her to the fleet.

The Lows were now out of the carrying trade to England, which British tea ships had almost entirely recaptured. Their last vessel to London was the clipper barque *Maury*, Captain Charles Fletcher, which had a curious race with the British iron clipper, *Lord of the Isles*. The idea of an iron clipper ship made all Americans wince, and much as they loved iron, the British found it sweated the teas, and dropped it for work in China. However, the iron clipper was England's fastest ship in the trade, and much larger than the *Maury*. The race was one of the closest in history, and several times the ships were in company, but the small American reached Gravesend with the *Lord of the Isles* several miles astern.

As for the *Great Republic*, coming back from the Crimea with a huge Russian dog to guard the Low warehouse, and smelling of unwashed poilus, she went forth in search of winds and sea room big enough for her. Her first voyage to California set records toppling. Under Captain Limeburner she reached the Line from Sandy Hook in 15 days and 18 hours, arrived off the Horn in 46, and stood off the Golden Gate after a passage of 89 days, very nearly matching the *Flying Cloud's* record. But thick fogs kept her out of the bay for three days, so she was chalked up for a 92-day run. Her best day's sailing was 413 miles, which put her in the choice company of six clipper ships going down in history with a day's run of more than 400 miles.

From San Francisco her first mate, Montgomery Parker, wrote Lieutenant Maury his opinion of what the *Great Republic* might be able to do about breaking the 89-day record down to the 85 days that Maury believed a clipper ship might one day accomplish. "Should she continue," Parker wrote, "to run between New York and San Francisco, she will one day make the trip within your possible 85 days."

Maury, reporting to the Secretary of the Navy, made an interesting analysis:

"This vessel did not have the luck to get a wind that could keep her on her mettle for twenty-four hours consecutively. Here and there she got into favorable streaks of wind, but she appears to have run out of them faster than they could follow.

"The friends of this noble specimen of naval architecture, however, can scarcely hope for a fair trial and proper display of her prowess until she shall be sent on a voyage to Australia. The brave west winds of the Southern hemisphere, which she will then encounter, will enable her to show herself; elsewhere, she can scarcely find a sea wide enough, with belts of winds broad enough, for the full display of her qualities and capabilities."

As Captain Nat had suspected, she was a little too large for this planet, at the outermost limit of human artifice against the resources of nature.

19

Hull Under

and

Far Away

"Do you recollect," Charles Low wrote his wife on May Day of 1859, "how I drove you out last year on the Boston Road, and we saw the children and young ladies coming home from Maying . . . driving down to Salem, stopping at Aunt Porter's and hurrying you away from ever place that I might be alone with you. . . . I can imagine I hear the old bell ringing in Blubber Hollow as we drive past the Engine House at two o'clock homeward bound. Oh how I wish I was with you behind the old roan mare."

But he was in the China Sea, commanding the *Jacob Bell* for one voyage, with nobody to keep him company but his dog Bruen. "He is a splendid fellow, when the bell rings for meals he always comes to table with the passengers and sits down by me and expects to have something as much as any of the rest."

Having wrecked Canton, the English and French forces had moved to the north, and the next year were to ratify a treaty that finally legalized the opium trade. At Whampoa Captain Low found everything looking familiar, the merchant ships at anchor, the sampans scurrying as usual, and he was heartily glad to be back. But when he was rowed up to Canton he was appalled: "whole acres of bare tumbling walls show the devastation made by fire and guns, it looks like the ruins you see in engravings. How many worthy Chinamen have been driven from their homes where generation after generation have found a living in peace and quietness."

The row of hongs had been utterly demolished, even the bricks had been pulverized, and the ground strewn with salt. He could not even tell where the factories had stood. It was the last of the familiar spot where his brothers had spent so many years, and which they loved best of all China. Canton was by nature an emporium, and her trade had by no means ceased, but this year it was going on under difficulties. The captain stayed with his nephew George Archer, who had moved his office to Honam, once the exclusive resort of the wealthy Chinese. He had built himself a comfortable house there among fishponds and verdant paddy fields.

After all these years the Fanqui could now move freely around the ruined city, and take sedan chairs if they liked. But there was little to see but humble houses and a few temples and missionary schools. On the whole, Captain Low was glad to get down to Hong Kong, almost as American as British when the tea fleet was in. You could get English groceries from Crosse & Blackwell, but Silas Burrows kept Goshen butter and New York State cider, and the very British *Daily Press* used as fillers tall tales and homespun jokes from St. Louis or Virginia City. The new Mark Twain brand of humor had already captivated Hong Kong.

William Hunter kept to his happy station in Macao, with small vessels for charter, but most of the American houses had headquarters in Hong Kong. Russell & Co. was far and away the largest, but Olyphant, Augustine Heard, and Frazar & Co. were active, and all of them had their own consignees among the clipper fleet.

As always Captain Low rowed among the ships to invite old friends to dinner or bring bouquets to their wives. In years of service he was now the oldest captain in the China trade and commodore of the fleet, with the duty of firing the morning and sunset guns for the others to follow. His ship had long been the social heart of any anchorage, and his celebrations of Washington's Birthday and the Fourth of July became a legend among the clipper captains. He always set a lavish table and shipped a culinary artist in the galley.

But he was lonely in Foochow, waiting two mortal months for teas. There was nothing to do all day but row ashore from Pagoda Anchorage and smoke on the veranda of Russell & Co., longing to be home.

"And when I get there," he wrote his wife, "hurrah boys, won't there be some fun. I tell you Sally I shall tear the house down, lug you off to sea and there we'll stay until I am able to live on shore. I know you will go with me, now won't you dearest, kiss me and say you will."

At home he found that his loved Harriet was recently widowed, which after all meant her release from the last few years of torment, watching John go to pieces under the weight of his business troubles. He had begun drinking heavily, and his brother sent him off for a voyage to China, the family remedy for troubles of mind or body. But John did not manage to pull himself together, so the marriage that had given Harriet many happy years was clouded at the end. Charles found her quiet and brave, and spent as much time as he could with her. Next to his mother, she was closer to him than anybody in the family.

A tall Westerner named Lincoln was running for the presidency, and the papers were full of "secesh" and rumblings the captain did not want to bother his head about. He was sorry that the *Flying Cloud* and three other famous ships had been sold to England, and that shipyard workers were now getting a dollar and twenty-five cents a day instead of four dollars. The country was nervous, quarrelsome, apprehensive.

But in South Danvers it was hurrah boys, for Sarah was coming out with him on the *Palmer*, and taking young Charles and Josiah. By great good luck the captain was inspired to take his cousin Ellen Porter along. In China she became engaged, and that involved her returning to Salem for the family blessing, and then going back to China to be married, with Sarah Low absolutely required as her chaperone. So with one inspiration Charles Low bagged his wife for two voyages.

She was pulled in two directions, sorely missing the twins and her mother, and yet enjoying the voyage in spite of herself. At Anjer all the old enchantment was waiting; to her, Java was "a perfect paradise." Charlie and Jose were seven and six, and they left Anjer heady with the loot presented by sailors and harbormaster—monkeys, birds, and a poodle bitch named Let. But as they went up the China Sea with its calms and baffling winds, worry and fret, and listened to the captain's reactions, they began to act like their father's sons. After all, they'd been born on the *Palmer*.

They set up their own clipper ship on deck, made from two long settees from the cabin, and shipped Dick the cabin boy as steward. They shortened sail a split second after their father bawled his orders, they tacked along with the *Palmer*, and nearing land, they sang, "Haul the bowline, the captain is a-growling."

Sally Low sat watching them as she wrote her mother. "Dear little chickens! Oh, how I wish we could stay at home! God grant the dear little boys will never have the desire to be sailors. Anything in the world but that."

Flagpoles were set up before the big houses on Brooklyn Heights the summer of Bull Run. Abbot Low flew a silk Stars and Stripes, given him long before by Houqua, until it was whipped to rags and replaced by bunting. The young men of Brooklyn were drilling near by on Montague Terrace, but Gus and Will were only seventeen, and Abbot Low managed to keep them home. Will entered Columbia College that fall, and Gus went to work at his father's office in Burling Slip.

A. A. Low was himself very busy with the war. He was president of the Union Defence Committee of New York, and made the Bank of Commerce, of which he was a director, the chief bulwark of the Treasury Department in financing the war.

All the spring and summer of 1861 Encke's comet was a magnificent sight with its long brilliant tail. In Brooklyn the Lows used to watch it glowing over Manhattan, and at Anjer it was dazzling, and the passengers on the *Palmer* broke out champagne enough to make the captain's lady more intoxicated than usual with the perfumed airs of Java. The Lows saw Ellen Porter married to her China merchant, and then, since there was no prospect of getting teas in Hong Kong, they took a load of coolies to San Francisco.

There they found that the war was serious. "And I had hoped," Sarah wrote her mother, "to hear that the whole affair was pleasantly settled." Charles debated whether to send her home with the ship or keep both in the Pacific and pick up what business he could.

"We shall always be poor," she lamented, "and will always be obliged to go to sea; for making money enough to stay at home is out of the question." Accepting that, she bore the separation from her four children bravely, and started back for China with the *Palmer*. They anchored off Honolulu, and Father Damon rowed out to pay a visit.

He may have given them news of their strange friend Walter Gibson, who had now arrived in the islands with his daughter Lucy. His errand was a fantastic one: he had convinced Brigham Young that the Saints should move in a body to some Pacific isle, and Young had actually sent him to Hawaii to spy out the land. There Gibson proceeded to build up such a powerful Mormon movement that the elders hurried out from Salt Lake City and dismissed him for taking too much authority on his own shoulders. By that time Gibson had mastered the native language and had the Hawaiians almost worshiping him, so he began his real career.

Within a few years he was premier and virtual one-man cabinet under King Kalakaua, leading a movement to free the islanders from domination by the American "Missionary Sons" who had

249

now established themselves as feudal lords. Since Gibson always went too far, he extended this movement to the whole Pacific, which he proposed to free from foreign overlordship. "Polynesia for the Polynesians" was the slogan of his vast campaign; he promulgated the Gibson Doctrine along the lines of the Monroe Doctrine, and got Samoa, the Tongas, and other islands into a federation led by Hawaii. Europe became alarmed, and Otto von Bismarck finally made Washington warn Gibson to stop this nonsense.

Meanwhile he had done at least as much good as harm in Hawaii by spreading ideas of health and hygiene in his native-language newspaper, importing colonists from the South Pacific to replace coolie labor, and in general restoring pride in the old traditions. He taught the Hawaiians to vote out the whites until in the 1886 election there was only one white man on the government ticket, and that was his son-in-law, Fred H. Hayselden. At this point the Missionary Sons organized a militia, got from King Kalakaua a virtual abdication and a "bayonet constitution," and after threatening to lynch Gibson and Hayselden, finally deported them stateside. Walter Gibson died a few months later, and before the century was out Hawaii was formally annexed by the United States.

Perhaps the real trouble with Walter Gibson was his embarrassing habit of being a century ahead of his time.

The Lows were finally home with a cargo of teas and silks, then the *Palmer* was soon out for Hong Kong on a curious errand, carrying a prefabricated steamer to China. The machinery and woodwork were stowed below decks, and the boilers lashed to the deck; a dangerous load for the long run in the Indian Ocean before westerly gales. But the captain delivered the detested teakettle in good order and went off to San Francisco with passengers and a cargo of tea, rice, and sugar.

He got out of the China Sea in time to avoid the Confederate privateer *Alabama*, on the prowl for Yankee beauties. She caught up with the *Contest* in the Java Sea, and until the wind failed the Low clipper gave the *Alabama* a race. Then the steamship got alongside and boarded and burned her. That same year of 1863 the *Jacob Bell* was captured and burned in the Atlantic by the Confederate *Florida*. Captain Frisbie of the *Jacob Bell* was tricked by the privateer's flying the Union flag until the capture was made. The Lows recovered their claims for both these ships after the war. Meanwhile the *David Brown* had been lost in a storm in the North Atlantic, so that the fortunes of war and weather cut down the Low fleet to the smaller size the times demanded.

By the time Captain Low reached San Francisco he had made a humiliating decision: he was going home on a steamship. He was sending the *Palmer* back to China to be interned until it was safe for her to venture out again, and that left him no choice but to take passage to the Isthmus in the steamer *Golden Age*.

As sailing time approached Captain Low often went aboard the side-wheeler, sizing her up and wondering how she would behave in a gale. The captain and mate assured him that high seas and head winds made no impression on a steamship.

They were on their way with a hundred-odd passengers and near Cape Corrientes when the mate woke him up one night.

"Captain Low, if you want to see a gale of wind, here's your chance," he called.

The captain looked out of his porthole, decided the gale was negligible, and went back to sleep. Early the next morning he was called on deck. Though the wind was still not strong, the barometer was falling, and the steamer was making bad weather of it, with decks awash. Then a heavy gust threw the steamer over and a flock of sheep on deck were washed overboard. The second mate was hurled across the deck and broke his arm.

"Your vessel is in a dangerous position," Low told the captain. "You must do something to bring her head to the sea, or she'll go over and drown us all."

"I can't get headway, Captain Low. The engine's on center."

The steamer carried sail, but none was bent. Low decided that only sail could save the steamer. He looked around and saw the deck awnings used in fine weather to give the passengers shade. He had them triced down to the deck, and at once this brought the ship's head around and held her steady. For the next few hours

251

Captain Low took the second mate's place and worked the awnings until the gale was over. The next day the passengers held a meeting to thank him for saving the ship from foundering.

"Thank the sails," he said. "Steam has no business on the seas."

Abbot Low never owned a steamship, but he knew steam had come to stay. Late in 1866 he took Ann and Gus on a trip around the world, starting in time for the opening of the Pacific Mail Steamship Line to Japan and China. He wanted to be on the first American steamship to cross the Pacific, the *Colorado*, commanded by Captain Bradbury, once of the Low clipper *David Brown*. The steamship took a northerly course and arrived in 20 days; communications were now so swift that mail reached Japan in 40 days from New York via San Francisco.

It was twenty-seven years since Abbot Low had left Canton, and he was welcomed back like a prince. By one of those coincidences always popping up in his life, he reached China just before the first Chinese embassy left for the United States to ratify a treaty of trade and friendship. In Canton Houqua's son gave the Lows a banquet that lasted even longer than those his father had given, and Ann was invited to visit the ladies in their quarters. Abbot Low made a warm gesture of his own; on the salt-strewn site of the old Russell quarters at Suy Hong he ordered the erection of a new building for the family firm of Smith, Archer & Co.

The China trade was changing fast. In 1869 the Suez Canal was finished and the old voyage around the Cape of Good Hope became a matter of choice. The telegraph and cables Abbot Low had supported so ardently also changed the ways of trade and sometimes worked against him. But until the house of Low was liquidated in 1887 its sons were at home in the country which had brought them riches and old friendships and adventures hull under and far away.

One by one their brave ships vanished from the China run:

The *Houqua* perished in 1865, caught in a typhoon in the China Sea.

The *Samuel Russell* was wrecked in Gaspar Strait, 1870.

In 1872 the *Great Republic* foundered, having already lost her identity; her British owners had renamed her the *Denmark*. The same year the *N. B. Palmer* was sold to Norway.

The *Surprise* was lost in 1876 on Plymouth Rocks in Yokohama Bay.

Last of them all, the *Golden State* was wrecked off Cape Eliza-beth, Maine, in 1886.

Captain Nat had long happy years of what he called retirement. He and his wife lived among their friends on Brooklyn Heights, where he was still the first to see a ship coming down the bay. One after the other he had no less than fifteen small yachts, and loved to gather up any young Lows who happened to be around the Heights, or summering at the new family resort of Newport, and take them for a sail, racing down anything under canvas that he encountered. He made one last voyage to China with his nephew Nat Palmer, hoping to cure the boy's lungs, but here he was defeated, as he almost never had been in his life, and himself died soon after he was back in San Francisco in 1877.

He was buried at home in Stonington, where small boys still are taught to sail. But what boy can sail from Stonington to discover a continent, and to evoke upon the seas its most entrancing fleet? Captain Nat was a great soul, with the luck to live in an age when one man could have more adventures than Odysseus himself.

The Tribe of Seth was diminishing; Mary Ann and Sarah and Haskell were gone, but the others appeared to be indestructible. Ned and his wife Lucy were still shuttling back and forth from China, keeping an eye on business in Shanghai while George Archer supervised the southern ports. Sarah Low had not managed to keep her firstborn out of the China trade, and Charles went out to Hong Kong when he was nineteen, "a most clever boy," his uncle Josiah wrote Smith, Archer, "we shall miss him at home very much."

At home Abbot, Josiah, and Edward Lyman were about ready to turn the business over to their sons and live out their long, contented, and prosperous days. At 40 Concord Street Mother Low still sat erect in a hard chair, doing the finest needlework. "I used to tell Mother all my cares," Charles wrote Harriet after Mary Low died, "I tell my wife as much as I dare to, but I cannot tell her *all*."

He could always tell Harriet, the warm bright spirit who was never daunted, never dull. She had lost her sons in infancy and two of her daughters, but the brilliant spinster Kate, and Mary and Harriet, who both married in 1872, were wonderful girls. Not, they declared, as wonderful as their mother, the really romantic figure in the family, the first American girl to enter China, the toast of Macao, and now a very great lady. For, after all, it is not only still waters that run deep. Harriet's bubbling mirth and coruscating moods hid real tenacity and courage.

Captain Low had moved his family down to Brooklyn, and Sarah's maternal heart was now appeased by her babes, Samuel and Rosalie and David. Her husband was off on the *Palmer*, racing with the *Game Cock*, the famous ship designed by Samuel Pook in 1850. She had left New York five days before the *Palmer*, but Charles had caught up with her early in the voyage, and had finally got her astern.

"It is the most exciting race I have ever had," he wrote in the special log he was keeping for Sarah. "She sails nearly as fast as we do in light winds. As soon, however, as we get a good stiff breeze we leave her. I am as happy as possible in sailing the ship . . . have hardly left the deck the last three days."

Sixteen days out, the *Game Cock* was still hanging about four miles astern, then they got a breeze and left her. Two days later, "the plaguy Gamecock is still in sight. Yesterday morning at 8 am she was about 7 miles astern of us, the weather squally and baffling, we were laying nearly becalmed, when she took a squall and went right up to windward and abreast of us at the rate of nine miles an hour. It was most provoking to lay there and see the foam from her bows, and our sails hanging against the mast."

Three weeks out, and he had the *Game Cock* out of sight astern, but they were in the doldrums, and it was raining. A month out, and the weather cleared:

"The Southern Cross nearly overhead, the Scorpion as large

as life in the east, my evening star still shows bright and clear in the west, carrying me back to my dear ones, my dear darling wife, Harriet standing on her doorstep, Kate riding out with Mr. Mills, Hooley's minstrels, the peanut stand, the old watchmaker, Boston carpet sweeping machine, Dr. Minton's and Gas House, and all the trees, paving stones, ash barrels and boxes . . ."

Later, "I am blue, the mate is blue, all hands are blue . . . it is cold and cheerless below deck and cold and wet on deck, with head winds and calm, bracing and hauling yards around, setting stunsails and hauling them in, standing by royal haulyards and flying jib down haul, squall, squall, rain, rain, calm, calm, so goodbye dearest, until I get a better wind."

He got a northwest gale and sailed under it at the risk of being dismasted, but now he had hopes of beating the *Game Cock* and the Low's *Golden State*, the fastest ships in the China trade. He beat them both five days to Anjer, and sped into the China Sea to make the record for the year.

"The old ship is staunch and strong as the day she was built. I am so infatuated with this exciting life I do not know how I can ever give it up."

He gave it up only to move his family to the cliffs above Santa Barbara, where every sailing ship that passed saluted Captain Low and the days now folded into legend, where he could look across the Pacific to the land that had taken the Lows as its foster children and lavished its gifts upon them. The golden day was ended now, and Cathay itself was ended as a shimmering dream that had pulled the wills of men and the snowy-winged ships across the seas.

(Continued from front flap)

a typhoon—dismasted, battered, and thrown on her beam-ends—he still fought through and made the port for which he had sailed, three thousand miles away.

The family's business—nurtured by their own luck and daring and men such as Houqua, the shrewdest of all the Chinese merchant princes—boomed till the arrival of the steamship and the subsequent decline of the clipper.

TALL SHIPS TO CATHAY is not only the fascinating story of a family unique in the long tradition of American trading, it is also an inspired history of China at the time of the Opium War—and of the glorious era of the clipper ships and the gallant men who sailed them.

THE AUTHOR

Helen Augur was born in Minnesota and received her degree from Barnard College in New York City. She has been special correspondent in Russia for the Chicago *Tribune* and staff correspondent in Rome for the New York *Herald Tribune*.

Miss Augur, a noted scholar, is the author of *American Jezebel: The Life of Anne Hutchinson, Passage to Glory: John Ledyard's America,* and has also published many short stories and articles in leading magazines. She now lives in San Francisco.